W9-AVM-105

In Katrina's Wake

New Perspectives on Maritime History and Nautical Archaeology

UNIVERSITY PRESS OF FLORIDA

Florida A&M University, Tallahassee
Florida Atlantic University, Boca Raton
Florida Gulf Coast University, Ft. Myers
Florida International University, Miami
Florida State University, Tallahassee
New College of Florida, Sarasota
University of Central Florida, Orlando
University of Florida, Gainesville
University of North Florida, Jacksonville
University of South Florida, Tampa
University of West Florida, Pensacola

University Press of Florida

Gainesville Tallahassee Tampa Boca Raton Pensacola Orlando Miami Jacksonville Ft. Myers Sarasota

In Katrina's Wake

The U.S. Coast Guard and the Gulf Coast Hurricanes of 2005

Donald L. Canney

Foreword by James C. Bradford and Gene Allen Smith

15 14 13 12 11 10 6 5 4 3 2 1

Library of Congress Cataloging-in-Publication Data
Canney, Donald L., 1947–
In Katrina's wake : the U.S. Coast Guard and the Gulf Coast hurricanes of 2005 / Donald L. Canney ; foreword by James C. Bradford and Gene Allen Smith.
p. cm.
Includes bibliographical references and index.
ISBN 978-0-8130-3510-9 (alk. paper)
1. United States. Coast Guard—History—21st century. 2. Hurricanes—Gulf Coast (U.S.)—History—21st century. 3. Hurricane Katrina, 2005. 4. Hurricane Rita, 2005. 5. Rescue work—Gulf Coast (U.S.)—History—21st century. 6. Gulf Coast (U.S.)—History—21st century. I. Title.
VG53.C36 2010
976.044—dc22 2010004734

Frontis: New Orleans flood response: A CG aluminum punt on a flooded street, with a CG helo in background. Hundreds of small boats trolled the streets, with CG personnel banging on roofs and searching for survivors.

The University Press of Florida is the scholarly publishing agency for the State University System of Florida, comprising Florida A&M University, Florida Atlantic University, Florida Gulf Coast University, Florida International University, Florida State University, New College of Florida, University of Central Florida, University of Florida, University of North Florida, University of South Florida, and University of West Florida.

University Press of Florida
15 Northwest 15th Street
Gainesville, FL 32611-2079
http://www.upf.com

To the men and women of the U.S. Coast Guard

Contents

Foreword

Water is unquestionably the most important natural feature on earth. By volume the world's oceans compose 99 percent of the planet's living space; in fact, the surface area of the Pacific Ocean alone is larger than the total of all land bodies. Water is as vital to life as air. Indeed, to test whether the moon or other planets can sustain life, NASA looks for signs of water. The story of human development is inextricably linked to the oceans, seas, lakes, and rivers that dominate the earth's surface. The University Press of Florida's series *New Perspectives on Maritime History and Nautical Archaeology* is devoted to exploring the significance of the earth's water while providing lively and important books that cover the spectrum of maritime history and nautical archaeology broadly defined. The series includes works that focus on the role of canals, rivers, lakes, and oceans in history; on the economic, military, and political use of those waters; and upon the people, communities, and industries that support maritime endeavors. Limited by neither geography nor time, volumes in the series contribute to the overall understanding of maritime history and can be read with profit by both general readers and specialists.

The twenty-first century has reminded us of the centrality as well as the uncertainty of the sea. During late August and September 2005, two awesome storms—Hurricanes Katrina and Rita—swept ashore from the Gulf of Mexico, pounding Louisiana and neighboring sections of Mississippi and Texas with destructive waves and winds unknown in that region. These storms rank among the most destructive natural disasters that the United States has ever faced, and not surprisingly their catastrophic results graced American televisions for weeks on end. The American public witnessed, firsthand, the failure of the government to provide relief to those most affected by the storms. No level of government could provide security for those who remained in New Orleans or efficiently evacuate the thousands who had lost everything. The reaction to Hurricane Katrina resembled a chaotic training exercise, in which the government failed. Amidst the incompetence and bureaucratic quagmire engulfing the region, as historian Donald Canney details, the U.S. Coast Guard became the only governmental agency with a significant level of involvement that could claim it successfully fulfilled its mission. From the very beginning, the Coast Guard swept into action, saving lives, providing relief, and establishing order in a chaotic situation.

Canney describes how the Coast Guard's success derived from the service's mission. The unsophisticated organizational structure of the service permitted a quick response without waiting for the panoply of military efficiency to be superimposed. Coast Guard personnel trained as small crews and the standardization of training permitted the interchangeability of crewmen, thereby giving the service greater flexibility than other governmental organizations. Operating in small units across the country with a decentralized organization, the Coast Guard was trained in a manner that allowed it to respond quickly to the disaster, and individual units fulfilled their life-saving missions without awaiting instructions from headquarters. Moreover, Coast Guard personnel reacted to the approach of the storms by repositioning their units outside the destructive swaths of those tempests; once the storms passed, they immediately took action as they had been trained to do. While other government agencies such as the Department of Homeland Security and the Federal Emergency Management Agency (FEMA) received warranted criticism for their inactivity or slow response, the Coast Guard moved quickly and effectively carried out its mission of saving lives. In fact, during the days after the storm, the skies over New Orleans were orange with Coast Guard aircraft, representing a model of efficiency during an incredibly trying time.

Most Americans watched the drama on television as Coast Guard rescue units—helicopters and small boats—pulled people from roof tops, from floating debris, or off water-surrounded high ground and ferried them to safety. During the storms some 5,000 Coast Guard members, 42 cutters, 131 small boats, and 62 aircraft rescued approximately 33,735 individuals. During an average year the Coast Guard rescues about 5,500 people—operations during the storms accounted for six years worth of rescues in only two weeks time. Once the immediate emergency had passed, Coast Guard units then employed their other "multi-mission" capabilities. They enforced law and order, responded to environmental hazards, and also restored hundreds of navigation aids that had been displaced or destroyed by the hurricanes.

Although this book focuses on the dramatic exploits of Coast Guard personnel during Hurricanes Katrina and Rita, it also evaluates the service's strengths and weaknesses during these crises. And while several other authors have tried to capitalize on the drama of these Gulf Coast disasters, they have not used the extensive Coast Guard records nor have they employed the critical eye that this study offers. As such, this book represents the first historical study to examine the Coast Guard during the storms, and in doing so it highlights the one federal organization that successfully fulfilled its mission during the crisis. The Coast Guard truly embraced it motto, *Semper Paratus*—Always Ready!

James C. Bradford and Gene Allen Smith
Series Editors

Introduction

"in keeping with the highest traditions of the United States Coast Guard."

It is pure boilerplate: the final phrase in every official citation and award given to individuals for meritorious action while serving with the United States Coast Guard. It is heard literally hundreds of times in Coast Guard units throughout the service—from fog-bound Maine and Ketchikan to Key West and Honolulu to vessels on the Mississippi to the Persian Gulf—usually in the monthly "All Hands" assemblies.

The neatly uniformed men and women stand respectfully and uncharacteristically still, usually in utilitarian assembly rooms or on painted steel mess decks. By the time these last words are spoken by the officer in charge, there are visible movements and surreptitious glances at wristwatches as the Coasties politely wait out the handshakes and final dismissal so they can return to work.

These men and women are not into ceremony, flash, or self-congratulation. Part of the service tradition, indeed, seems to be self-effacement. Spoken or implied, they thrive on doing their job, and are slightly embarrassed by public hoopla and "press." No matter that their "job" may routinely call for extraordinary efforts, often in life-threatening situations at sea or ashore. "No big deal" is often heard from Coasties of every age and description. Oddly enough, they mean it.

Indeed, the "All Hands" meeting, with the unaccustomed formality and military correctness, is from another time and place—totally alien from the twenty-first century in both appearance and attitude. Passé and stilted, slightly corny, the words and actions seem to be out of an old war movie. The assembled Coast Guard personnel often wonder: Why not forego it all and just do the work of the Coast Guard?

However, there are debts to pay. To paraphrase Sir Winston Churchill: the many owe the few. And with what currency do we render these obligations?

In the late summer and fall of 2005 the debtors were seen, thousands of them. We saw them clinging to battered rooftops, floating on closet doors, and waving old shirts: desperate people reduced to the basics of life and often beyond. The city of New Orleans and a swath of the American Gulf Coast fell under a storm of monumental size and intensity, declared by many to be the most destructive hurricane in American history. Indeed, even today, five years after the event, the future of the Crescent City remains uncertain.

Of course, Hurricane Katrina alone is not the story. No positive effect could be expected from the storm itself. No human hand or agency could stay the winds or withhold the waters. The real story is in the response and aftermath. Were necessary pre-arrangements made and carried out? Were people in the storm's path subject to danger or death which reasonable efforts could have ameliorated? Did government and private agencies respond effectively, appropriately, and in good time? The answers to these questions form the basis for the real story of Hurricane Katrina, and later, Rita.

This book attempts to answer these questions. Specifically, this is the story of the role played by the U.S. Coast Guard in the stormy cataclysm and its aftermath.

It is a story which must be told.

The men and women who risked all and expected no more than their monthly pay deserve—and indeed ought to be—repaid in other ways, with words and respect. This book is part of that recognition.

Donald L. Canney

1

Round One

Katrina Slams Florida

Wrong.

He had read the storm wrong. In commercial fishing the stakes are always high and all it takes is some bad weather to ruin an entire trip, but in the Gulf of Mexico during hurricane season a storm can be fatal. As skipper Mark Gutek hung on to the rail—whatever solid part he could reach—he realized that the storm had outwitted him. Ruefully he shook his head.

The day before he'd listened to the spotty storm reports coming through the VHF radio and taken the risk. He figured the hurricane would veer north after slicing through south Florida, leaving him and his two crew members free to finish the grouper catch—another ton in the hold would get them a decent return in Key West.[1]

Through the night Gutek told himself the storm would let up by morning, but in the grim light of day the scene was frightening: waves he could not see over, winds pulling at his eyelids, thunder drowning out all other sounds. *Mary Lynn* was a 41-foot longliner, as solid of a boat as Gutek had ever captained, but in these waves she was a cockleshell.

The VHF crackled and sputtered in the storm, making it impossible to get a clear weather report. Gutek and his crew, Anita Miller and Charles White, had no idea of the depth of their abyss. Because they could not receive a complete weather report, they could not hear the warnings, advisories, and calls to head to port. They did not know they were running directly into what would become the most destructive hurricane in American history. Gutek did not need official reports to know it was the worst he had ever seen. They battened down everything and abandoned their fishing line.

By mid-morning the winds were at sixty-five miles an hour and swells of forty-five feet towered over the vessel. Things started to go. The hatch over the hold flew off; they weighted it down. It went again, flying off to be swallowed by the ocean. Their steering gear—essential to keeping the boat in control—was leaking fluid and failing.

When the rudder no longer held, Gutek went for the last resort and put out the anchor. The storm made short work of it and they were now wallowing broadside to the waves, out of control. Gutek, Miller, and White sat and prayed.

Then came the big ones: smashing through the wheelhouse door, carrying away 300-pound bait barrels like matchwood. Gutek gave in. At 8:00 P.M., the most horrendous night of his life still ahead of him, he pulled the emergency beacon switch and prayed some more.

◎

The struggling *Mary Lynn*'s EPIRB (Emergency Position Indicating Radio Beacon) bounced a signal via satellite to listeners at Coast Guard stations in Miami and Clearwater. CG helicopter pilot Lt. Craig Massello found himself staring at the radar screen in the semi-darkened operations center at Clearwater. The rescue of the three sailors had looked "doable" while the initial reports showed 40 mph winds and ten foot seas, but now the maps and charts showed the boat no more than ten miles east of the eye of the storm.

A CG C-130 Hercules had already been dispatched to the scene, but the airplane was not equipped for a rescue mission. Despite the generally accepted idea that helicopters could not "withstand the severe turbulence encountered" in hurricanes, it would take Massello's helo to get the crew of the *Mary Lynn* out of the water.

"Impossible," he thought. "There's no way. No good way, at least." Nevertheless, he assembled his team: copilot Lt. jg. David Sheppard, flight mechanic AMT2 Robert Cain, and rescue swimmer AST2 Kenyon Bolton.

At 9:00 P.M. their twin-engine helo, a HH-60J Jayhawk, was thrashing through the increasingly intense and unpredictable winds between them and the *Mary Lynn*. Normally a ninety-minute flight, it would take them two and a half hours to get there.

It was not easy. Later, flight mechanic Cain would remember, "The winds just kept building and building and you could just feel us constantly being blown off course."

Meanwhile, only furious bailing with five gallon buckets kept the *Mary Lynn* above water. When the winds grew unbearable they huddled in the wheelhouse with the radio, watching water spray around the plywood sheet they had jury-rigged over the smashed door. Gutek realized the odds that they would survive were not good. Miller and White were surely thinking the same thing.

Then came the first hint of relief: the C-130 was on the radio, overhead. "Help is on the way," said the voice on the other end.

Thanks to the circling C-130, finding the little boat was easy, but by the time the helo was in place there was less than fifteen minutes of fuel available for the rescue attempt. They would be forced to return to base. In any event, Massello was fighting winds in excess of ninety miles per hour, making any kind of stable hover impossible. The conditions were wrong. This was not the time to save the three people on the *Mary Lynn*.

At about 2:45 A.M., the bad news reached the *Mary Lynn*: the helicopter had to break off and return to Key West for fuel. Even then the numbers were scary. In these winds Massello might not even reach Key West.

Things were only getting worse for the soaked and battered crew: their life raft had imploded and flown out of sight. If the boat sank now, they would be in the water with only lifejackets.

It sounded like it was all over.

On the runway at Key West, Massello's team could hardly walk in the wind. They refueled and Massello reminded them that even regulations could not force them into an impossible situation.

"No go is an option," he said, but Sheppard, Cain, and Bolton got back in the helo, ready to head out once more and finish their rescue mission

It was 5:30 A.M. when the Jayhawk was again over the *Mary Lynn*, but it was too dark to safely drop Bolton, the rescue swimmer. On the *Mary Lynn* Gutek, Miller, and White waited. It was eerily quiet. Their engine had died, and soon their battery power would end as well.

With the murky grey of daylight came the "orange frogman" from the sky. Bolton swung down on the wildly gyrating cable from fifty feet above, hoping to avoid the twenty- to forty-foot waves. His first "contact" was not the water. He slammed up against the boat's stern. Flight Mechanic Cain tried again, handling the hoist cable, and finally putting Bolton in the water.

Still attached to the cable, Bolton swam to the pitching, rolling boat, close enough for Anita Miller to jump in and swim to him. He attached the harness strop around Miller and then they rose into the sky, snatched out of the water as Massello backed above.

Next came Gutek, but the skipper jumped into the water with a life ring that was still attached by rope to the boat. Inevitably, the rope and the hoist cable tangled. Now the tossing boat was attached to the rescue helicopter. Charles White, the last of the *Mary Lynn*'s crew, saw the danger and frantically assisted Bolton in untangling the mess, before he was also lifted into the Jayhawk.

It took twenty minutes to get Gutek, Miller, and White to safety.

Massello and crew had risked an eight and a half hour ordeal to bring back the crew of the *Mary Lynn*. For Gutek, White, and Miller, it had been nearly twenty-four hours since their battered boat had ceased to be a vessel likely to survive Hurricane Katrina.

Later, Kenyon Bolton, who had also flown through Hurricane Frances, said: "It was nothing compared to Katrina." As for the *Mary Lynn*, the little boat was never seen again.

⊙

The prologue to the Gulf coast landfall of Hurricane Katrina is often overlooked—the storm had already traced a deadly path across south Florida. The tropical disturbance had first officially incubated on August 23, southeast of Nassau in the Bahamas, some 300 miles from the tip of Florida. From "Tropical Depression" it transmuted to "Tropical Storm" on the 24th, receiving the next name on the hurricane list: Katrina. Late that day her winds reached hurricane force and warnings went out as she approached Florida, moving at about 6 mph.[2]

The storm made landfall near the Broward County, Dade County line at about 6:30 P.M., August 25. Fortunately, Katrina was carrying winds of only around 80 mph when she struck this highly populated area—just north of North Miami Beach. And by this time the Coast Guard had pre-set emergency measures in place. The first was setting up an Incident Management Team (IMT) in Miami to deal with the emerging storm, as well as placing liaison officers at emergency operations centers, specifically in Broward, Brevard, and Dade counties. Then four Miami-based helicopters, two 110-foot patrol boats, and the cutter *Valiant* were sent elsewhere to wait out the hurricane. All ports in the area—Miami, Miami River, Port Everglades, Port of Palm Beach, and Fort Pierce—were closed to shipping. Only the Coast Guard COTP (Captain of the Port) could authorize their reopening.[3]

The storm tore across the tip of the state, over the Everglades, and emerged in the Gulf of Mexico north of Key West. Its 80 mph winds, heavy rain, and 3–5-foot storm surge resulted in flooding.

Fourteen deaths were attributed to the storm in South Florida. In addition to the *Mary Lynn*'s crew, Coast Guard helicopters rescued nine people off three vessels in distress: five were removed from *Sea Note*, three from *Rita K*, and another from fishing vessel *Maria Rita*.[4]

Local Coast Guard units sustained minor damage. Part of a hangar roof was mangled at Air Station Miami, and there was water damage at Station Fort Lauderdale and Station Miami. One 41-foot CG utility boat was battered by a falling tree.[5]

The most memorable event of this early stage of Katrina was the air-sea rescue of the crew of fishing vessel *Mary Lynn*, recounted at the beginning of this chapter. The story later had its own series in the *St. Petersburg Times* and represented the classic Coast Guard nautical rescue scenario.

The rescue—though later overshadowed by Katrina's devastation of the Gulf Coast—gained its own notoriety. It was taped by a Discovery Channel team in a second CG helicopter hovering nearby. Additionally, all four crewmen from the Jayhawk (CG6019) received the Distinguished Flying Cross: Lt. Craig Massello, aircraft Commander; co-pilot Lt. jg. David Sheppard; Flight Mechanic AMT2 Robert Cain; and rescue swimmer AST2 Kenyon Bolton.

⊙

It was a morale party at New Orleans' Southern Yacht Club and Capt. Frank Paskewich, the commander of the newly established CG Sector New Orleans, had just wished his people a relaxing weekend. Coming off the microphone he was shown the latest predicted storm trajectory. Now a Category 2 storm with 96–110 mph winds, it had veered west from an expected landfall on the Florida Panhandle. It would strike the coast of Louisiana, and the city of New Orleans was in its projected path.

Paskewich had to retract the "liberty" he had offered earlier. His Coast Guardsmen were not likely to get any relaxation, much less liberty, until the storm passed.[6]

Paskewich would find himself the key man in the developing story as commander of Sector New Orleans, the largest portion of the Coast Guard's Eighth District. Paskewich was a twenty-four-year veteran in the service, mostly working in marine safety and port operations roles. He had been stationed in the New Orleans area since 1997.[7]

With the storm bearing down and intensifying, Paskewich immediately set in motion the pre-planned Coast Guard responses. To handle the administrative end, he ordered a command post set up in Alexandria, Louisiana, about 150 miles northwest of New Orleans, and an advance team was dispatched there early Saturday morning. At the same time District Eight set up an incident management team in New Orleans. Closer to home, Paskewich ordered all the smaller stations in the expected hurricane path to prepare for evacuation to their assigned safe havens. Finally, the New Orleans staff began notifying the local maritime industry—shippers, tug companies, and oil platform operators—that they should implement their hurricane plans.[8]

By late Saturday, August 27, Katrina had intensified to a Category 3 storm with winds from 111–130 mph. In the Saffir-Simpson Hurricane Scale, this indicated a storm surge of 9–12 feet above normal, and an expectation of flooding up to 8 miles inland in areas less than five feet above mean sea level.

To put the Coast Guard preparations in perspective, at 6:00 P.M. Friday, governor Kathleen Blanco had declared a state of emergency in Louisiana. On Saturday, governor Haley Barbour did the same for the state of Mississippi. The Federal Emergency Management Agency had also activated rapid response units in Baton Rouge.[9]

Saturday and Sunday were hectic with activity. On the ground, the Coast Guard units began evacuating. All personnel from New Orleans, Venice, and Grand Isle, Louisiana, as well as Gulfport, Mississippi began pulling away to points north, west, and east of their bases. Simultaneously, all "floating assets"—patrol boats, river tenders, and small boats were dispersed to safe areas.

At CG Station Grand Isle, on the only inhabited barrier island in

Louisiana, there was clear and imminent danger: the isle is so low-lying that even a 3-foot rise above normal tide can cut off the island's access road. The men and their families were notified at 11:00 P.M. on Friday night that they were to evacuate as soon as possible. They had about six hours notice to pack their belongings and be on the road, moving. Most went to Meridian, Mississippi and some to Baton Rouge. The two 41-foot utility boats and their crews were to head up river as far as Baton Rouge.[10]

At Station Gulfport, the Coast Guardsmen had been active up to the last moment responding to two distress calls from local sailboats attempting to regain the harbor in advance of the storm. The station, which had been destroyed in hurricane Camille and rebuilt on a different site, was a mere five and a half feet above the high water mark, so there was no question that even a Category 3 storm would inundate the place. The station commanding officer, CWO Steve Lyons, ordered the station's two 41-footers to Baton Rouge for the duration of the storm and the 87-foot patrol boats CGC *Pompano* and *Razorbill* sailed to Sabine Pass, Texas.

On the same day, most of the station's personnel convoyed to the Air National Guard base about 5 miles north of the city, leaving seven people at the station to respond to last-minute needs and search and rescue cases. It was decided that the station building was more secure than many homes and several pets—four dogs and a cat—were placed in what was thought to be a secure room in the station. "Mayday" the dog, the chubby station mascot, joined this group and they were the only living things at the unit on the evening before the storm. The last seven men held out until around 10:00 P.M., when most of their communications failed.[11]

Meanwhile, other Louisiana units made similar preparations. The Coast Guard Air Station in New Orleans had retained their five helicopters as long as possible, but finally dispersed them: three to Lake Charles, two to Air Station Houston. Station New Orleans and Station Venice, the latter located near Southwest Pass some 15 miles from the mouth of the Mississippi, evacuated all personnel. Venice dispatched its two 41-footers to Baton Rouge and its personnel to Meridian, Mississippi; the 160-foot construction tender CGC *Pamlico* moved north to Baton Rouge. Also evacuated were Aids to Navigation teams at Dulac and Morgan City, Louisiana.

When the dispersals were done, the Coast Guard had a fleet at Baton Rouge. Thirteen vessels had congregated there: eight 41-foot boats (one of which was out of commission and being towed), three 55-foot aids to navigation boats, two inland construction vessels, and the 75-footers CGC *Clamp* and *Pamlico*, with the latter pushing a construction barge. By virtue of senior rank, the commanding officer of *Pamlico*, Chief Warrant Officer Robert Lewald was suddenly in charge of one of the largest flotillas in the Coast Guard.[12]

Farther east, Coast Guard units fell under Sector Mobile, and storm preparations there were equally intense. Under sector commander Capt. Edwin Stanton, evacuations began. Most of the 500 active duty personnel were sent to Maxwell AFB, Alabama. The port of Mobile was closed, as were sections of the Intracoastal Waterway.[13]

The Coast Guard's final preparations for the storm fell into place on Sunday, August 28. By this time, the temporary command post was in operation at Alexandria. The city had been selected because of its convention center and convenient hotels. Some 250 personnel would be housed there during and after the storm. Meanwhile, back down the river, the Coast Guard closed the entrance to the Mississippi to incoming traffic and ordered all oceangoing vessels over 200 tons to depart for deep water. Sections of the Gulf Intracoastal Waterway were closed at New Orleans and Morgan City.[14]

By late Sunday, the storm was within 150 miles of New Orleans and still intensifying. More significantly, the storm was immense, measuring about 460 miles in diameter. At this point, almost regardless of its exact path, New Orleans and points eastward were in for a massive hit.

In New Orleans, on Sunday, mayor Ray Nagin had at last—after consulting with the city lawyers—issued a mandatory evacuation statement. By this time Katrina had been upgraded to a Category

5—the highest level possible—with winds in excess of 155 mph and a storm surge greater than 18 feet above normal. The National Weather Service warned that the storm would leave the city and surrounding area "uninhabitable for weeks . . . maybe longer." Only three Category 5 storms had ever made landfall in the United States since record keeping began: the "Labor Day Hurricane" of 1935, Camille in 1969, and Andrew in 1992. The 1935 storm had been relatively contained and struck lightly inhabited areas. Camille had created a 25-foot storm surge. Andrew had been the most destructive hurricane to date, with an estimated $25 billion in damage.[15]

By late Sunday, traffic was jammed exiting the city, and local shelters were filling quickly. It was estimated that 80 percent of the city population had fled New Orleans, leaving around 50,000 to endure the storm. The Superdome became an uncomfortable home for about 13,000 New Orleans residents.[16]

The question was no longer "if" the storm would come, but "how bad will it be?" Prepared or not, the city and the Gulf Coast were hunkering down for the impending blow. The Coast Guard, leaning on its experience and expertise, was on point and ready.

Round Two

Katrina Flattens the Gulf Coast

It is in some sense superfluous to detail here the path and career of the storm itself, in that the Coast Guard response began in the wake of the hurricane. It is, however, necessary to paint a picture of the extent of the tragedy geographically as well as in terms of the human and physical destruction it left behind. Indeed, one of the key characteristics of this hurricane was its nearly unprecedented diameter. That, in conjunction with its path across many heavily populated areas, set it apart from many storms with comparable wind and storm surge levels. And, of course, the New Orleans levee breaks completely redefined the situation as well as the response required by the Coast Guard. Finally, looking at the extent of the storm will remind the reader that, in addition to the headline-grabbing events in the Crescent City, Katrina's destruction scoured an entire coastline from Louisiana through Mississippi and Alabama, and left damage as far east as Panama City on the Florida Panhandle, over 200 miles from New Orleans.

Hurricane Katrina made landfall at 6:10 A.M., August 29, near Buras, Louisiana, dropping rain at the rate of an inch per hour. By the time it struck land, the storm was deemed a Category 4, and indeed registered 161 mph gusts at Buras and nearby Triumph, both of which were some 30 miles from the river's mouth and over 60 miles southeast of New Orleans. The entire population of both towns—some 3,300 people—had evacuated inland, leaving the storm to demolish the 1,146 households and drown livestock and wildlife. Coast Guard Station Venice, on the river about 10 miles southeast of Buras, remained standing but was submerged in 6 feet of water and sustained a 10-foot hole in the station roof. There were no casualties as the personnel had evacuated before the storm.[1]

Further west, across Barataria Bay at Grand Isle, the storm's eye passed about 10 miles east of the island; Barataria Bay saw 130–140 mph winds. The entire population of Grand Isle—around 1,000 people—had evacuated. It was said that only two men remained to ride out the 125 mph winds of the storm. Both survived, one clinging to a tree. The 6-foot storm surge violated the Coast Guard station building, which sustained over $8 million in damage, for the most part to the ground floor. Likewise, the walled ground level storage areas beneath the dependent housing units were washed away. The power of the storm was highlighted by the relocation of a forklift parked at the station. It was found 600 yards from its original position.[2]

As the storm moved northward, it swept all before it, in particular hitting the bulk of Plaquemines Parish which straddles the Mississippi River all the way from the river's mouth northwest to New Orleans. It devastated famous sport fishing communities such as Port Sulphur and Point a la Hache. The former (elevation 3 feet above sea level, population around 3,000) listed three deaths due to winds and a levee break. The parish's most famous landmarks, the two Civil War era forts which had battered Admiral Farragut's fleet, did not escape. Fort Jackson, on the west bank some 2 miles from Triumph, was inundated and remained so for six weeks. Most of the fort's historical displays and artifacts were lost. On the east bank, at Fort St. Philip, much of the older brick structure was gone, leaving only the post–Civil War concrete buildings.

In all, Plaquemines Parish, which covers 844 square miles, was entirely covered by the storm surge. Of a population of around 29,000, most had been evacuated and there were three deaths.[3]

Moving north, Katrina next battered through St. Bernard Parish, a large peninsula sandwiched between Plaquemines on the south and Lake Borgne on the north, and bordering on east New Orleans. The 125 mph winds and 20–25 foot surge topped the Lake Borgne levees and covered urbanized areas of the parish. Farther east, beyond the "protection" of the levees, entire fishing communities were wiped out. The entire housing stock of the 465 square mile parish was submerged, some in water 14 feet deep. A portion of the flooding in the western reaches of the parish was from the Industrial Canal levee break in New Orleans. In the aftermath, nearly 20,000 of the 25,000 homes in the parish were severely damaged and uninhabitable.

Adding a man-made element to the St. Bernard parish calamity was a major oil spill. Over a million gallons of crude oil escaped from the Murphy Oil Company's Meraux refinery during the storm, leaking from a storage tank which was dislodged and lifted from its foundation on the east bank of the Mississippi, some 5 miles east of the St. Bernard/Orleans Parish line. The spill tainted over 1,700 homes in a one square mile area.[4]

In all, most of the population had evacuated and the parish authorities listed 127 deaths attributable to the storm. The most astounding figures of all were the "before and after" population statistics: from a pre-storm population of over 65,000, to fewer than 16,000 people in 2006—there was a 76 percent decline in St. Bernard Parish.[5]

Fortunately for New Orleans proper, the storm's path had altered before coming ashore, making a slight turn from due north to a more easterly direction, eliminating the possibility of a direct hit on the city. Had the storm maintained its northern path from Barataria Bay, the eye would have passed directly over New

Orleans East and Lake Pontchartrain. Another mitigating circumstance, in hindsight only, was the final determination by the Weather Service. The agency later restudied the event and concluded that Katrina was in fact a strong Category 3, with up to 130 mph sustained winds, when it hit the southeast Louisiana coast. Few victims of the storm would have been relieved to know this. The storm's second Gulf Coast landfall would be at the Louisiana, Mississippi border, at the mouth of the Pearl River.[6]

Before reaching the Mississippi coast, Katrina's western reaches made New Orleans the largest American city to sustain major damage by hurricane winds and storm surge.

New Orleans proper is composed of Orleans and Jefferson parishes. The former includes New Orleans East, running along the bank of Lake Pontchartrain, as well as the central business district and the French Quarter—all north of the Mississippi. Six blocks west of the French quarter is the Louisiana Superdome. It is some 7 miles from Lake Pontchartrain south to the river across downtown New Orleans.

Of course, the levees are a major part of the New Orleans landscape, both those along the Mississippi as well as those along Lake Pontchartrain. Additionally, levees line four drainage canals which reach due south from the lake into the city. Levees also line the Intracoastal Waterway which enters the city from the east and debouches into the Industrial Canal, the farthest east of the four north-south canals. Yet another water inlet for the city is the Mississippi River–Gulf Outlet Canal (MR-GO), which flows nearly due west from the Gulf into the Intracoastal Waterway, and thence into the Industrial canal. The Industrial canal runs the entire width of the portion of the city from Lake Pontchartrain to the Mississippi. The storm surge essentially made each of these waterways funnels carrying flood waters into the heart of the city. Since some 75 percent of the city is in the flood plain, the critical nature of the levees is difficult to overstate.

Jefferson Parish abuts Orleans parish on the west, and extends some 25 miles southward past the suburbs into the low lying country of the upper reaches of Barataria Bay. It includes, in the municipality of Kenner, bordering on Lake Pontchartrain, Louis Armstrong International Airport. It is about 10 miles from downtown New Orleans to the airport and it is 12 miles from the city center to the eastern border of the city. The north-south 17th Street Canal (otherwise known as the Metairie Relief Outfall Canal) forms part of the Orleans/Jefferson Parish border. After the storm Jefferson parish flooding along the lake was less than 2 feet deep. However, in the rural southern reaches of the parish, there was a 15–20 foot storm surge. Fortunately the parish president had ordered mandatory evacuation on August 26. It is estimated that the permanent population of the parish plummeted by about 10,000 due to the storm.[7]

For New Orleans proper torrential rains were reported as early as 4:30 A.M. Monday morning. From then through late afternoon, New Orleans was under a wind and water maelstrom. Category 3 force winds battered the city for around six hours and a 12-foot storm surge pushed the waters of Lake Pontchartrain and Lake Borgne into the city, by way of the four drainage canals as well as the Intracoastal Waterway and the Mississippi River–Gulf Outlet. As early as 7:45 A.M. levees along the Industrial Canal were breaching and by around 10:00 A.M. much of the city was inundated to the level of the surrounding lakes. Four sections of the city saw over 10 feet of water in their streets and houses. The first two sections were the east side of the Industrial Canal, which is New Orleans East and also forms Pontchartrain's shore, and the Lower 9th Ward, which fills in the angle between the south part of the Industrial Canal and the river. The third and fourth areas of the city with over 10 feet of water were the two neighborhoods sandwiched between the Industrial Canal and the 17th Street Canal: Lakeview and Gentilly on Lake Pontchartrain. The city proper, south of Lakeview and Gentilly, had flooding ranging up to 8 feet, gradually shoaling up to the south. The northern reaches of the French Quarter had less than 4 feet. The other areas on the river itself—the Garden District and Central Business District were also relatively dry. About 80 percent of the city was flooded. Westward, Jefferson Parish reported some 2 feet of water on its Pontchartrain verge. It is noteworthy that, because of the orientation of the storm, the Mississippi River levees withstood the onslaught; only the lake and waterway levees failed or were overtopped.[8]

It was estimated that 90 percent of the city's population evacuated beforehand, but the death toll was over 800 and 55 percent of the parish's homes were damaged. More traumatic to the city's future, the Orleans Parish population dropped dramatically: from over 454,000 to less than 180,000. As of the date of this writing the population has rebounded to around 250,000.[9]

Leaving a devastated New Orleans, Katrina next moved north across the eastern end of Lake Pontchartrain, nailing St. Tammany Parish with winds ranging from 61 mph in the west to 125 mph in the east. After 20 hours under nature's siege, the 12–18 foot storm surge aggravated by up to 18 inches of rain had devastated the town of Slidell. Over 1,000 people had evacuated to higher ground in the northern part of the parish, which helped limit the death toll to six, though some 5,000 were injured.[10] This was chronologically the last coastal Louisiana parish affected by the storm.

⊙

While Slidell and St. Tammany Parish writhed under the moving storm, Katrina made its second Gulf Coast landfall. The target in sight was dead on the Mississippi/Louisiana border, which happens to be the Pearl River and its town, Pearlington, a few miles up from the Gulf. According to one source the storm surge here measured over 30 feet. That, as well as 10 inches of rain and 125 mph winds meant horrific damage to the small community. According to one source every building, home, and vehicle in Pearlington was destroyed. The storm surge brought 20 feet of "toxic stew" over 4 miles inland.[11]

This set the disastrous pattern for the Gulf Coast from Pearlington east across Waveland, Bay St. Louis, Pass Christian, Long Beach, Gulfport, and Biloxi, Mississippi. Waters overran the entire

Mississippi coast a half mile inland and in some places over 24 feet deep.

Waveland, Bay St. Louis, and Pass Christian sustained the greatest damage. Their location with St. Louis Bay to their rear, the Gulf on their front, and absolutely no high ground in between, was untenable. Water first funneled into the bay and took the towns from behind, then the storm surge hit from the Gulf side. Waveland, which had been scoured by Camille in 1969, again succumbed. Brick buildings 2 miles from shore were simply washed away and 28 feet of water was reported in some areas of the town. As with Pearlington, nothing was left undamaged.[12]

Bay St. Louis, on the west side of the bay, and Pass Christian, on the east, faced similar scenarios. In the former, the surge from the bay covered all but a 20-foot bluff on the bay side of the town; then the surge from the Gulf *overtopped that.* Pass Christian had no comparable high point. The surge from the bay slashed through the town, and then the Gulf waters finished the job. There were piles of wreckage over 30 feet high where the two surges converged and did their worst.[13]

Farther east, Long Beach, Gulfport, and Biloxi hardly fared better. At the former, the devastation could be gauged by the remains of the local Wal-Mart. The building was gutted and the back side blown out. The entire inventory was elsewhere: a pile of rubble and sale signs over 50 yards away.[14] Gulfport's size worked against it. As a port city, shipping containers were its stock in trade. Hundreds of them sat on wharves and along the quays, no match for the incompressible water which slammed them head- or side-long, plowing them into and across any obstacle. A 40-foot container had no chance against a 10-foot wall of moving salt water, weighing in at 1,700 pounds per cubic yard—each yard about the weight of an old Volkswagen. Later photos show the containers scattered like toys up to a half mile inland. They moved to the tune of the watery master, as did objects more securely attached to foundations, piers, or concrete. Things entirely unattached found no mercy whatsoever: a 40-foot fishing boat was dropped unceremoniously between two trees several hundred yards inland.[15] Highway 90 along the coast, formerly an avenue of substantial old Southern homes, became the southern boundary of a narrow wasteland of scraggled trees punctuating the interstices of forlorn concrete slabs and brick stair steps to nowhere.

The Coast Guard station at Gulfport was typical of the destruction in that area. When the Coast Guardsmen returned from upcountry, all that remained was the steel skeleton; the rest was not much more than hand-sized rubble. The nearby Marine Life Oceanarium was also demolished; its dolphins and other nautical denizens gone or dead.[16] Probably the most publicized loss in Gulfport was the gambling industry. Nine of ten floating casinos along the shoreline were on dry ground. Harrah's Grand Casino was astraddle Highway 90 and the President Casino had its surge-inspired overland odyssey cut short by a collision with the local Holiday Inn.[17]

Finally, Pascagoula, Mississippi, near the eastern border of the state, received a 20-foot surge. Katrina disrupted operations at Ingalls Shipbuilding, the state's largest employer, and destroyed the home of Trent Lott, former Senate Majority leader.[18]

In Mississippi, Katrina was blamed for 220 deaths. The Gulf littoral, as one writer put it, looked like the product of W. T. Sherman's Civil War march through Dixie.[19] There was a major difference, though: Katrina played no favorites; she was the enemy of all.

The Gulf coast of Alabama was the last major target of Katrina. Even Mobile, at the north end of its bay, registered 80 mph winds and a 16-foot storm surge. Downtown Mobile was under several feet of water. It was 5 P.M. before Katrina's winds dropped below 60 mph. By then the Coast Guard training center had sustained a partial loss of a hangar roof. Offshore, the famous Dolphin Island resort was heavily damaged and the island was nearly bisected by the storm surge. Some 56,000 people were ordered evacuated in Alabama's Gulf coast counties, and the death toll from the storm was 24.[20]

⊙

This was Hurricane Katrina, in summary. The storm bent the U.S. hurricane statistics: it was by far the most expensive hurricane, with property loss valued at around $81 billion, an estimated 200,000 homes destroyed, and over 1 million people displaced. It resulted in the third highest death toll, at 1,833, while an estimated 90,000 square miles of the Gulf Coast fell under the scourge of the storm—an area about the size of the state of Kansas.[21]

And, for the purpose of this book, I have limited this survey to areas which would become the battleground for the U.S. Coast Guard. This is not to slight or underestimate the other areas, which include parts of the Gulf states where the storm moved north beyond the coastal destruction. And this summary has necessarily skimmed the surface: it is simply to orient and prepare the reader for the overwhelming task presented to the U.S. Coast Guard as the winds calmed and the waters receded.

"There's thousands of them"

The Afternoon of the Storm

The wait was interminable to the Air Station New Orleans helicopter crews on the ground at Lake Charles, Louisiana and CG Air Station Houston. There was a job to be done and they were impotent until the graph said Katrina's winds coincided with the flight capabilities of the search and rescue HH-65. Although the printed specs on the little Dolphin helo's capabilities were rigid, they knew weather reports could be inexact. And, in any event, the five helos and crews had allowed the storm its due and a little weather never discouraged Coast Guard fliers much anyway.

It was time.

Captain Bruce Jones, commander of the New Orleans aircraft, was at Lake Charles with three of his birds. They had vacated NOLA (New Orleans, Louisiana) the day before and the crews met for breakfast on Monday, August 29 to discuss the situation. At that point, they estimated they could safely enter New Orleans airspace by four that afternoon.[1]

Fuel, however, was the next problem. Lake Charles was over 150 miles from New Orleans and no one knew what to expect in the disaster area. After fruitless satellite calls to the New Orleans naval air station, New Orleans International Airport, and Lakefront Airport, they finally raised someone at the CG station at Houma, Louisiana, about 35 miles southwest of the city. Confirming that fuel was available at Houma, Jones contacted the two Houston aircraft and directed them to rendezvous there that afternoon. They would use Houma as a jump off point into what was then the unknown.[2]

Conditions on their arrival at Houma that afternoon were not encouraging: at two o' clock there were 65-knot gusts, the sky was overcast at 3,000 feet, and there was 2–5 mile visibility. Worse, local power was down as well as the radar transmitters, so no weather reports were available from anywhere in the hurricane's path. If they flew into the ravaged city, they would be, in many ways, on their own.[3]

Waiting out another couple of hours was not something they cared to tolerate, particularly if any meaningful rescue attempts could be mounted before nightfall. However, they determined that if they flew out immediately and headed southeast, skirting the south end of the storm as it moved north, they could be on scene following the wake of the hurricane. They could then check out the condition of the CG stations at Venice and Grand Isle, as well as survey for people in distress as they flew northward toward the city. It was a plan not without risks. Gusting, unpredictable winds still whipped through the area and the pilots would be deliberately positioning their helicopters as close to the winds as their machines would allow.

At 2:20 P.M. two helicopters were launched to the southeast. The sights that met them were to become the norm. As Captain Jones later put it: "It looked like an atomic bomb had hit the place: houses just shredded into bits; boats everywhere up on top of the levee, on top of bridges, in the woods; heavy, heavy flooding; none of the pumping stations were working; homes underwater."[4]

The first Dolphin launched, CG6514, caught a faint MAYDAY on

VH-FM. Aircraft commander Lt. David M. Johnston followed the signal to Port Sulphur, a river hamlet about 35 miles southeast of New Orleans and not more than 10 miles from the storm's landfall, where he and his crew found a small aluminum boat caught under a tree in a confusion of fallen power lines and debris. The survivors—a grandmother, mother, and four-month-old infant, three generations of a Plaquemines Parish family—hung precariously onto the boat with their three dogs.

When the water level had reached the upstairs window of their home, they had escaped onto the roof. The daughter dove into Katrina's waters and swam to find their boat, bringing it back to the house. The grandmother literally threw the baby to her daughter before making the jump herself and boarding the tiny boat. On the wildly wallowing boat, in the implacable wind, they waited seven hours for someone, anyone to rescue them. Finally, Johnston's helo arrived.[5]

Johnston and his co-pilot, Lt. Craig Murray, fought the controls to maintain a steady 100-foot hoist (to clear the trees and power lines) in 50-knot wind, rain, and wind shear. With Aviation Electronics Technician Warren Labeth operating the hoist, they let down rescue swimmer Laurence "Noodles" Nettles. Despite full power, the severe downdrafts dropped the aircraft precipitously, and twice Johnston and Murray recovered the helo scant feet above trees and power lines.

The first hoist rescued the mother, her infant, and two dogs from the unsteady boat. The second hoist brought the grandmother and the last canine safely into the helo, but the third hoist, to recover Nettles, nearly failed when a gust snagged the cable in a tree. Labeth mediated between the aircraft and Nettles. He served out enough slack in the line to allow Nettles to break the branches and free the life line. Only then was he able to bring his fellow Coast Guardsman to safety.

This was the first Coast Guard rescue of Hurricane Katrina in the New Orleans area and, by all accounts, the first air rescue by any service after the storm.[6]

In the following days, this would be the pattern for hundreds of rescues on the Gulf coast. This one in particular was, appropriately, comparable to a rescue at sea: three survivors, a small boat in distress in high winds and roiling water, no place to land, and no other help at hand . . . plus obstructions and dangers not seen in the open ocean: trees, power lines, and floating and unstable debris.

But the crew of CG6514 was not done yet. They saw another survivor on the nearby levee, and they let down Nettles again to recover the man.

Lt. Johnston worked his way northwards through the devastation, setting Nettles down to deal with more survivors and leaving him to set up a collection point and attempt triage for the distressed and injured. Before this sortie was over Johnston, Nettles, and crew had moved as far as Chalmette and New Orleans' Lower Ninth Ward. They rescued 43 survivors.[7]

Not the least memorable rescue was of a 300-plus-pound individual trapped in an attic. Nettles was again on site, and, using the aircraft's small camping axe, he hacked through plywood and joists to enlarge a two by two foot hole to sufficiently allow the survivor through. The victim, however, was unable to lift herself out. In desperation, Nettles attached the hoist cable to the lady and repositioned her directly under the aperture so Labeth could hoist her to the helicopter. And all of this was at night.[8]

While Johnston and crew worked their way, rescue by rescue, northward, their companion aircraft, CG6522, commanded by Lt. Cmdr. Thomas F. Cooper flew southeast toward Grand Isle, searching for any survivors in their flight path.

The total breakdown of normal communications forced Cooper and his crew to fly to places they normally would simply have contacted electronically, so they turned north toward the city to determine the conditions back at home base, CG Air Station New Orleans. At 3:10 that afternoon, they landed at the Coast Guard facility, located on the naval air station at Belle Chasse, some 20 miles south of the city in Plaquemines Parish. They found it relatively intact, and with the welcome sight of a fuel truck on the tarmac. Cooper immediately reported back to Houma with this news, clearing the way for the dispatch of the other three helos to the station.[9]

This part of their mission accomplished, Lt. Cmdr. Cooper and crew flew to West Jefferson hospital, located about a mile south of the Mississippi in Jefferson Parish, to determine if MEDEVAC patients could be brought there, specifically the survivors picked up already by Lt. Johnston and his crew. It took less than five minutes on the ground there to determine that the hospital was viable and would accept survivors. Then Cooper had CG6522 back in the air, over the city.[10]

Cooper and his crew manned the first aircraft over New Orleans that day, and obtained the first video footage of the destruction. In the ninety minutes after lifting off from the hospital, Cooper and his crew rescued twenty-four survivors, all the while fighting gusty 50-knot winds. One survivor, an expectant mother, was the first person rescued in metropolitan New Orleans. Cooper, making several sorties, delivered all two dozen to the Superdome by 5 P.M.[11]

Perhaps one of the more difficult operations for Lt. Cmdr. Cooper, co-pilot Lt. Roberto Torres, and crew that day was a pinpoint vertical rescue. A 400-pound, non-ambulatory man was attached by the rescue swimmer directly to the hoist cable and lifted from his bed, through the damaged roof, to the helicopter.

When not rescuing survivors from the flooded city, Cooper and Torres performed another crucial task while overflying New Orleans. From overhead, they noted points of high, dry land and infrastructure which would make appropriate drop and collection points for survivors of the catastrophe. These were: Lakefront Airport, the University of New Orleans campus, and the Interstate 10/Lake Pontchartrain Causeway Interchange (commonly called the Cloverleaf). These would become familiar places to many of the distressed and their rescuers in the next several, intense days.

Around four o' clock in the afternoon of that unforgettable day, Coast Guard Sector New Orleans commander Capt. Frank Paskewich and deputy sector chief Capt. Robert Mueller flew in from Alexandria on a HH-60 Jayhawk piloted by Lt. Cmdr. Mark Vislay Jr. They were the first to get some idea of the extent of the catastrophe, taking stock of the ships tossed on shore and a city "completely inundated," before setting the aircraft down at the Superdome to pick up FEMA representative Marty Bahamonde. Paskewich, Mueller, and Bahamonde were anxious to survey the destruction wrought by the storm. Bahamonde was to report his findings to FEMA director Michael Brown. Brown, in turn, was to relay the information to the White House. The reports made by these men would be the first look at the city's plight for the outside world.

Capt. Mueller reported that it was "absolutely stunning." He found himself saying, "Oh my God, this is the worst I've ever seen." But it would not remain the worst for long. The "next place" he saw was even worse.

While in the air they picked up the Air Station New Orleans pilots' radio chatter: "There's thousands of them. There are people all over the place. We're picking them up. We need everything. We need more helicopters." Coast Guard ethic kicked in and, according to Paskewich, Vislay, the pilot, "sort of asked and said 'I can fly you around or I can go rescue people.'" There was only one answer to that and the three ranking men were dropped back at the Superdome. Vislay and his HH-60 went on to rescue seventeen people that afternoon.[12]

However, the three officials felt they had not completed their information gathering flyover, so they commandeered Lt. Cmdr. Thomas F. Cooper's CG6522, which had stopped at the Superdome only to refuel. Cooper was directed to fly the three observers over the city. Despite his protests, he was soon heading east with Paskewich, Mueller, and Bahamonde aboard.

This sightseeing and fact-finding survey would remain in their consciousness forever. Mueller saw "the yacht club on fire . . . and boats piled everywhere. Coast Guard helos were starting to make rescues and they were being buffeted all over the place . . . in horrendous winds. You know 65s aren't that big and they're just getting hammered but they're hoisting people off roofs . . . We kept going east and the water kept getting deeper and [when] we saw the I-10 Twin Spans [crossing to Slidell] it was collapsed. It was just gone."

Cooper flew them as far as Slidell, northeast of Lake Pontchartrain, completing the picture of an entire city devastated. Once back on the ground, Bahamonde called Secretary Brown with the first eyewitness accounts of the city from the air. The Coast Guard officers knew this was "total devastation of proportions never seen before in the Coast Guard . . ." and that a massive effort would be required—as quickly as possible.[13]

It was nearly midnight before all Air Station helos shut down for the day. The five aircraft and crews had rescued 137 people in some nine hours since the first lift at Port Sulphur. All aircrew members had exceeded the CG standards for flight time and crew missions. Earlier in the day, at around 3:45 P.M., three Air Station HH-65s, CG6507, CG6593, and CG6598 had returned to the city from Houma, landing at the Air Station to drop off two officers and Petty Officer EM2 Rodney Gordon. All three helos lifted off, in search and rescue mode, within ten minutes, but Gordon and the two officers began to put the station back into operation.[14]

And it is with Petty Officer Gordon that the saga of the first day of Katrina, and the heroic deeds of these first five Air Station New Orleans aircraft and crews, closes. Gordon, with less than three years in the Coast Guard, found himself alone and charged with restoring the Air Station power and operations. As the prime location for all CG air operations in the city and area, it was imperative that some semblance of "normal" conditions prevail as soon as possible. The key was to restore electrical power. On this depended the vitals: communications, tower operations, and fueling. Gordon, with only a handful of tools and parts, first restored a failed generator system, powering up the operations and communications center on base. Then, with a front end loader, Gordon cleared the mass of debris from the landing areas around the station. Finally, by late evening, he had obtained emergency lighting units and set them up to enable 24/7 aircraft maintenance. Petty Officer Gordon's day did not end until around two o' clock the next morning.[15]

It would be almost four days before complete power and food and water was available, but the station itself was capable of supporting basic air operations by the next sunrise.

As August 29 drew to a close, Petty Officer Gordon and the men racked out on the floors of the Air Station's administration building, in makeshift accommodations, should have known that they would soon not be alone. The plight of New Orleans and the Gulf Coast was known in the upper echelons of the U.S. Coast Guard. It had been seen firsthand, graphically described by Capt. Paskewich and Mueller, and passed up the chain of command.

While Gordon had been scraping debris off the station flight ramp, a single Coast Guard Falcon jet could be seen crossing over the miles of desolation. On it was Rear Admiral Robert F. Duncan, commander of the Coast Guard's Eighth District. He came in from Houston, by way of Alexandria, as he put it "at 800 feet, following the 60-knot wind band." He would later say there was a Petty Officer on that flight "who runs when he sees me . . ."

It was a real white-knuckle sleigh ride, but the overview from altitude told enough of the story: destruction as far south as Venice and as far east as Mobile. Another passenger on the flight described Pass Christian as "foundations and matchsticks," and Waveland, it seemed, was even worse. They had attempted to land at Mobile, but high winds prevented that, and so they returned to Houston. There was no way to exaggerate what they had seen. The Coast Guard response was plain: Admiral Duncan pulled out all the stops and the CG began "ramping up" with everything available to throw into the fray.[16]

Besides calling up security, electronics, communications, and administrative emergency support units from all over the Coast Guard, there were the all-important search and rescue workhorses—aircraft and boats. And decisions had to be made about priorities: how far to cut back normal operations elsewhere in order to relocate men and machines to the Gulf Coast; what types of airplanes, helicopters, and vessels to retain at their home stations; and what types were most appropriate for the taxing operations in the disaster area.

The types of helicopters available made the choice obvious. The HH-60 Jayhawks were significantly larger than the HH-65 Dolphins, with the added advantage of longer "legs"—the ability to stay in the air for longer missions. Both these factors made them more appropriate for carrying large numbers of survivors out of harm's way. However, the new "Charlie" (third generation) version of the

HH-65 was coming into the CG inventory. These had been re-engined and were capable of carrying up to ten people at once with a full load of fuel—in sharp contrast to the earlier '65s which could only airlift about three survivors in addition to the crew.[17]

As to how many aircraft could be relocated to the disaster area from the various CG units, those decisions were made by negotiations among the district commanders and, in particular, Admiral Vivien Crea, commander of the Coast Guard's Atlantic area. In effect, when it was a choice between retaining a particular aircraft at its home station "in case it might be needed" or sending it to the place where the need was immediate and obvious, the latter consideration was the trump hand. In the end, as a senior officer put it, "We responded with everything that we could . . . We didn't have anything else to respond with without shutting down units."[18]

The first results of these efforts were quickly seen. Normally in the immediate New Orleans area there were four helicopters, four fixed wing aircraft, and sixteen cutters. Within twelve hours of Katrina's landfall there were 21 CG helicopters, seven fixed wing aircraft, and 24 cutters assigned to support rescue operations in New Orleans and environs.[19]

In fact, the first of the outside aid had already arrived. Six additional helicopters would fly into the New Orleans area that afternoon and evening—four from Mobile and two from Houston.[20] The HH-60 piloted by Lt. Cmdr. Vislay has been mentioned above. Another HH-60 under Cmdr. Patrick Gorman arrived shortly afterwards and immediately set to work. His crew included rescue swimmer Joel M. Sayers. Sayers made a direct deployment to a roof where a woman indicated that her husband was trapped in the attic, unable to use his legs. The hole through which she had crawled was too small for her husband, so Sayers attempted to enlarge it by hand. When this did not work he opted to break off the attempt until he could find an appropriate tool. To identify the house from the air, Sayers left a brightly colored cloth attached to a vent pipe, then hoisted the woman off the roof. When they landed at the drop-off zone, Sayers located a fire axe—apparently from an abandoned fire truck—reloaded the woman, and returned to the house. Sayers said:

"I looked back into the hole in the roof, and the husband looked surprised to see me." Sayers yelled for him to stay clear, and then he chopped through the roof and extricated him.[21] This scenario, including the use of fire axes, became a common one as the Katrina rescues continued. Part of this rescue was videotaped by another crewmember and a fifteen-second clip appeared on national television. Sayers was later named Person of the Week by ABC News.[22]

The third Jayhawk was commanded by Lt. Cmdr. Scott Langum. Langum's distinction was the first use of night vision goggles. He was also met with distinct handicaps: he had arrived after dark, had performed no daylight reconnaissance, and was faced with a city nearly blacked out by power failures. His aircraft made at least three successful rescue hoists that night, maneuvering among darkened towers, power lines, and 1000-foot antennae guywires.[23] Langum's accomplishments point to another factor in the Coast Guard's successes in the following days: only Coast Guard aviators were regularly trained in the use of night vision goggles.

On one of the Air Station Houston helicopters that arrived shortly after the storm cleared was AST2 Chris Monville, rescue swimmer, in a crew led by Lt. Olav Saboe, and Lt. jg. Shay Williams. Their flight mechanic was AMT3 Mike Colbath. Flying at 300 feet, they at first saw nothing but subdivisions full of houses with water "all the way up to the shingles," Monville recalled. Their first hoist was a man who had cut his way through the roof, and his dog. After that, "other than for sleep, for the next four days we didn't stop."[24]

One of Monville's next rescues was a woman on board a shrimp boat with a broken femur and six-inch gash to the bone. The trick was to carefully get her into the basket and hoist in such a way as to avoid the tangle of rigging. Colbath and Monville worked smoothly, each anticipating the other's needs and the hoist went smoothly "in not-so-perfect conditions."[25]

Monville's next job was on the ground: they had flown to St. Bernard High School and found over 400 people there, along with firefighters and local volunteers. Monville ended up doing triage, determining who needed immediate medical attention, then physically moving them to a hoist point. He said, "We'd carry them out of a window or off the roof to hoist them into the helicopter. People who could not walk, we'd carry them."[26]

Priorities became necessary, and Monville was in the unenviable position of making life and death decisions. "I'd have to explain that we could only take so many at a time, you're walking, breathing, talking—you're fine. We have to take the sick first. Everyone comes to you, and they all have a story . . . You . . . take the worst out first." The sick were taken from the high school to a nearby hospital or other dry location, in this instance, Belle Chasse High School where there were EMS services. Monville stayed at this task until the pilots told him to quit for the day.[27]

Another Houston helicopter was piloted by Lt. Jason Smith, a former Army officer and Bosnia, Afghanistan, and Iraq veteran. Smith flew into New Orleans Air Station, refueled, and opted to search in the northern part of the city, with his helicopter still bucking 50–70 knot winds and unpredictable gusts—all of which meant that constant split-second decisions were the rule, simply to maintain lift and airspeed. Hovering with a basket-load of people added yet another challenge to the job.[28]

Smith made many hoists that afternoon and evening, but one stood out and illustrated some of the quandaries the CG pilots and swimmers met on a minute-to-minute basis through the early days of the emergency. In this instance, in the dark, Smith lowered the swimmer, AST3 Charles "Chuck" Medema, to assess two men in a small boat tied to a tree next to a flooded house. It turned out their situation was less critical than that of their mother, who was on life sustaining equipment and floating on a mattress nearby. Furthermore, this lady's mother was trapped in the house. The men had attempted to coax their grandmother into the boat, but she could not swim and refused. These complications were compounded by the helicopter's fuel situation: there would not be enough airtime to prepare and lift all these people.

Smith left the swimmer in place and returned for fuel. Additionally, he would have to obtain permission to complete the rescue because he and his crew had long passed their maximum allowable hours (six) in the air.[29] Meanwhile, Medema assessed the situation and decided he needed to bring the mother out of the house and onto the boat. He swam all the way around the home, shouting until he found her. After reassuring her that he would not let go, she climbed out a window, braved the water, and Medema buddy-towed her to the boat.[30]

When Smith returned with the helo, having explained the situation to the Operations Officer, Medema opted for the "double lift" method for the older lady. He wrapped blankets around her and attached two strops for the lift. After securing the life support equipment to the rig, he signaled for the lift and successfully brought the lady up to safety.[31]

The next dilemma was where to take her—it had to be a hospital, yet most of the hospitals were without power or were otherwise unable to take another patient. Eventually they landed at an unlit hospital, only to learn that the power outage included the elevators. The swimmer and flight mechanic carried her down several flights of stairs to reach the emergency facility. This did not complete their day: they had to return for the other two men in the boat.[32]

It had been an unforgettable day for the crew, but it was particularly memorable for AST3 Medema. It was literally his first day as a Coast Guard rescue swimmer. His commanding officer had signed Medema's official certification letter only hours earlier, while the swimmer was in the helicopter en route to the disaster area.[33]

⊙

While the Coast Guard's aviators were en route from Houma and elsewhere, another small drama was occurring at Coast Guard Station New Orleans, located at Bucktown just west of the 17th Street Canal on Lake Pontchartrain. Station commanding officer Chief Warrant Officer Dan Brooks and others had evacuated their small boats to Covington, on the north shore of Lake Pontchartrain, before the storm. They were joined by some of the displaced boat crews from Station Grand Isle. This latter group, trailering a 17-foot jet drive boat and a 23-footer, had been ordered into New

Orleans to do search and rescue rather than immediately return to their home base. The night after the storm passed, the CG personnel from both units searched for several hours for a debris-free launching site on Lake Pontchartrain, finally locating one at Lee's Landing on the northwest side. No one had much sleep that night, and in the morning they launched their boats. They gingerly navigated through the debris and fallen trees to reach the lake, carefully avoiding hazards which could have snagged and holed their lightly built boats. By the time they had reached the lake's south shore, it was mid-afternoon.[34]

As they approached the station, they received a taste of the destructive power of the storm. As one of the crew remembered, "I'm looking for my visual references and I don't see them. I'm looking on radar and I still don't see them [sic] there is nothing but pilings." The dock itself had washed away, so they tied the boats to the seawall.[35]

Immediately they were met by a civilian stranger at the station, who explained that he had been airlifted from a roof. Soon the returning Coast Guardsmen were confronted with some sixty people, some of whom had been dropped off by rescue helicopters. Their rescuers obviously did not know the building was empty. The rescued were desperate for food and water and were in the process of looting and vandalizing the station. They were caught with pilfered computers and phones in hand and had destroyed the crew quarters and kitchen, spreading filth and feces on the walls and floors. They had even allowed their pets to relieve themselves on the carpets. Fortunately, the crowd had been unable to break into the unit's ammunition locker.[36]

Despite being outnumbered by about eight to one, control had to be established in this volatile atmosphere. CWO Brooks first stationed a security guard at the broken-down front gate, thus preventing more interlopers from entering. When the station personnel noticed someone throwing something out a window, they investigated and found drugs.

The Coast Guardsmen rounded up all the civilians into one area and, after a tense facedown, instituted a thorough search and frisk. They turned up and seized a plethora of contraband: five bags of marijuana, two handguns, fifteen knives, and twenty-five bottles of alcohol. Once control was established, Brooks and his people were able to attempt to meet the basic needs of the survivors. They would be allowed to remain temporarily at the station. Food and water would be provided, though the latter was in short supply and had to be rationed out for the next two days. The group was later evacuated. Meanwhile, the station personnel and the crew from Grand Isle managed to return to their primary mission.[37]

It would be the next morning before serious search and rescue could begin, after emergency power was established as well as rudimentary communications. Station New Orleans would become one of the major hubs of water-based rescues in the next few days.

⊙

At this early point in the narrative, it is appropriate to discuss the evacuees themselves. At one point in researching this work it was suggested that a more balanced approach would include numerous evacuee accounts of their rescue and assistance from the Coast Guard.

The first problem was not that there was no venue where survivors publicly told their stories: there were numerous websites for this. However, there was no efficient way to locate Coast Guard–specific narratives and discuss the evacuees' storm stories.

Other problems soon became obvious. First, many people simply did not remember who or what agency actually rescued them. In the stress of the moment all they recalled was someone in a harness and work uniform and a few harrowing seconds hanging between land and a noisy helicopter. By the same token, the evacuee narratives were rarely detailed or specific. While many had much to say if they had been stranded without water for days, all they had to say about the rescue was that they were grateful to be out of danger, and "thanks" to the individual who carried them to safety.

These factors led me to reconsider the use of evacuee stories. This is not to deemphasize their role or importance. However, the real story in this book is that of the people—and the organization—that worked to and beyond their potential to bring rescue and relief to thousands who were essentially helpless.

4

The Maritime and Environmental Disaster

Hurricane Katrina, on the national stage, was a cataclysm involving thousands of ordinary people, homes, and possessions. The stories of human suffering, pain, heroic rescues and, unfortunately, miscalculations and incompetence on the part of various agencies and individuals, dominated headlines and other media for weeks.

For the U.S. Coast Guard, the story went far beyond the search and rescue operations, though these gained the service a matchless reputation with the public. There were, however, other facets of the storm and aftermath that were uniquely Coast Guard responsibilities. Though not the stuff of headlines, these were vital to public safety as well as the economic wellbeing of the entire Gulf Coast.

Historically, the Coast Guard has been the caretaker of the entire national maritime environment. This entails keeping the sea and coastal lanes open and free from hazards, as well as providing and maintaining all the necessary aids to navigating these lanes. In more recent years, as exemplified by such events as the *Exxon*

Valdez oil spill, the service gained significant responsibility for hazardous material containment and cleanup on the coasts and rivers. In practical terms, the storm left the Coast Guard with literally hundreds of jobs: ships, boats, and offshore drilling platforms, wrecked or disabled, grounded or washed ashore; buoys and navigation markers missing, damaged, or inoperable; and, not least, hazardous and health-threatening oil and chemical spills. Thus there were weeks and months of hard work ahead, scattered over hundreds of square miles of the Gulf and inland waterways.

It is appropriate to delineate the extent of the job they faced. The Mississippi Gulf Coast maritime environment is the largest and most important in the United States; New Orleans itself is the fourth largest port in the world, in terms of tonnage in and out.[1] Furthermore, four of the eleven largest U.S. ports were affected by the hurricane. These were: ports of Southern Louisiana, New Orleans, Baton Rouge, and Plaquemines. The port of Southern Louisiana is the second largest in the nation in terms of tonnage handled, slightly behind the port of Houston. These four Louisiana ports handle over 400 million tons of cargo annually.[2]

The Gulf coast is the site of the confluence of the shipping lanes to the United States from all over the world, with the outflow of traffic from the largest river basin in the country, the Mississippi. Thus there were hundreds of barges, mostly on the river and tributaries, plus large numbers of container ships thrown into the mix. Finally, one has to add the oil industry contribution: tankers, hundreds of oil and gas platforms, and the support infrastructure—including refineries and pipelines from Texas to the Florida Panhandle. In total, the storm endangered over 250 miles of the Mississippi River and 200 miles of the Gulf Intracoastal Waterway.[3] Thus there was immense potential for economic dislocation and hardship from this hurricane.

Oil industry statistics emphasize the importance of the area's oil and gas resources. Before the storm about 29 percent of the nation's crude oil and 20 percent of its natural gas came from Gulf coastal waters.[4]

Specifically, Chevron oil's largest refinery, at Pascagoula, Mississippi, took a major hit from Katrina, and the facility did not regain normal production for six weeks after the storm. This, plus the destruction of 121 oil platforms and rigs and other damage reduced Gulf crude production by over 77 percent and gas output by over 64 percent.[5]

Of course the oil industry was not the only entity wrenched by the storm. The shipping industry itself required major waterways for huge oceangoing container ships. The barge traffic required clear passage via the Mississippi to New Orleans. The burgeoning aviation and shipbuilding enterprises on the Gulf coast had vital interests in the maintenance of the waterways. And, finally, the large commercial and recreational fishing industry was severely hurt by Katrina.

Thus there was much pressure on the Coast Guard to reopen the ports closed by the storm and to ensure that the waterways affected by Katrina be available and safe for navigation as soon as possible.

Safety on the waterways requires accurate and highly visible marking. Therefore there are hundreds of buoys, range lights, day markers, and fog signals. These mark water depth, hazards, shoals, shipping channels, hazards to navigation, etcetera. Before the storm there were 3,268 aids to navigation in the affected area. These ranged from major lighted buoys weighing up to six tons, to small land-based signs and lights.[6]

The storm destroyed or damaged beyond repair approximately 1,800 buoys and beacons. (This statistic applied to the total for Katrina and Rita).[7] It would be the Coast Guard's task to determine the condition of, and repairs needed for, each navigational aid, and prioritize repair and replacement according to the relative importance of the waterway being marked.

Of course, the maritime assets most vulnerable to the fury of the storm were the ships, boats, and barges afloat in its path. Some 3,000 vessels of all types were "displaced" by the hurricane. They were seen everywhere: between trees far inland, smashed together in groups against bridges and abutments, and piled on top of houses, vehicles, and roads. And this did not include those vessels that had vanished entirely, lying at the bottom of rivers, inlets, and the Gulf waters.[8]

Some approximation of the numbers can be deduced from a mid-September, 2005, Coast Guard salvage response report. Nearly three weeks after Katrina, 688 fishing vessels, motor vessels, and barges were listed as casualties. Of these, 166 were sunk. The remainder were damaged, aground, partially submerged, or adrift and therefore hazards to navigation.[9]

A short list of some of the larger individual cases includes: 27,500 ton tanker M/V *Team Leopard,* on top of barges on the Mississippi near New Orleans; oil platform *Mobil Gem Thompson,* adrift; sixteen empty barges adrift a mile from the above tanker; an eighty-barge breakaway near Port Sulphur; a 655-foot freighter, *Polyhronis,* aground; and Parker 21 oil rig wedged against a railroad bridge in Mobile.[10]

The Coast Guard responsibility for these vessels entailed monitoring and enforcing their salvage, refloating, and repair, as well as marking waterways where the vessels created hazards to navigation. Though no major waterways were completely shut down by these vessels, it would be months before the waters were completely free of hazards and wrecked boats.

Finally, the environmental impact of the storm was significant. There were approximately 4,800 small oil spills. There were seven major spills (defined as releasing over 100,000 gallons of contaminants) due to the two storms, five of which released over 1 million gallons each, including the Murphy oil spill mentioned previously. Additionally, there were five medium spills, defined as releasing over 10,000 gallons into the waters. It is estimated that over 9 million gallons of various contaminants went into Gulf and river waters during the two storms. For comparison, the *Exxon Valdez* deposited 11 million gallons of oil into Alaskan waters in 1989.[11]

These statistics make it clear that after August 29, 2005, the Coast Guard was faced with the most challenging aids to navigation and waterways management task in its history: the rectifying of the maritime environment in all its manifestations. From buoys to oil spills to damaged shipping, these infrastructure repair missions would form a large part of the Coast Guard's workload for literally years to come.

First Responses

Mississippi and Alabama

Katrina moved northward at around 15 mph, so its eastern half swiped through the Gulf coast a bit later on August 29 than it had through the New Orleans area. Consequently, Coast Guard air operations centered at Mobile—in particular at the CG air training center there—were impossible until around 5 P.M. that afternoon when wind velocities dropped below tropical force levels.

At that point Sector Mobile, which bordered Sector New Orleans on the east, had two priorities. First was to launch their own aircraft and boats for local and area search and rescue. Second was to prepare the air base at Aviation Training Center as the staging area for the massive influx of CG aircraft flying in from elsewhere, en route to New Orleans. As the largest CG air facility close to the stricken city and adjacent coast, Mobile would become the major nexus for fueling, maintenance, and repair of Coast Guard aircraft during the coming weeks.

The latter tasks involved adapting the existing hangars and flight line to handle as many aircraft as possible, as well as beefing up communications and air traffic control to deal with hundreds of flights, in and out, every day. Secondly, increased demand for aircraft maintenance and repair—far beyond the normal needs of Mobile—would require a constant source of parts and material, so a system of replenishing supplies was necessary to ferry parts from wherever in the CG they could be found. In practice this meant regular and ad hoc shuttles to other air stations, in particular to the CG aircraft repair and supply center at Elizabeth City, North Carolina. Finally, the base itself had to prepare to house and feed hundreds of new personnel, men and women on site specifically for the emergency on the Gulf Coast.

While these mundane but time consuming tasks were in process, Mobile-based helicopters launched into hazardous winds and rain in the late afternoon of August 29, seeking the victims of the storm. The first off the line was Lt. Cmdr. William E. Sasser, Jr., in an HH-65, flying low with night vision goggles along the Alabama/Mississippi coast. The first rescue was in 50-knot gusts, which certainly hampered, but did not prevent it from succeeding. The rescue swimmer was lowered to a flooded home, and Sasser maintained his position for some twenty-five minutes while the swimmer brought two survivors out through a hole in their roof. At least four other helos from Mobile were in action that night. Two of them rescued fishermen from shrimp boats washed far inland. Cmdr. Michael McGraw extracted three survivors from a boat nearly a mile from the coast, while Lt. Cmdr. Thomas S. Swanberg's helicopter rescued eight from a pair of boats equally distant from the shore. The rescue was complicated by close-in trees and tangled ship's rigging, which forced Swanberg to thread the basket and swimmer down from over 100 feet.[1]

Lt. Cmdr. David W. Edwards probably had the most arduous flight of this first evening. On approaching a demolished apartment complex in the dark, he lowered the swimmer, who learned that among the survivors was a woman in near-fatal diabetic shock. The woman and swimmer were immediately lifted and the patient flown to Biloxi Regional Hospital. Then Edwards and his crew returned to assist the remaining survivors.[2]

In all, by around noon the next day, Mobile had fielded five HH-65s and seven HH-60s, as well as three Falcon HU-25 jets, the latter to provide communications for the helos. Use of night vision goggles had enabled round-the-clock sorties and contributed to the rescue of 150 survivors of the storm.[3]

Meanwhile, on Tuesday, August 30, the displaced Coast Guardsmen began to filter back from their safe havens upcountry. Most of them were not prepared for the scope of the damage to their workplaces and homes. At Station Gulfport, where they had confidently shut their pets in the most secure area of the admin building, the Coasties returned to find only the structure's steel skeleton—presiding over rubble and shards little larger than what one could carry in one hand. The power of the storm had displaced a 1,700 lb. weapons storage safe and a 6,000 gallon fuel tank found 70 yards from its original location. There was no sign of the cats and dogs. CWO Steve Lyons, the station commanding officer, returned to what had been his office, looking for anything salvageable. He found only two items: one was the ceremonial shovel used for the building's groundbreaking; the other was his coffee mug. He had left the mug on his desk before evacuating. The desk was gone, but the mug was where the desk had been. Appropriately, the shovel would be used again for dedicating the new station structure. And Mayday, the unit doggie, eventually turned up. He had been found by someone living inland and was returned to the station in October—somewhat dazed, but healthy.[4]

The shock of the destruction was particularly felt by those who had sailed their cutters west to Sabine, Texas before the cataclysm. They were anxious to see their home base again. When the boats came over the horizon and the binoculars came out there was dead silence on deck. It was eerily quiet: the post-storm sea was calm and the skies were, as one meteorologist put it, the "prettiest blue . . . you've ever seen."[5] It seemed a cruel irony that those same skies could have been responsible for the scene before them. The shoreline looked like a scene from a post-apocalyptic movie. Only gaunt steel girders marked where the station and outbuildings had been; the rest was rubble.[6]

Seven of the men and women from the station had lost their homes to the storm. With the station gone, they had no place to go. Eventually they returned to the temporary housing at the Air National Guard base north of town. It would be weeks before anything resembling normality would return to the station.[7]

However, a different view of the station, from the air, was symbolic of better things to come. Capt. David Callahan, commander of the training center, on a flyover from Mobile, was shocked by the total destruction of the site. Then Callahan noticed another lone survivor: a single light pole remained upright on the pier. Someone had rigged a line to it and raised the U.S. and Coast Guard flags. Over the destruction, the flags were still there.[8]

The morning of August 30 saw a frenetic pace at Mobile. On the operational control side, the storm had damaged a large part of the main hangar roof, making the second floor unusable. All the administrative and communications staff had to be relocated.[9]

The communication and accompanying air traffic control problem was still unresolved when the first of the many CG aircraft began arriving from other units to assist in the disaster response. At 2:30 A.M., HH-60 CG6038 landed on an unlit field with no approach or tower control. Cdr. Bill McMeekin and crew had come in from Clearwater, encountering Katrina rain bands for two hours of their three-and-a-half hour flight. On the ground, they were given a briefing on conditions in New Orleans as they were known at the time, which was, by dint of lack of communications with the beleaguered city, exceedingly sketchy. By 4:00 A.M. they were in the air and en route to New Orleans.[10]

Meanwhile, as air operations were getting underway at the training center, other coastal Alabama CG units were also struggling to get back to business, patrolling the coast and, when necessary, rescuing people. The CG small boat station at Dolphin Island, a few miles due south of the entrance to Mobile Bay, was launching search and rescue boats by first light on August 30. There was little else to do on the island: electricity was being provided by a generator, and food was limited to a stash of Meals Ready to Eat (MREs), on which they would subsist for several days to come. Their 41-foot utility boat and two 25-footers—just back from Mobile where they had waited out the storm—were joined by two 47-foot motor lifeboats and additional 25-foot high speed boats, arrived from CG stations at Destin, Panama City, and Pensacola, Florida—areas less damaged by the storm. Fortunately, at least for the crew of one of the 47-footers, this day and its mission was uneventful. The four-member crew, under the command of Bosun's Mate 1st Class (BM1) Michael Alexander, was to maintain a Coast Guard presence and assist mariners. The latter was particularly critical in the post-hurricane waters. The storm had displaced or destroyed buoys and channel markings needed for deep water vessels transiting the otherwise shallow waters of Mobile Bay.[11]

The 47-footer's patrol area went as far as Gulfport, and they found the waters relatively free of traffic. Certainly the usual pleasure boaters were nowhere to be seen, and small commercial fishing boats were no doubt in port, or worse, with their owners surveying the storm damage. The closure of 290 miles of the Intracoastal Waterway and all the ports from New Orleans to Panama City likewise limited the waterborne traffic on this day. The 47-footer's approaches to the shore were limited as well. At Biloxi, for instance, the debris field extended miles into the Gulf, making it hazardous to attempt an approach to the shore. Clear water was only assured over 5 miles out. The crew's patrol lasted eight hours and put them back at Dolphin station that afternoon.[12]

Elsewhere along the Mississippi/Alabama coast, Coast Guard stations and crews were returning to find their lives changed forever. At the CG station in Pascagoula, half of their personnel and many on CGC *Shamal*, a 179-foot coastal patrol boat, had lost everything to the storm.[13] Damage to CG facilities proportionally decreased as the power of the storm abated on its eastern reaches. Station Destin, Florida on a barrier island east of Pensacola was on generator power but remained in commission. Panama City reported no significant damage.[14]

At Mobile, on the second day after the storm, search and rescue flights were intensified over the Mississippi/Alabama coast, as well as over New Orleans proper. Furthermore, another four helicopters arrived from air stations at Atlantic City, Clearwater, and Elizabeth City, North Carolina.[15]

As the aircrews ramped up their search and rescue flights, the pressure on them grew as daylight revealed the massive impact of the storm. The commanding officer at the air station, Capt. David Callahan, was aware of the growing mental and physical pressures, but the reality hit home when a veteran HH-65 pilot returned from a mission and, whether from exhaustion or the horrors he had witnessed, threw up.[16]

Flights that day emphasized search and rescue, particularly evacuation of the seriously ill or injured to local hospitals. Early on the August 30, Lt. Joseph W. Klatt, in an HH-65, encountered a group of survivors on a debris-strewn beach. The rescue swimmer was deployed to assist nearly 150 survivors there, and later another eight with severe burns and other injuries.

At Waveland, one of the hardest hit neighborhoods, there were at least two urgent rescues. Lt. Cornelius Cummings piloted his HH-65 over a flooded forest to hoist three women who had been treading water for eight hours. One was elderly and diabetic; the other two were her daughters. Cummings maneuvered the rescue swimmer among the trees to the top of a nearby boat. The swimmer hoisted the women to the boat, and then Cummings lifted them to safety. A second group rescue was handled by Lt. Charles E. Webb and another HH-65, along the devastated Waveland shoreline. Five panic stricken survivors were trapped by debris, and Webb dropped the rescue swimmer to calm and prepare them for rescue. Once they were on board, Webb made the bold decision to dump his extra fuel to allow him to bring out more survivors—this in spite of not knowing if alternative fuel sites were nearby. In nearby Bay St. Louis, Lt. John F. Durelle dodged his HH-65 repeatedly through high pines to bring eight survivors to safety.[17]

As the Mobile-based aircrews wrested survivors from danger on the Gulf shores as well as in New Orleans, the Air Training

Center was being converted for emergency operations. One of the priorities was to restore the communications interrupted when the operations center had succumbed to wind damage. The center was then moved to the Bachelor Officer/Enlisted Quarters building. In the interim, a local radio station had lent its VHF facility to enable contact between dispatch and aircraft in flight. However, by early Wednesday, August 31, the communications center was up and running, though still on generator power.[18]

On the aircraft support and maintenance front, CWO3 Kenneth Hardenbrook, head of the aviation engineering division, was implementing procedures and assigning people to deal with unprecedented levels of high priority work. This involved adding new maintenance personnel into schedules as needed, and assuring that fuel as well as parts and supplies were available when called for, twenty-four hours a day. The latter involved coordination with other Coast Guard parts depots to maintain a stockpile of parts for all types of aircraft being used for the emergency: HH-65s, HH-60s, HU-25s, and C-130s. Simultaneously, he supervised the repairs to the storm-damaged building.[19]

These activities were only a portion of those in progress at the Air Station as the demand for labor, equipment, and supplies ballooned beyond all precedents. In these early days of the Katrina emergency, few Coast Guard personnel—whether aircrews, boat drivers, enlisted men, officers, or civilians—escaped the tyranny of the immediate. Leisure time would not exist, officially, for days to come.

6

Wet Tuesday in New Orleans

Monday, August 29, will be forever inscribed in New Orleans history. All day the city was hunkered down in the unrelenting winds and rising waters. Only scattered rescue efforts were possible before sunset that day. A few preliminary flyovers had only served to put the Coast Guard and other agencies on notice of the magnitude of the work to come.

Tuesday morning, rescuers began to converge on the city from all directions and by any means: land, water, or air. The task was complicated by the flooding, nearly eliminating possible rescue by land. Fortunately, the Coast Guard was in its element on water and in the air, and, by virtue of speed and access, the CG's helicopters had begun their work the afternoon and night before.

On the water, small boat search and rescue operations began early on that watery Tuesday. Boat crews from Marine Safety Unit Morgan City, MSU Baton Rouge, Integrated Support Command New Orleans, Station New Orleans, and Station Grand Isle were on scene that morning, as well as Disaster Assistance Response Teams from Sector/Group Upper Mississippi River.

The group from Integrated Support Command, an administrative unit providing computer support, personnel administration, dispensary services, et cetera, had evacuated to the Coast Guard LORAN (Long Range Navigation) Station at Grangeville, Louisiana before the storm. According to their "normal" hurricane plan, their first responsibility was to return to their facility and restore their computer systems and administrative infrastructure, then return to regular operations. However, in this instance, on Monday night when they contacted Sector New Orleans and relayed their intentions to do this, the plan went by the board. As Lt. Cdr. Darryl Schaffer, the unit's disaster response officer, put it, Sector told them to "bag the computers, we don't care about them. Go pick people off rooftops."[1]

And so Tuesday morning found Lt. Cmdr. Schaffer not in an office sitting in front of a refractory computer, but on the Interstate 10/610 split interchange, about 2 miles south of Lake Pontchartrain and east of the Industrial Canal, overseeing the launching of two small boats into the waters of the devastated city.

Acquiring the boats had been an ad hoc activity as well: one was an 18-foot "morale" boat ("morale" boats were not owned by the CG, but were purchased with recreational funds raised by members of the individual units), borrowed from the LORAN station. The second vessel was a 16-foot flat-bottomed boat fitted with an outboard motor belonging to the New Orleans CG aids to navigation team. It had been stored at Grangeville to be retrieved after the storm. Shaffer commandeered both boats.[2]

The ten Coast Guardsmen operating the two boats (designated ISC Boat Number One and ISC Boat Number Two) were a diverse lot of unseasoned mariners: an Electronics Mate, a Fireman, Damage Controlman, Information Systems Technician, Health Service Technician, Electronics Technician, three machinery technicians, and only one Seaman. Led by Lt. Cmdr Schaffer they drove as far as the dry road would allow and halted at the interchange to look around.

One of the petty officers shouted, "Hey Mr. Schaffer, there's somebody waving a shirt over there!"

Schaffer immediately gave the word: "Go, launch both boats. Let's go."

So they launched into the uncertain waters at 9:30 A.M., and returned with their first survivors less than ten minutes later.[3] This informal contingent of men and one woman made the first Coast Guard waterborne rescues in New Orleans after the storm.

The ten mismatched Coasties, untrained in search and rescue, unarmed, and equipped with only lifejackets and sunblock, rescued around fifty survivors in their first hour on the scene.[4] It was a typical Coast Guard response: the lifesaving mission is first priority; go with what you have and make do.

The early rescues were in the vicinity of the 17th Street levee break. The survivors, who had assumed that the wind was their only serious worry, had been shocked at the sudden deluge and had fled to their roofs with little more than the clothes on their backs. Schaffer remembered one lady in a nightgown and slippers, with no identification, breaking down. "She didn't have a house. If I remember it, she was even the one that watched her mother die."[5]

These two CG boats were soon joined at the "Split" by FEMA task forces from Texas, Virginia, and California as well as other volunteers. A joint command was set up and about forty boats were soon operating from that location. By the end of the day an estimated 340 survivors had been brought to safety by the combined Coast Guard and FEMA rescuers at the I-10/610 Split.[6]

Among the other Coast Guard first responders in New Orleans waters that morning were the personnel from Station New Orleans, already frazzled by their dangerous confrontation within their own walls. There was some delay early on as they awaited instructions, but an hour passed and all they heard from the Incident Command Post in Alexandria and the authorities in Baton Rouge was a suggestion that they continue to wait until the situation "clarified." Exasperated and without formal instructions, the Coasties finally walked out and launched into the job.[7]

The first to go were Boatswain's Mate Second Class Jessica Guidroz and two others who trailered a 17-foot jet-drive boat, accompanied by the Grand Isle crew under BM2 Christopher Hebert and a 23-footer. They launched from the I-10/I-610 Split into Metairie and Lakeview. These areas were among the hardest hit by the overflow from Pontchartrain.

Trolling through these neighborhoods was a hair-raising ride. BM2 Hebert, who had gone to school in New Orleans, was boating on streets where he had driven as a teenager, running over at least six submerged autos.

Eventually, the two boats had to separate because the superstructure of the larger 23-footer could not pass under overhead power lines. While the Grand Isle crew worked to lift the lines, the 17-footer went on through the street-cum-canals, with the crew banging on roofs, looking for open attic windows, and yelling. They were directed to a house where a couple had refused earlier rescue attempts, saying they had heard FEMA was not allowing dogs to be rescued, and they were not leaving their two pets. Besides, they said, they had enough supplies for a couple days. Guidroz said they would probably need more than two days' worth of supplies. As for the pets she reassured them, "Just bring the dogs and we'll figure out something to do with the dogs." The couple asked for time to pack so Guidroz hove off and returned later, this time with a larger boat, and picked them up. Not long after, she landed them safely at the I-10 collection point.[8]

The next rescue was more complicated, but still typical of the situation in the engulfed city. The Coast Guardsmen were told that an old lady was trapped in an apartment building so they made their way to it. It was a particularly bad street. Guidroz said, " . . . like every tree and power line had fallen into the water and then cars everywhere. You couldn't see the cars so we were running over cars and we'd hit something and we were like 'What was that?'" Slowly they picked their way along, but eventually decided it did not matter what they hit. They had no communications except occasional text message service, and besides, they concluded, even if they had communications, if they sank the boat there would be "nobody to come get us anyway."[9]

"So we just kept going," remembered Guidroz.

The crew of the 17-footer found a three-story building with the first floor completely flooded. After tying up, they began a door-banging search for the rumored survivor. Soon they resorted to busting in doors all through the structure, but still, they could find no old lady in distress. Instead, they discovered an "old guy" on the top floor who refused assistance. It took forty-five minutes to convince him to leave. He was taken to the CG station and then trucked to the FEMA collection area.[10]

Guidroz and crew then refueled, trailered the boat to the Jefferson Highway, and re-launched. The little crew then encountered a group of evacuees who had been dropped off in a dry median area and now wanted to be taken to a FEMA collection area. But Guidroz and her crew were not taking people who could move on their own. Even if the water was waist deep they could have walked. Guidroz reported that some of the men got "really rowdy and all upset" and began advancing to force themselves onto the boat. She was armed and thought, "For the first time in my life I will have to shoot somebody."

Instead, Guidroz and her two crewmen pushed their boat off to a safe distance. If their would-be attackers would not walk to FEMA, they were also unlikely to chase them through the water.[11]

Once out of danger, the boat crew resumed their work, picking up several older people, including one lady so frail they could not determine if she was alive. They first attempted to drop all of the survivors at the local hospital. But that facility would only take the one obviously critical lady—who at last, when being put in a wheelchair, showed some signs of life. The rest were taken to the FEMA drop off point at I-10.

The crowded scene at I-10 was not encouraging. Guidroz recalls, "... that place was just mass chaos." People were running all over. They fought to get their family members into ambulances. Apparently without weapons, the National Guard was unable to maintain order. It was Guidroz's and crew's last stop before returning to the CG station. It had been a long, harrowing day.[12]

BM2 Guidroz's sortie was, unfortunately, typical of the first day in the drowned city. The most basic communications were nonexistent. Her crew went from situation to situation literally by word of mouth. Much time and motion was wasted searching in places which may well have been visited before they arrived. For instance, buildings already searched were yet to be identified or marked. And, no one knew whether a shelter or health facility would accept survivors until the rescuers and their evacuees physically arrived at the door.

The dangers were too numerous to list: debris, downed trees and power lines, submerged cars and other objects—all inimical to safe passage for rescue boats and their crews. And the objects of the search presented their own obstacles: reluctance to leave their homes, or, conversely, people attempting by force to take precedence when offered rescue.

Meanwhile, the 23-footer crew from Grand Isle, which had been delayed by the power lines, cruised in the vicinity of Veterans Highway which parallels the south shore of Lake Pontchartrain. They rescued some twenty to thirty survivors and worked until 9:00 P.M. that evening, returning to the station for barely palatable MREs.[13]

The Coast Guard contingent from Marine Safety Unit Baton Rouge had a more productive day, with a dangerous ending. Lt. Cmdr. Shannon Gilreath, their commanding officer, contacted the CG Incident Command Post at Baton Rouge and learned that Louisiana Fish and Wildlife was in charge of search and rescue in New Orleans, and any Coast Guard responders should coordinate with them, first at Baton Rouge, then in the city. Gilreath rounded up a three-man crew—BM2 Ryan McKay, BM1 Eric Gonzales, and Marine Safety Technician Second Class Richard Forte—and a 24-foot utility boat, CG 247113, and dispatched them early Tuesday. They arrived at the city and joined a Fish and Wildlife-coordinated convoy from the I-10/Causeway interchange to the St. Claude Street Bridge in the Lower 9th Ward and Arabi. From there they launched the boat, dodging dislodged homes, cars, and power lines as they negotiated the treacherous streets and pulled people from flooded houses.[14] Often they could only navigate the streets by noting the location of light poles—the only objects tall enough to be visible.

One of the more difficult rescues involved two people trapped on the second floor of their home. Downed power lines, cars, and trees, prevented Gilreath's crew from approaching the house from the front. They used their boat hooks to lift power lines high enough to allow the boat between the house and the one next door. Both survivors jumped the 8 feet from their windowsill to the boat.

After the MSU crew had rescued sixty-five survivors they began shuttling them—including residents of the nearby St. Rita's nursing home—from smaller rescue boats to the St. Claude Bridge pickup point. From there a National Guard unit was carrying them to another collection point, thought to be the Superdome.[15]

They worked tirelessly through the day, but at 5:00 P.M. the National Guard unit departed from the St. Claude Bridge location. The crowd of survivors, already frustrated, was left behind without supplies or shelter, and night was coming on. For another hour the unarmed Coast Guardsmen remained in the midst of the increasingly hostile crowd until finally they reloaded the boat and joined a Fish and Wildlife convoy out of the area. However, the situation went from bad to worse when their truck and trailer could not negotiate the abandoned vehicles that partially blocked the road. Gilreath and his crew were separated from the remainder of the convoy and the Fish and Wildlife officers did not wait for them. They were on their own, with nearly nonexistent communications.

Unfortunately, that was not the end of their problems. Gilreath's truck soon developed transmission problems and finally broke down outside of Baton Rouge. They called in requesting not only a replacement truck, but also weapons and body armor. A group of CG reservists came to their rescue, but the exhausted crew of CG247113 was unable to rest until almost three o' clock in the morning when they finally reached a stopping point near Gramercy, Louisiana.[16]

One of the more distant CG units to arrive was a group from Marine Safety Office/USCG Group Upper Mississippi River, based in St. Louis. The two Disaster Assistance Response Teams (DARTs) set up in the city around 2:00 P.M. with thirty-six personnel—thirty-three CG, two CG reserve, and one CG auxiliarist. This group contacted the next of kin of those who refused to leave their dwellings so that they might convince their endangered relatives to evacuate to safety.[17] One DART group worked with New Orleans Police Department officers at St. Claude Avenue and rescued seventy-five people in that area. The other team deployed near Causeway Blvd. and rescued about forty survivors from rooftops.[18]

BM2 Kevin E. Biami, coxswain of a flood punt, was among the DART team rescuers who found 2,000 people in a flooded housing complex. Unable to rescue them all, Biami evaluated the survivors, assessing the priorities. Those with medical problems were taken to safety first.

Later, his crew caught sight of a very pregnant woman who was exhausted from swimming and delirious. Given her condition, they could not pull her into the boat, so Biami led her to the roof of an otherwise submerged car. Only then was he able to slide her into the punt. Her water broke as she fell into the boat. Biami immediately rushed her to the launch point for MEDEVAC.[19] It is estimated that the DART teams rescued about 500 people during this first day on the scene.[20]

After standing down for the day, the DART teams elected to go to the Naval Support base on the East Bank for the night, but they arrived to find near-riot conditions at the facility entrance. The volatile situation prevented one team from entering the base and they resorted to Baton Rouge for the night. Conditions at the Naval Support base were such that the base commander gave instructions for an evacuation plan in the event that the base was overrun by rioters. Fortunately this did not occur.[21]

Another small Coast Guard contingent arrived later that day from the Marine Safety Unit at Morgan City, Louisiana: a 23-foot and a 24-foot boat, along with three trucks, a travel trailer, and a motor home. They arrived at Station New Orleans, where their first job was to patrol the area around the station, and then they pushed off into the city where they worked with the Louisiana Fish and Wildlife personnel and rescued thirteen survivors.[22]

The last major waterborne Coast Guard contingent to arrive that Tuesday was the famous "flotilla," sometimes referred to less seriously as the CG "Armada," which had gathered on the river at Baton Rouge. Chief Warrant Officer Lewald—designated PATCOM (Patrol Commander) by Sector New Orleans—had thirteen vessels on hand, one of which was out of commission and being towed, plus a construction barge. On Monday evening he contacted the state and Coast Guard at Baton Rouge and, as Lewald put it, they said " . . . why don't you go on back downriver and see what you can do."[23]

CW03 Lewald may not have been trained as a fleet commander, but he was a quintessential Coast Guard sailor. Most of his twenty-year career as an enlisted quartermaster and then a warrant-officer boatswain had been spent at sea or on the rivers. A large portion of that had been on the "black hull" fleet, the CG's aids to navigation boats. He had been on the Mississippi for two years, commanding *Pamlico* and in charge of the buoys and markers on the lower Mississippi. He had substantial practical knowledge of the river on which he was about to descend with his mixed flotilla.[24]

Moving a large group of ships down a debris-filled river at night was unsafe to say the least, so the fleet got underway at first light Tuesday. It was about 100 miles from around MM235 (Mile Marker 235) on the river to New Orleans, and though the sense of urgency was felt by all, Lewald's flotilla could do no more than 10 knots throughout the passage, having to conform to the slowest of his vessels. As they moved further and further southeast, even that pace was increasingly difficult to maintain. As Lewald remembered it: "It was like coming down in the middle of winter and all those trees that were 30 and 40 feet are now 10 feet because they're all broken over. So [sic] went from being very green to being very brown and . . . all the tugs and barges and ships up on the levees."[25] They were down to 8 knots or less by the time they reached the city.

The flotilla had left behind Aids to Navigation Boat 55119, and its commanding officer sent out a vehicle to Baton Rouge to make a store run and purchase locally the supplies needed for an extended stay in the ravaged city. Once loaded, 55119 ran down river at speed, caught up with the convoy just above New Orleans, transferred the stores to *Pamlico* while underway, and fell back in line.[26] It was a good example of foresight on the part of these practical senior enlisted members of the service.

They arrived at the Crescent City Connection Bridge, near the Central Business District of New Orleans, after dark. Two of the 41-foot utility boats were the first in. With massive power outages and streets mostly underwater, the entire city was dark and supernaturally quiet, but fires in the distance and emergency flashlights blinking in high rise buildings belied the people still trapped and frantic for rescue.[27]

Almost as soon as he had moored, Lewald was contacted by the Naval Support Activity personnel for assistance: they had 100 people who needed to be moved from their east bank location to the west bank of their facility. The east bank, of course, was contiguous to the breeched levees; the west bank was relatively dry. Lewald later learned that the crowd consisted of forty Navy personnel and sixty civilians. The latter group had showed up at the Navy's gate desperate to get out of downtown.

Lewald immediately dispatched three of his 55-footers and four 41-foot utility boats to the scene. Once the crowd was on the west bank facility, Navy security personnel ushered the civilians out the gate. Later that night, the Coast Guard was taken to task for "dumping" the civilians on the west bank and Lewald had to explain what had actually occurred.[28] It appeared that the Navy personnel at NSA were more preoccupied with their security than assisting refugees.

Once the transfer from East Bank to West Bank was accomplished, Lewald received another radio request. A ferry boat captain from Crescent City Connection Ferry was hoping for assistance: "Would you be willing to help out with the evacuation of St.

Bernard Parish?" The situation was desperate. As parish president A. J. Rodriguez told Louisiana lieutenant governor Mitch Landrieu, "We have only one shelter . . . We have 2,000 people that need evacuating from Chalmette . . . tomorrow it will be 5,000 people."[29]

"Absolutely" was Lewald's immediate response to the ferry captain. He contacted the Navy for permission to use their West Bank area as the drop off point for the St. Bernard Parish evacuees, but to his astonishment the Navy's answer was "no."

The next morning, when the operation began, the Algiers ferry landing, near Algiers Point, became the destination for evacuees collected from Chalmette in St. Bernard Parish. It was further up the river than the Navy facility, but it would have to suffice.[30]

Tuesday, August 30, was a day of preparation and somewhat inchoate activity for the many Coast Guard contingents on the waters about the city, even as the airborne rescues carried on with increased intensity, as will be seen in the following chapter.

Before moving on, we must turn south to the little station at Grand Isle whose commanding officer, Lt. Comdr. Gibbons, as already mentioned had deployed all his ships but one to New Orleans. He turned his remaining vessel, a 23-footer, toward home, but they were only able to approach by road as far as Leeville. Still some twenty miles from their station, they realized the bridge to the island had been washed out, forcing them to launch and make a 65-mile roundabout voyage via Barataria Bay to reoccupy their devastated home base.

What they found was discouraging: everything up to six–eight feet above the ground was destroyed, and the winds had heavily damaged roofs everywhere. None of the family housing units were habitable. There was no power, water, or communications. A total of seventy-eight people—Coast Guard and dependents—were displaced by the storm. A small moment of relief came when someone noted that Nextel direct-connect could be had from a single point on base, alleviating the communication problem slightly.[31]

As Commander Gibbons recalled, it was one discouraged group, sitting around on the remains of a brick wall, gazing at rubble and devastation, cut off from families with no way of learning how they were faring after the storm, and wondering what to do next. " . . . on an island with no road access, electricity, water, sewage or any other basic functions, was like we had gone back in time," he remembered.

At that moment, when all hope seemed lost, Chief Boatswain's Mate George Williams scavenged an American flag from somewhere and raised it above the wreckage. They began the work of rebuilding their station.[32]

By evening an out-of-commission electric generator was repaired, set up, and running. Normal or even minimal operations were impossible until the buildings were again habitable, so temporary facilities were leased at Lockport, about 50 miles northwest on the peninsula. This included housing and a temporary operations center.

Despite their own homes still lying in ruins, the unit was soon involved in local assistance. While the bridge to the island remained unusable, the Coast Guard provided ferry service to the mainland. In the three weeks following the storm some 4,000 island residents and emergency workers, as well as food and supplies, were transported by this temporary expedient.[33]

In spite of the obstacles, the station was back to somewhat normal operations two weeks after Katrina. Lt. Cmdr. William Gibbons attributed much of the credit for the station's rebound to Chief Boatswain's Mate Williams. Because of his actions after Katrina, the Navy League of the United States presented Williams the Douglas A. Munro Award for Inspirational Leadership in 2006.[34]

What was in the Water

From the time the news broke that the New Orleans levees had been overtopped, and then breached, horrific predictions were made. The "toxic soup" was proclaimed a potential environmental and health disaster.

Within a week of the storm, the U.S. Center for Disease Control sent a team and evaluated the floodwaters in the city. Their test results seemed to support the dire predictions: bacterial levels were ten times higher than normal, there were high levels of E. coli, lead from pipes, and fecal matter, plus general pollution and decaying bodies in the water. Some experts feared the "world's largest sewage spill" in the standing water. Furthermore, five deaths were attributed to "contaminated flood waters."[35] As one Coast Guard rescue boat driver put it: "When you see cockroaches dying in New Orleans in the water you know it's not good." Another officer explained: "You tried not to get in the water. . . . But if you're pulling somebody out of the water you're going to get wet. During the first day maybe there weren't quite as many contaminants out there but you could still smell the raw sewage. . . . The rotting food hadn't really started yet. That came a couple days later when the waters receded. [Then there were] the oil spills; remember there are cars underwater there, oil is going to leak and you could see the sheens on top of the water . . ."[36]

Of course the Coast Guard contributed to this charged atmosphere with its reports of numerous and substantial oil spills. These amounted to an aggregate of over 9 million gallons of oil released over a widely scattered area.

The Coast Guard personnel would have been particularly vulnerable. It is probably fair to say that the average survivor of the storm spent little time in the water itself. Most of them seemed to have been able to escape vertically to await rescue—on roofs or in upper stories of their dwellings. Conversely, the U.S. Coast Guard rescue swimmers probably spent more time—over a period of more than a week—in the "toxic soup" than any other specific group in the city.

Despite the danger, there were few actual instances of chemical-related health issues. Rescue Swimmer Lawrence Nettles, for instance, spent four days nonstop on rescue operations, took a twenty-four-hour break, and did another four or five days. During his second deployment he spent an extended time in his wetsuit, passed out from heat exhaustion, and suffered chemical burns from contact with the water. His skin turned red and began to peel off and chemicals ate through his wetsuit footwear. None of these injuries kept him from his duties.[37]

Of course there were other hazards in the water, but these were typical of the situation: debris of all kinds, including broken glass, house insulation, jagged aluminum windowsills, etcetera. There were also more "natural" problems as rescue swimmer Kenyon Bolton (from the *Mary Lynn* rescue) discovered when he spent a half hour with a survivor, waiting for the return of his helicopter, all the while removing hundreds of fire ants from his own and the survivor's bodies. Bolton was later medically evacuated, though against his wishes.[38]

Related to the water problems were airborne hazards. There were many reports of helicopter hoists performed despite nearby fires and their attendant fumes and ash. Additionally, dangerous hydrogen sulfide gas was encountered by at least one Coast Guard pilot and helicopter over New Orleans.[39]

Moreover, the fear of toxic chemicals affected the Coast Guard's use of ice-boats for rescue operations. Several of these aluminum vessels, powered by a rear-mounted engine and large aboveboard propeller, were sent by District 9 (Great Lakes units) to work in the city. They were later taken out of service when it became apparent that the exposed propeller aerosolized the water, and thus made it possible for the water to be inhaled.[40]

After the initial fears were expressed and the waters had receded, press reports began to cast doubt on the extent of the dangers from contaminants in the floodwaters. In September, 2006, an article proclaimed that the environmental pollution was "not as bad as expected." Another article stated that dead and decaying bodies were not really dangerous, particularly if the victims had drowned.[41]

At any rate, the scare quietly abated. At this writing, I have not learned of any long-term medical or health problems stemming from the hours Coast Guard men and women spent in the unsanitary waters of the Crescent City or elsewhere.

7

Wet Tuesday II

The Air Rescues Intensify

We left the air and waterborne rescue operations in New Orleans as they stood the Monday afternoon and night after Katrina passed through. We also moved on to describe the increasing pace of water rescue activity in the city on Tuesday—the first full day of operations after the storm. Now we complete the picture of the ravaged city by describing the air rescue operations that same day.

The fact that the air and water portions of the Coast Guard effort can be separated into two different narratives for the same time period points to two significant factors in the operation. First, the two arms of the effort were starkly independent of each other. At least in the first few days, it was unusual for the two activities to intersect. In many instances, this only occurred when CG helicopters were flagged down, usually by hand signals, to airlift a seriously ill or injured survivor from a rescue boat to a hospital. Of course, there is no way to know how many of these rescues occurred, or, more critically, how many did *not* happen when needed.

The second factor that played a significant part in keeping the air and waterborne operations separate was the communication problem. In general, as has been mentioned, the communications net broke down in the wake of the storm: cell towers were knocked down, local phone service was out, and the Coast Guard satellite phone system was out or plagued by dropped calls. As Capt. Robert Mueller, deputy New Orleans sector commander put it: "I couldn't call. I was carrying five cell phones and I couldn't talk to anybody. The best thing that worked was the Nextel Direct Connect." But few people were lucky enough to have those. "You know it was just you had to go places to talk to people because you couldn't talk to them on the phone . . ." In the field, coordination between air units and boats was "extremely difficult," said Mueller, " . . . a lot of our boats had no way to talk to the helicopters." So aircraft/boat communications were haphazard to say the least. Mueller continued, "But with the helicopters . . . they'd circle, and as somebody heard them they'd come out and stick out a hand or something. Then they'd put the swimmer down and where he thought there were two people, there'd be fifteen . . ."[1]

Of course, the ad hoc nature of some of the CG waterborne efforts did not lend itself to successful or systematic communications with anyone, whether it was helicopters, other boat crews, or even commanding officers. Fortunately, the lack of communication did not prevent the rescuers from going out and saving lives. However, it has since been acknowledged that one of the major shortcomings in the Coast Guard's Katrina effort was the communications breakdown.

Two factors are noteworthy regarding communications during the rescue phase. First, one of the few relatively consistent avenues of radio communications was between and among the aircrews over the city. The helicopter and other CG pilots had no problem relaying rescue information among themselves, even though they may not have been able to communicate with the staging areas on the ground. In fact, the downside of this was when the number of aircraft in the area multiplied, the radio traffic, both directed and "radio chatter," soon became too dense for the system. Secondly, the aircrews' shared information was critical to directing the rescue efforts—they would return from flyovers and report in at the air station or elsewhere with rescue and survivor information for the next crews being sent out.

Another oddity of the situation was that after the first day or so, the local area codes 504, 225, and 318 were either disabled or overtaxed with calls. Conversely, calls to St. Louis, for instance, were more likely to succeed, provided the cell phone provider's towers were still standing. Also, people in the disaster area carrying cell phones with nonlocal area codes were more likely to be able to make and receive calls. These inconsistencies resulted in instances where emergency calls were made from the "street level" to the Department of Homeland Security in Washington, giving specifics such as "My sister-in-law is trapped" that included street addresses. These were then funneled back on-scene for action by CG or other rescuers.[2]

Another communications quirk was text-messaging. It was found that in some instances, this method was the only way to communicate out-of-area.[3]

In all, the communications breakdown was nearly total, or at least so pervasive that there was no single reliable method of electronic contact between parties. This was a circumstance no one anticipated, and which certainly hampered the effectiveness of the Coast Guard response—as well as that of other agencies.

And the volume of communications traffic would only increase as the days wore on. On August 30, Coast Guard aircraft from air stations at New Orleans, Clearwater, Mobile, Cape Cod, Corpus Christi, and Houston were doing search and rescue over the city. In addition, a C-130 from Clearwater was positioned as a communications hub for the SAR helicopters. At this point there were twenty-one CG aircraft supporting the operations in New Orleans.

The CG aircrews and others were flying into a maelstrom of a different sort now. When dawn broke, those citizens who were still in the city realized the extent of the flooding and destruction as well as their predicament: waiting out the storm was one thing; trapped on a roof or in an attic without food or water, and with no way to know when the waters would recede was an entirely unexpected development.

It was a typical sultry New Orleans August with temperatures soaring into the high nineties and humidity nearly at the saturation point. These were horrendously appropriate conditions to bring on heat prostration and aggravate all manner of respiratory distress, but for the aviators this meant yet another problem. High heat and humidity (low pressure/air density) translates into less lift for a given amount of power. Under normal circumstances, these conditions could be dealt with as a matter of course. However, these helicopters would be pushed to their power and load limits while attempting to quickly rescue as many people as possible. Thus, the aviators found themselves with little power reserve where sudden changes in loading or superheated air currents could swiftly put a helicopter into emergency conditions—potentially endangering aircraft, crew, and survivors on board.

Human desperation and depravity added another layer to the disaster. Finding that any regularly constituted authority was unlikely to either exist or arrive when needed, hoodlums and gangs took advantage, and the looting began. Of course, there were noncriminal aspects of the thievery: the struggle to get water, food, or other necessities was sufficient motivation for creative shoplifting. Making lawlessness more blatant was the availability of guns, and soon gunshots were part of the ambience in the city. Coast Guard rescuers may have often braved storms, heavy seas, sinking ships, and desperate survivors, but now they faced entirely new challenges in this inundated metropolis.

It was reported that over 350 distress calls were fielded by the Coast Guard on this day in New Orleans, and the pace of air operations stepped up markedly. The following are examples of the work the CG helicopters and crews accomplished. These are only slices of the scene: a mission by mission, aircraft by aircraft account is beyond the scope of this book.

⊙

On August 30, three of the crew of CG HH-60 Jayhawk CG6017 were already part of the Katrina story from when it began in Florida. The aircraft commander, Cmdr. Bill McMeekin, co-pilot Lt. jg. Catharine Gross, and Aircrew Survival Technician Third Class Bret Fogle, had ridden in company with the storm in CG6018, providing a backup helo for the *Mary Lynn* rescue west of the Florida Keys. They returned to base at Air Station Clearwater late on August 27, and then, on August 29, joined by AMT2 Randal Ripley, they flew aircraft CG6038 into New Orleans at night. They were the first crew to deploy to the city by way of Mobile. After three rooftop hoists in the dark and in less-than-optimum conditions, they returned to Mobile around 9:00 A.M., August 30.[4]

That evening, after meeting the minimum crew rest requirements known as "bag limits," McMeekin, Gross, Ripley, and Fogle returned to the air, carrying three HH-65 crewmembers to drop off at New Orleans. They landed at the New Orleans air station and were immediately directed to locate forty firemen reported to be stranded "somewhere" downtown. A search of the area revealed no such group. Instead, they found fifteen to thirty people stranded on a high rise pool deck. A crewmember was hoisted down and ascertained that the group was in no immediate danger. Their position was relayed to the air station and listed for a daylight pickup.

Next, McMeekin and crew were sent to Baptist Memorial Hospital to MEDEVAC 200 patients. After landing on the unlit and cramped helipad, they learned that the patients had already been evacuated—but there were 200 visitors and staff in need of transportation. Again, their situation was not critical, and arrangements were made for daylight evacuation.

However, the Coast Guardsmen were approached by paramedics who needed to have medical supplies sent to Tulane Hospital for life support there. About 1,000 lbs. of emergency medical gear was loaded, as well as three paramedics. But there was a snag: it wasn't clear whether Tulane had a helipad. If there was no helipad, the crew agreed to drop the gear at the Superdome. Once over downtown en route to the hospital, one of the EMS techs directed them to a parking garage among high rise buildings, marked with a small "H." However, the "pad" was surrounded by light poles and elevator shaft entrances, with 150–200-foot high rise buildings limiting access on three sides. Another high rise stood on the fourth side, but across a street, allowing the only clear access to the spot. "Clear" is a relative term, considering the 54-foot diameter rotor blade and 65-foot length of the Jayhawk, vis-à-vis the width of a city street. With the flight mechanic and rescue swimmer positioned as lookouts, McMeekin literally flew down the street until adjacent to the deck, then made a "sliding, 180-degree pedal turn to [a] steep approach, no hover landing." In other words, a really tight turn while simultaneously pulling away from the building opposite, accompanied by swift loss of altitude. There was no room for error and no time to settle into a standard hover before set-down. After the crew no doubt unclenched their white knuckles, the medical cargo was unloaded and the paramedics dropped off. McMeekin was not done yet, though. His piloting skills would again be required to clear the buildings with a high power vertical takeoff before heading for the comparatively wide open spaces of the Lakefront neighborhood.[5]

In that water-soaked area their first rescue was a man hoisted from his roof despite the power lines and trees that threatened the rescue. They then learned of a house full of survivors nearby, but this time trees and other obstructions prevented them from dropping the hoist. Luckily, McMeekin spotted a small boat on the flooded street and signaled the boat crew with a searchlight, directing them to the survivors.

The Coast Guard helicopter was now nearing "bingo" fuel (the minimum needed to return to base), and McMeekin and crew made for the Cloverleaf to drop their charge. Even landing was a challenge: McMeekin avoided at least two other helicopters nearby and dodged light poles to bring the aircraft to rest on a grassy area. The survivor disembarked and joined hundreds of others on the site awaiting transportation elsewhere.

At midnight, back at the New Orleans air station, McMeekin and crew refueled their helo, grabbed water and MREs, and resumed the mission. Returning to Lakefront, they spotted a man on the roof of his garage. The flight mechanic was hoisted down to rescue the lone man only to find that he was not alone—five more family members were inside. Holding the basket steady, the flight mechanic waited as the survivor brought out the group. Six people, including one elderly woman, were lifted out in five hoists.[6]

After dropping this group at the Cloverleaf, CG6017 returned to Baptist Memorial Hospital, where there was reportedly a critical patient to MEDEVAC. After again landing on the makeshift helipad, it appeared that one of the crew would have to literally search the facility to find the patient. However, the 200 visitors and staff encountered earlier were becoming unmanageable and demanding evacuation. Such a foray into the building would be extremely unsafe.

Flight mechanic Ripley attempted to convince the crowd that conditions at the Cloverleaf were worse than those at the hospital. Meanwhile, nurses climbed the vertical ladder on the back side of the building carrying the patient—who was being manually ventilated and had coded once on the way up. The staff physician directed the patient be taken to a hospital at Baton Rouge, but unfortunately McMeekin's aircraft had insufficient fuel to reach that city. The weary and distressed doctor then threatened to leave the patient unattended on the pad if McMeekin did not take her. A compromise was reached: McMeekin flew the patient and a nurse to Air Station New Orleans where they were transferred to another CG helicopter for transport to Baton Rouge.

McMeekin and his crew left Air Station New Orleans around 5:15 A.M. and were back at Mobile about an hour later. They had put in 7.6 flying hours during the night.[7] By this time, McMeekin, Gross, Ripley, and Fogle were ready to find a calm place to de-stress.

⊙

On this day in the deluged city unique and individual stories abounded, ranging from spur-of-the-moment disaster response management to hair-raising rooftop rescues to rescue swimmer encounters with hostile and armed survivors. Some of the more noteworthy of these heroic tales follow.

Lt. Cmdr. Thomas Swanberg, a HH-65 pilot, found himself and his crew in the midst of the first wave of Department of Defense helicopters over the ghastly scene of the city. He immediately took on aircraft controller duties, directing twelve aircraft as needed throughout the city, facilitating evacuation from two local hospitals and the saving of over 500 lives. Even as Swanberg oversaw this work, he and his crew continued nighttime rescue hoist operations.[8]

The rescue swimmers continued their extraordinary feats. Petty Officer Timothy Fortney freed two elderly women trapped in their home, but first, to gain access, Fortney had to make use of the only battering instrument available: his hoist basket. While hanging upside down from the eaves, he swung his basket and slammed it into the window to break it. Then, while still upside down, he steadied the basket near the broken window to allow the ladies to climb aboard.[9]

Third Class Aviation Survival Tech Mitchell Latta found a similar use for a sledgehammer that morning. An amputee diabetic was in shock and trapped in her attic. Latta first hammered through the roof and ceiling, making an aperture large enough for the 400-pound lady—though not sufficient for the rescue basket. He attached the hoist strap to the lady and, coordinating with the flight mechanic in the aircraft, winched her out of the house.[10]

AST1 Jason A. Shepard had a unique situation on his hands. He spied a young couple with a small baby on top of a car—with the car in imminent danger of being submerged in the waters. Shepard knew a direct approach would probably result in the couple and child being blown into the water by rotor wash. As an alternative, Shepard was dropped onto a nearby home. He jumped some 12 feet down onto the car hood, where he was able to steady and position the three for hoisting. While in the water, Shepard saw hundreds of survivors scattered on nearby rooftops.

Shepard swam house to house, navigating through debris and

waste. He scaled walls to reach survivors. As soon as one group was handed off and hoisted to the helicopter, he swam on to the next group of survivors, repeating the cycle.[11]

Survival Technician Jay M. Leahr searched the streets from above and located several survivors in a flooded home. The flight mechanic lowered him to the roof, where he found three people trapped in the attic, including an unconscious woman and an infant. Using a chainsaw and an ax, he broke through to the attic and lifted the unresponsive woman—who was at least twice his weight—onto the roof for hoisting. Then he took the infant in his arms and positioned himself for hoisting to the helicopter. Later that day, without the aid of ax or saw, Leahr physically ripped a small window out of its frame to make an opening large enough for the rescue of a trapped woman.[12]

In at least two instances on this day, the rescue swimmers faced volatile, life-threatening situations beyond "simple" life saving—situations they were not trained for and certainly did not expect. Jason Shepard, whom we last saw swimming house to house, was let down to a levee to treat a survivor with arterial bleeding, and close to death. Suddenly he found himself in the midst of 200 angry survivors who demanded immediate relief and rescue. He faced down the crowd and took charge. Taking note of the most belligerent of the would-be rioters, he used the force of his personality to re-channel their hostility and put the rowdiest of the group in charge of the more critical survivors. Then he was able to return to assist the original victim—who survived, thanks to Shepard's efforts.[13]

One of the more unusual events of the night operations occurred in the cabin of an HH-65 which had airlifted a family of five and their pet cat from a tiny veranda, despite tree branches and rubble obstructing the lift. Something set off the cat—probably the noise and din of the helo—and it escaped from its owner, scrambling across the helo and attacking the aircraft pilot. Flight Mechanic James M. Guidry managed to catch the animal before much damage was done.[14]

It might be appropriate here to note the status of pets in the CG rescues. Rescues of cats and dogs can be seen throughout this narrative. In most instances which I have encountered, there was no reluctance to rescue these animals. On the other hand, one of the rescue swimmers left behind two Rottweilers, one of which was sick, and the other of which had attacked him.[15] There were other instances of animals being left behind, and I assume the situations for the most part resulted from time or weight constraints, and where the choice was between saving humans or the animals.

In a crowd control situation similar to rescue swimmer Shepard's, AST1 John C. Williams was lowered into the ruins of an apartment complex and came up against a group of angry survivors, demanding immediate evacuation on their terms. Williams reminded them that he was their only chance at rescue and that it would be done *his* way. He gained their compliance and the hoisting began. The calm was short-lived, however, and soon they again rebelled, rushing the rescue basket. Williams again halted the rescue process until the crowd backed off.[16] In this and many other situations during Katrina, the rescue swimmers were astute enough to use their authority effectively, even when faced with enormously disadvantageous odds.

While the rescue swimmers were the foot soldiers meeting the expected and unexpected on the ground, the helicopter pilots were having their own bouts with wildly changing scenarios in the air. Lt. Cmdr. Scott Langum, flying an HH-60, was first given incorrect directions to Baptist Memorial Hospital. There was no alternative but to fly at nearly street sign level. He finally located the facility only to learn that the landing site would not support the full weight of his aircraft. He landed "wheels light"—maintaining enough lift to keep the full weight of the helo off the surface—and evacuated thirteen critical care patients. Later that night, he continued hoist operations, rescuing thirty-two survivors while maintaining 100-foot hovers. He made the final lift despite total breakdown of the helicopter's internal communications.[17]

Lt. Cmdr. Christian Ferguson, also commanding a Jayhawk,

found a family of seven on the roof of a rapidly collapsing building. With the structure literally "sinking" from sight, Ferguson maintained a 110-foot hover, rescuing all seven as the floodwaters destroyed the building. Later, during the same mission, he rescued another four survivors from a second story balcony. An extraordinarily dangerous 160-foot hover was necessary due to the proximity of powerlines.[18]

Finally, Lt. Cmdr. Eric S. Gleason, flying an HH-65, rescued critically ill survivors from a balcony, the approach to which was strewn with choking debris. He threaded the rescue swimmer through the morass to effect the rescue. After picking up another critically ill individual, he learned that the local hospitals were not accepting patients. Gleason would not take no for an answer: he hunted down an ambulance on Interstate 10, landed, and delivered the patient into their care, saving the individual's life.[19]

The words of rescue swimmer Matt O'Dell probably paint as vivid an account of the scenes in New Orleans that day and night as can be had:

> Took off early evening, and flew all night. . . . We did directs and baskets. Rooftop evacuations were the most common. While on rooftops I could see the hands and arms of people coming from attic vents, and being left on-scene, I could hear people screaming from what seemed like everywhere. [It] was very unnerving. On several occasions I utilized the aircraft's crash axe to enter homes. . . . On one occasion the survivors were unable to climb out of the roof, so I had to physically lift them out while I was standing on the roof, none of whom were small people. . . . A lot of this day was a blurr [sic] to me, I think mostly due to exhaustion and maybe some residual "shell shock" to the massive destruction that I was witnessing. We flew into and well beyond a flight time bag.[20]

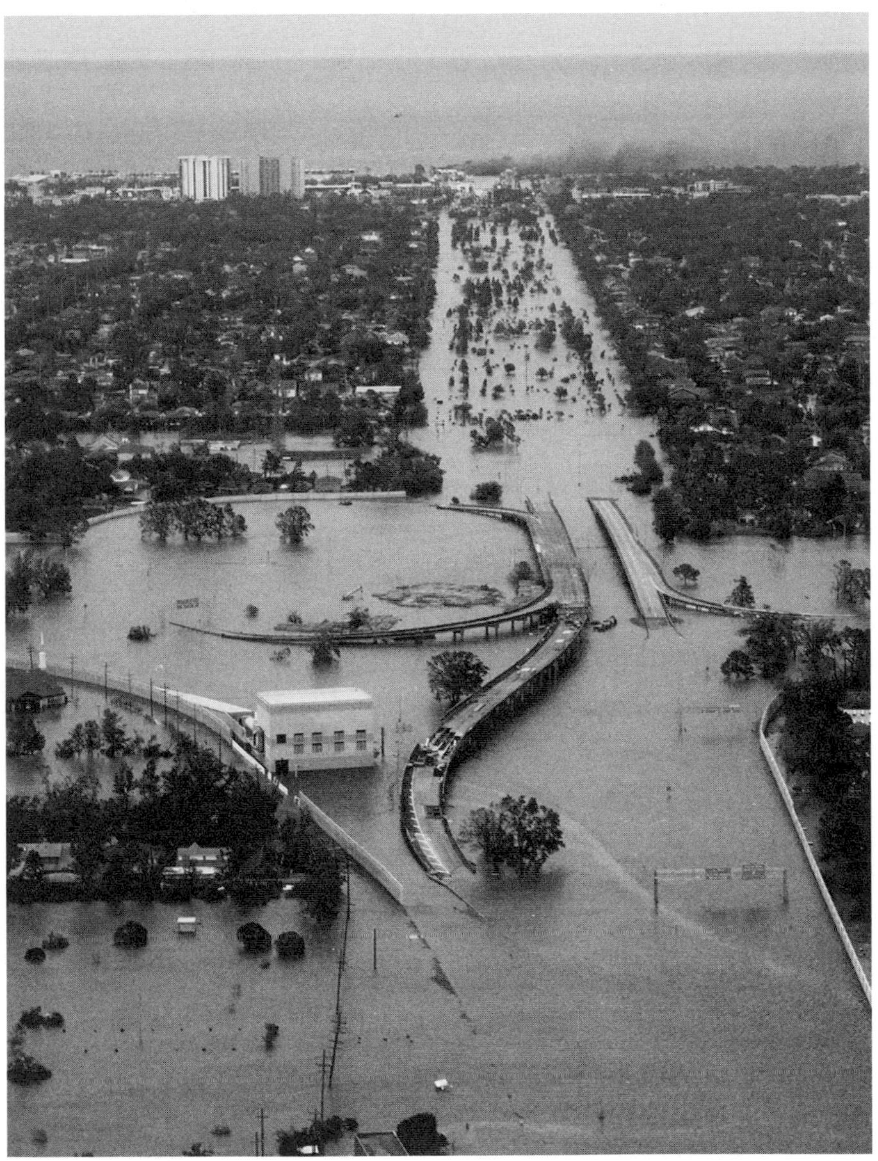

New Orleans, the afternoon after Katrina: View looking north, with Lake Pontchartrain in the distance and the University of New Orleans in the left background. Note the inundated interstate interchange and pumping station in the foreground, and smoke from fires along the lake shore.

Levee Breech in New Orleans: View looking southward from Lake Pontchartrain along the Industrial Canal, with the Mississippi River and central New Orleans in the background. In the right foreground is the Gentilly neighborhood, site of major flooding from both Lake Pontchartrain and the levee breaks.

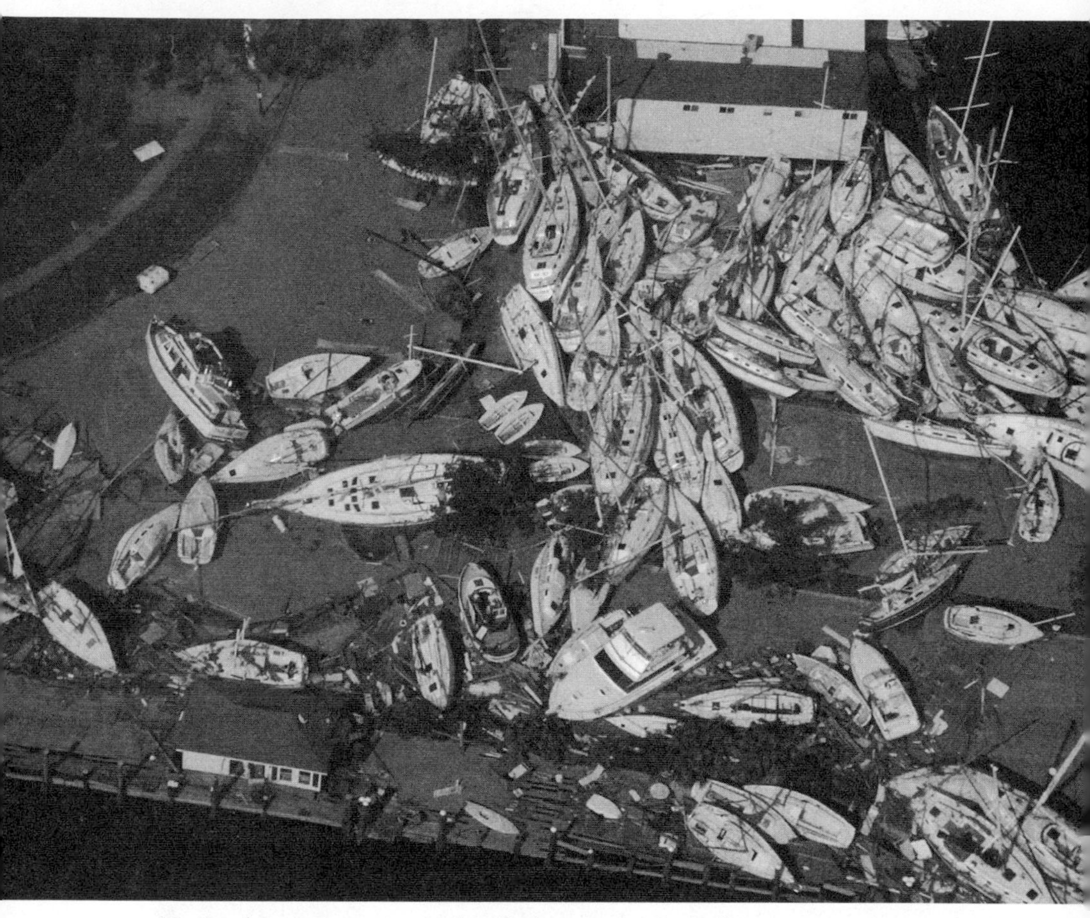

Marine devastation at an unidentified marina on the Gulf coast. In a scene repeated ad infinitum from south Louisiana nearly to Mobile, this image shows over sixty vessels piled ashore, the result of the Katrina storm surge and winds.

U.S. Coast Guard Station Gulfport, Mississippi, after Katrina. Remains of the main station building are in the background. Many of the Coasties stationed there lost all but what they were wearing or carrying when they evacuated before the storm.

Coast Guard cutter *Pamlico*, a work-a-day construction tender commanded by CWO3 Robert Lewald, became "flagship" and a center of operations for CG vessels moored in the Mississippi near central New Orleans. In addition to working search and rescue in the city, Lewald's team organized barge evacuations of thousands of survivors to the south side of the river.

Barge load of survivors en route from flooded Chalmette to Algiers Point on the "dry" side of the river. Thousands of evacuees were organized, loaded, and unloaded by CG personnel during the week following the storm. The Coast Guard also provided security at collection points on both sides of the river.

A Coast Guard HH-65 preparing to take off. Piloted by Lt. Cmdr. Thomas Cooper, this New Orleans–based helo (CG6522) was among the first five helicopters to begin search and rescue over the city, battling 50-knot winds and making the first rescues before 5:00 P.M. the afternoon of the storm.

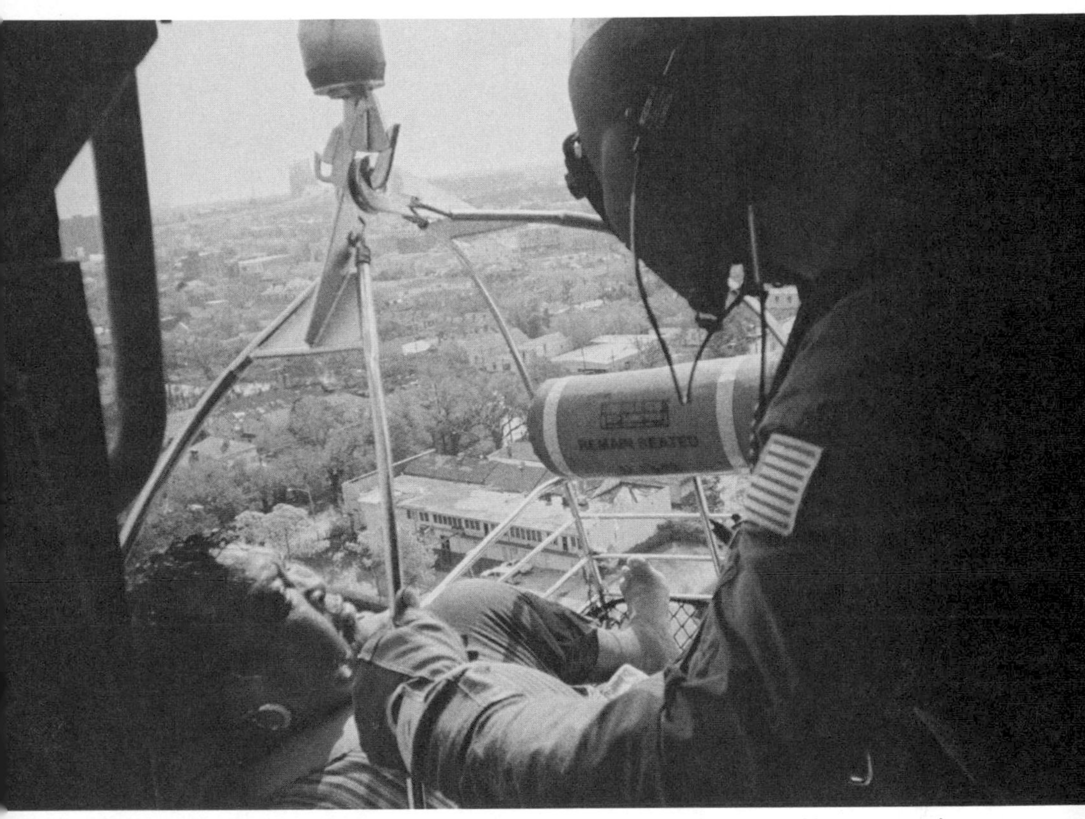

Woman and infant rescued over New Orleans: note the rescue basket and hoist, viewed from within the helicopter.

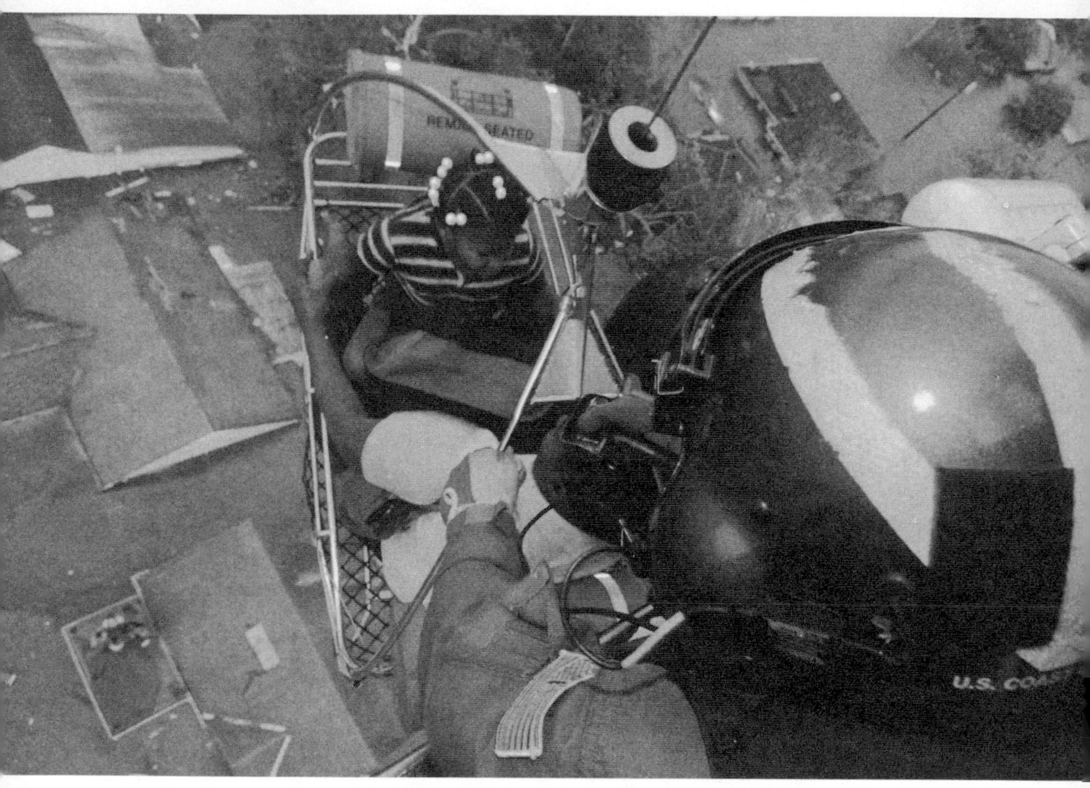

Rooftop rescue: a dizzying view straight down from the helo. Note the helo rotor wash below and the hole broken through the roof. In this instance the pitch of the roof probably made use of the rescue basket problematic.

Hospital approach: a Coast Guard HH-60 over a flooded hospital: note the rescue basket (*circled*) directly below the helo, several feet of water surrounding the facility, and the second CG helicopter in distance. There is no helipad in the photo.

A Coast Guard aerial rescue fleet of ten CG helos—five HH-60s and five HH-65s—at Aviation Training Center, Mobile, participating in Katrina operations. Katrina concentrated nearly 40 percent of the entire Coast Guard aviation fleet for the operation.

The U.S. Coast Guard flies over New Orleans as the city emerges from Hurricane Katrina.

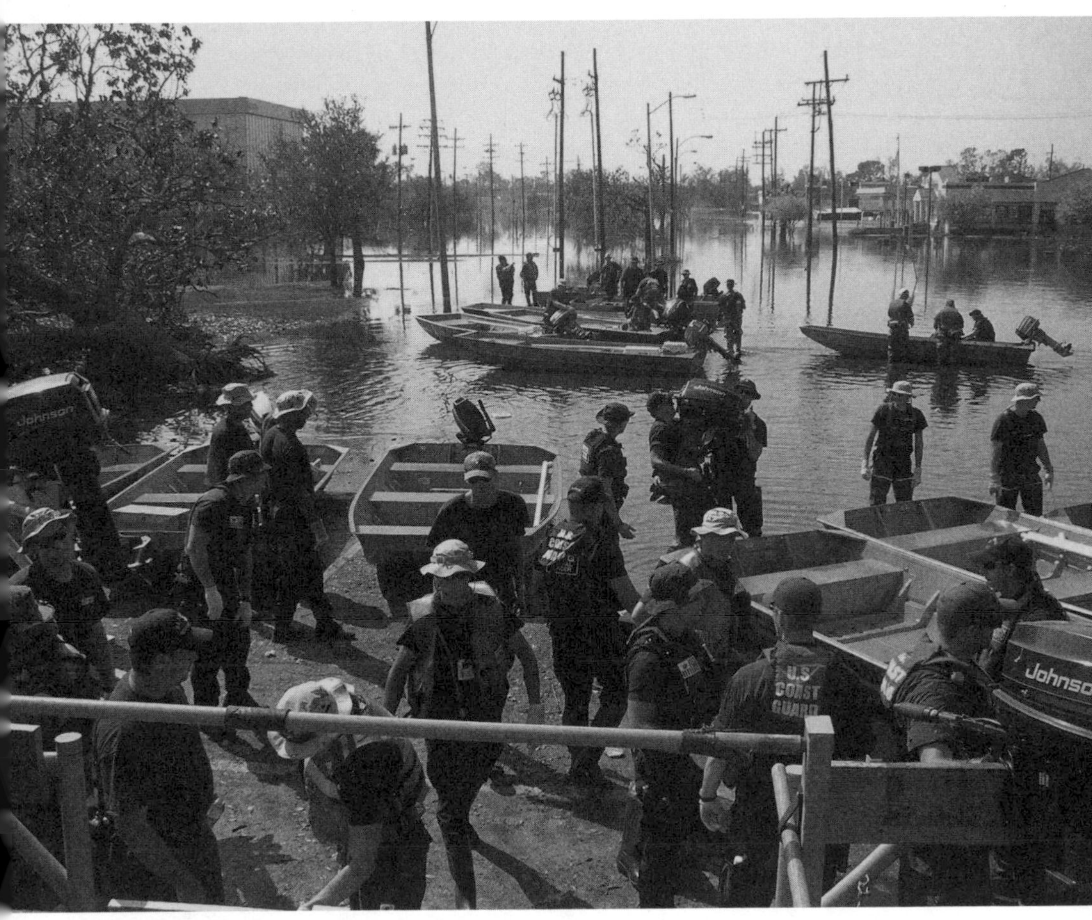

CG flood rescue boats preparing to move out into the city. Over thirty Coast Guardsmen are in the photo, along with a dozen boats. Note the Coasties carrying an outboard motor in the center.

President Bush greets rescue swimmers and other CG personnel at Aviation Training Center, Mobile, September 2, 2005. Captain David Callahan, commander of the center, is on the president's left.

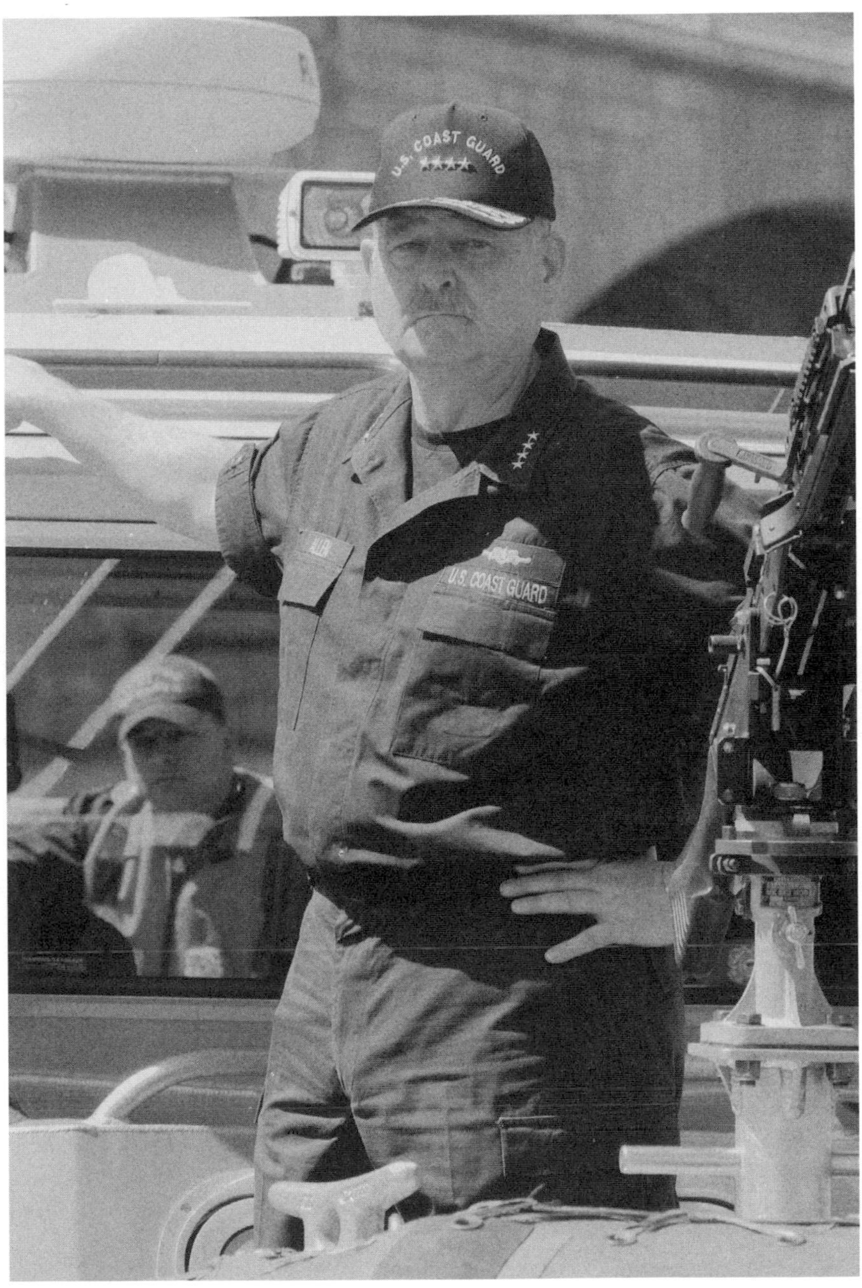

Coast Guard Admiral Thad Allen, appointed primary federal official for Katrina by President Bush on September 6, 2005. Adm. Allen became commandant of the Coast Guard in mid-2006. Credit: FEMA.

In post-Katrina New Orleans, CG helicopters became jacks of all trades. Here an HH-60 drops a huge sandbag into place at a levee breech.

Pallets of water and other supplies on site in front of the hangar at CG Air Station Mobile. Early on, CG flyers noted the need for water and other essentials for those stranded at interchanges and other pickup points. From that point on, CG aircraft regularly carried such supplies to drop off as needed.

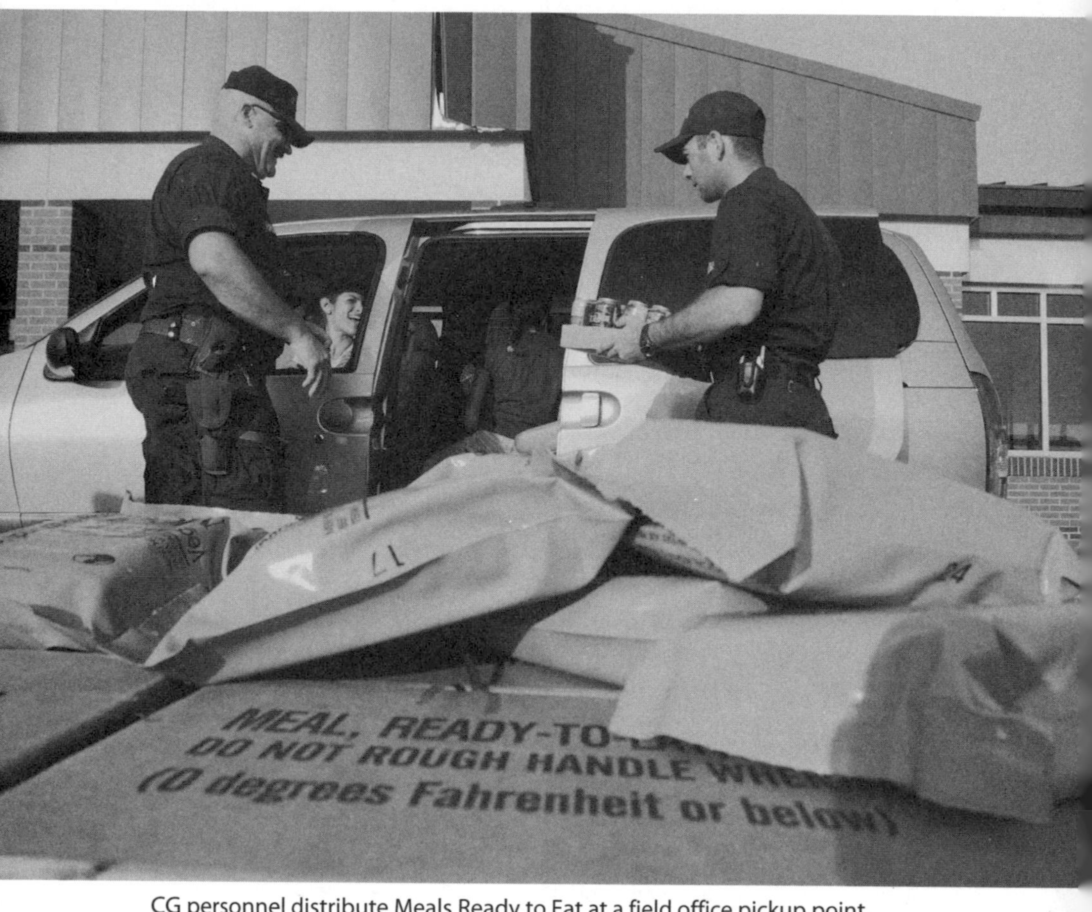

CG personnel distribute Meals Ready to Eat at a field office pickup point.

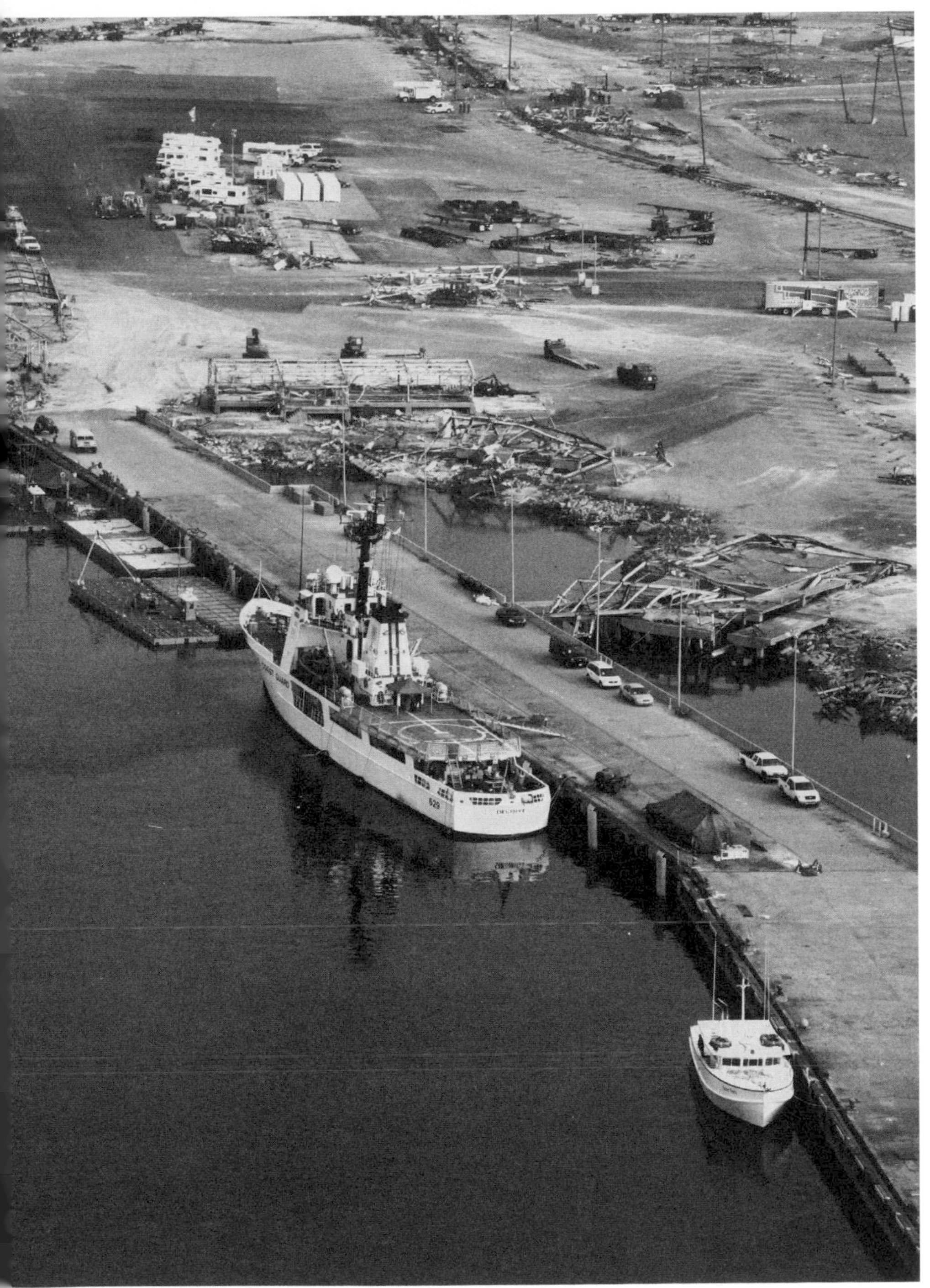

CGC *Decisive* in place at Gulfport, serving as communication and coordination center for CG and other agencies' relief efforts after the storm.

Alligator being cleaned by CG and other personnel. Katrina and Rita played havoc with all forms of wildlife, not only due to the storm itself, but due to many small and large hazardous material spills. CG environmental teams dealt with many of these issues.

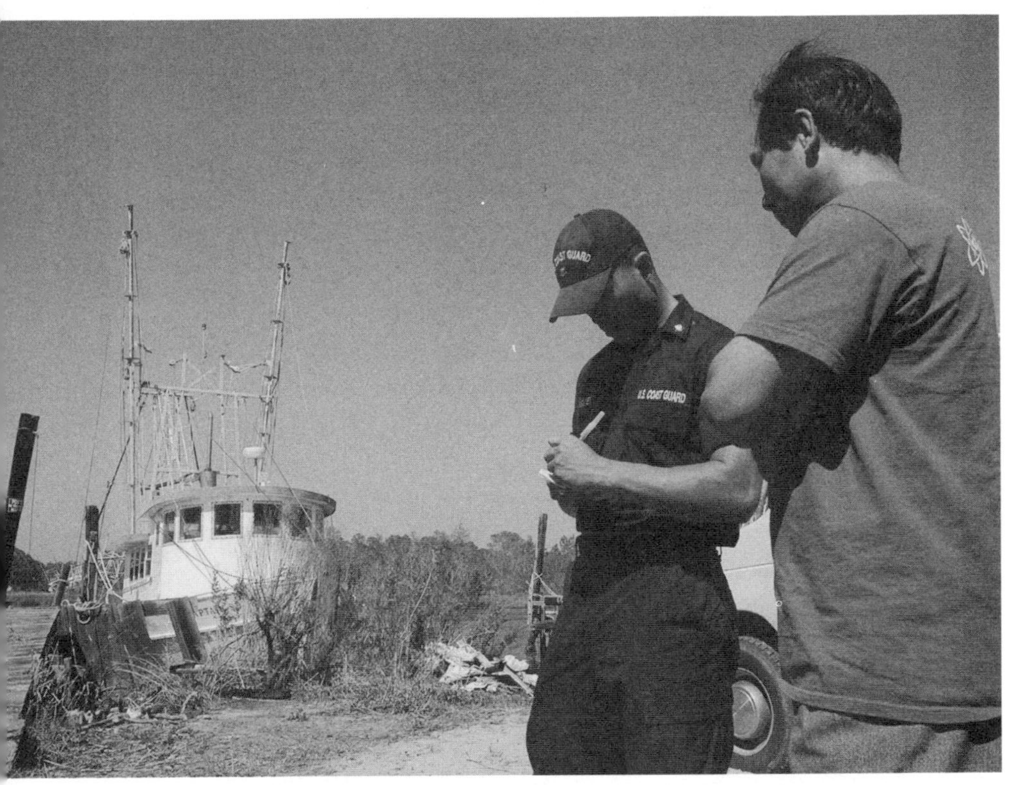

Along the Mississippi coast, a large Vietnamese fishing community was hit hard by the storm. Dozens of their boats were destroyed or run ashore, many with their owners still on board. CG teams quickly lent aid where needed. Here, petty officer Huyhn A. Nguyen translates for one of the fishermen, with a grounded boat in the background.

Two CG HH-65 Dolphins in very close proximity over New Orleans: as more and more CG and other agency helos came onto the disaster area, hair-raising scenes such as this were not rare enough. Only professionalism of the highest order prevented close calls like this from turning into nightmare scenarios.

Wednesday, August 31

Operation Dunkirk, Zephyr Field, and Station New Orleans

As the skies filled with Coast Guard aircraft, as well as National Guard and state agency helicopters, the watery streets of New Orleans saw the bottoms of dozens of CG boats along with those of other state agencies. As the days progressed, centers of operations emerged for both aviation and small boat efforts. Aviators staged in and out of the Coast Guard air station and boats operated out of three locations: Station New Orleans, Zephyr Field—the large, dry, training facility for the New Orleans Zephyrs AAA ball team—and CGC *Pamlico* and consorts on the river. We follow the boat operations in this chapter.

We left Mr. Lewald, commanding officer of the *Pamlico* flotilla, on late Tuesday night when he was asked to assist the evacuation of Chalmette, St. Bernard Parish. The Crescent City Connection ferry company provided three vessels, each able to load 150–200 people. In addition, a deck barge capable of handling 500 evacuees at a time was located, along with a tug to move it. With the use of these as well as the CG vessels of Lewald's ad hoc flotilla, substantial numbers could be removed to safety. This was the beginning of what some dubbed Operation Dunkirk.[1]

Early on Wednesday morning Coast Guardsmen working in cooperation with the St. Bernard parish authorities began the process. At first the ferries and barge were not available, so the seven 41-footers and three 55-footers were dispatched to begin evacuations. St. Bernard Parish survivors sheltered in the Chalmette High School were advised to move to the ferry landing or to a warehouse at the Chalmette Slip, about a mile up the river from the landing, for evacuation. By the time the Coast Guard arrived to begin moving them, it was estimated that there were already thousands at the warehouse. At first people were taken by CG small boats from the ferry landing to the Chalmette Slip, placed on a convenient floating dock, then picked up by the ferries and barge for the move to Algiers.[2]

Safety was of particular concern with the barge passengers. Unlike the ferryboats, there were no facilities or beltlines on the barge, so CG 41-footers escorted the barge and tug for each trip. In addition, Lewald's crew located a grounded ferryboat on the levee and its supply of life jackets was commandeered for the barge passengers' use. The task was time consuming—coordinating the loading of 500 people on a barge was no easy matter.[3]

But the hardest part of the job for the CG personnel was still to come, on the Algiers side. It began poorly: when Lewald first notified the Jefferson Parish sheriff of the plan, the man balked, saying he did not want "those people from Chalmette" in his jurisdiction, despite the fact that Chalmette was under 12 feet of water at the time. Lewald did not specify in his Katrina archive interview how the dispute was settled, but it was, probably based on an agreement that the Coast Guard would impose a security perimeter around the ferry terminal.[4]

On the Algiers side, the two main challenges facing the Coast Guard were security and tending to the physical needs of the burgeoning and increasingly restive crowd. Security was the top priority. Lewald recalls: "There were bad people everywhere; people with guns." As a rule, aids to navigation personnel were not required to have weapons or body armor, nor were they issued any, but Coast Guardsmen from small boat station Venice had brought their armory when they evacuated. Also, a boat crew from MSO Baton Rouge had arrived—having lost the use of their boat earlier in the day—and added their arms and assistance to the mix. Earlier the MSO team had been asked by the Fish and Wildlife officers to provide security for their vehicles, but they had politely refused, noting that their primary mission was search and rescue. They were roundly cursed by the state officers so they simply left to find a more appropriate job.

Lewald ordered a perimeter set up with sentries at each end of the road to the ferry terminal, plus roving guards moving through the crowds and a couple of sharpshooters. It was sufficient for daylight operations but during the night the Coast Guard personnel returned to their vessels and moved the fleet off the bank.[5]

The security force was soon challenged. Lewald recalls: "Several police cars were stolen . . . They would drive up, you know, and once they got closer it definitely wasn't a policeman in that police car . . . and we would have to draw, and they'd see that we were serious and they would turn and go."

When this didn't work, they tried a different approach. The "bad guy" would approach and say there was a survivor needing help nearby, attempting to get the guards to leave the perimeter. "They wanted the weapons . . . and [to] overwhelm us," said Lewald.

A new rule was established: no sentry could leave sight of the ferry building.

The evidence of gun violence was overwhelming. Lewald estimated that through the week about a dozen individuals came into their "lines" with gunshot wounds. He speculated that they were looters and/or criminals. And of course, spurts of distant gunfire, particularly at night, were not uncommon.[6]

The question of weapons became particularly alarming when Lewald and his contingent learned that the Chalmette police were not searching the individuals boarding on their side of the river. To avoid unnecessary confrontation and ensure safety for evacuees and the Coast Guard rescuers, amnesty boxes were set up on the Algiers side. As the evacuees disembarked they were told, "Alcohol, illegal narcotics, and weapons go into the boxes, no questions asked." Pointing at uniformed, armed Coasties stationed at the top of the landing, they added, "And up there we're going to search you."[7] This was sufficient incentive to obtain cooperation from the survivors.

The eventual haul was appalling: Lewald estimated 500–600 firearms were collected, plus knives, alcohol, and drugs. "It was the wild west," recalls Lewald. The alcoholic beverages and drugs were disposed of in the river. The guns were at first handed off to the local police, but when Lewald saw them dividing up the contraband with their cronies, he ordered all firearms moved to CGC *Clamp* for safekeeping. The weapons were later turned over to the Galveston police department.[8]

With measures in place to deal with external and internal threats, the physical condition and needs of the evacuees had to be met. Once on the west bank, the crowd was without immediate transportation elsewhere—there was no regular source of buses and the number of survivors in various collection points increased.

As Lewald put it, "we did triage there, because these folks were in a bad way." People had left most or all of their possessions at home, including, in some instances, their insulin. The heat was overwhelming, there were minor cuts and scrapes, many had not eaten recently, and some were in diabetic shock. The Coasties did their best with what was on hand—water, candy for the diabetics, bandages, etcetera. They were able to MEDEVAC the worst cases with CG or other service helicopters, usually signaled by hand.[9]

Professional medical help was essentially unavailable, with one exception. Lewald spoke highly of a nurse from Charity Hospital, a Ms. Cindy Fourman, who showed up each day at dawn and remained until sunset. She lived nearby and refused Lewald's offer of an armed escort home. She felt that this would draw the attention of the "bad guys." Lewald called her a "true hero" and credited her with saving 250 lives from August 31 through September 4.[10] Later attempts to locate the nurse and recognize her contribution were unsuccessful.

The sheer number of evacuees and the rate at which they were arriving at the Algiers terminal was highlighted on Wednesday night. At 5:00 P.M. the National Guard and Wildlife and Fisheries officers departed, leaving nearly 2,000 restive evacuees still awaiting transportation under the nominal supervision of two New Orleans police officers and six Calcasieu Parish officers. Taking matters into their own hands, the policemen located and commandeered twenty school buses. Assisted by the Coast Guard MSO contingent, they had all the evacuees moved out and on the way to Baton Rouge by 11:00 P.M.[11]

⊙

The operations at Zephyr Field, located south of Interstate 10 in Jefferson Parish, had their Coast Guard origins on Wednesday, August 31. Lt. Cmdr. Darryl Schaffer, who had been in charge of the little ISC New Orleans contingent with their borrowed boats, was asked late on Tuesday by the FEMA representative to check in at the Emergency Operations Center at Zephyr Field the next morning. There he joined the unified command structure being set up and consisting of FEMA personnel, state Fisheries and Wildlife officers, and Jefferson Parish authorities. All were under the ostensible direction of the Louisiana Office of Emergency Preparedness, in Baton Rouge, which in turn was in contact with the mayor of New Orleans.[12]

In actuality, for the first few days, there was little contact with the state OEP. Communications were almost nil. Schaffer recalls: "Nothing worked, nothing at all worked. No cell towers were up. All landlines were cut off. Courier pigeons would have been better." Typically, there would be one phone call a day or they would literally have to drive to Baton Rouge to communicate. Consequently, rather than the OEP directing actions locally, the Zephyr Field on-site intermediaries were reduced to simply reporting what was being done, as well as requesting additional personnel and supplies.[13]

At Zephyr Field, Schaffer was designated the Unified Command Representative for the Coast Guard, and thus Zephyr Field was designated a CG Forward Operating Base (FOB). Schaffer was immediately struck by one of the shortcomings of the other agencies involved: lack of knowledge of the local area. He had, while waiting at Grangeville, been using a New Orleans tourist map to cross-reference with CNN, FOX, and MSN news broadcasts. He and his crew knew enough of New Orleans to identify particular areas shown on the aerial rescue sequences. They would sticky-note the map with annotations—mostly "Flooded." When Schaffer brought out this map, the other agency representatives were immediately interested. He was apparently the only one with knowledge of specific locations where operations were blocked or where access could be gained to the flooded areas. Other valuable information was also made available: areas which were flooded but relatively prosperous were less likely to need assistance because those citizens probably owned vehicles and could have evacuated before the storm; vis à vis poorer sections where few had cars.[14]

Schaffer's knowledge was immediately put to good use. While the ISC boat crews went out again to the I-10/610 location for surface rescue work, Schaffer was at Zephyr Field coordinating the efforts of CG, FEMA, and state and local forces being launched into the disaster area. Even at this early stage there were some 600 people in this rescue task force.[15]

CG forces under the FOB command included Marine Safety and Security detachments from New Orleans, Galveston, Houston, Port Arthur, and Morgan City. Additionally, the local USCG Auxiliarist Mike Howell showed up with his boat, the *Manana*, bringing potable water and toilet facilities. "Housing" for the incoming CG personnel was purely makeshift: in storm-damaged buildings, in government vehicles, and in the open air. MREs were often the only menu choice and toilet and bathing facilities were insufficient.

Many of the Coast Guard members themselves had lost much to the storm; some had only what they were wearing when they evacuated before Katrina's landfall.[16]

The third nexus of the CG small boat effort was the now-settled Station New Orleans at Bucktown. After defusing the confrontation with the squatters/looters in the building, CWO Brooks was able to organize a thrust into the flooded community, and selected BM2 Jessica Guidroz to direct the group.[17]

Guidroz was relatively new to the Coast Guard, having joined in 2002, but had a solid background—with experience as a coxswain (small boat skipper) and as a law enforcement boarding officer. Her home was on the north shore of Lake Pontchartrain, giving her invaluable knowledge of the area. She was put in charge of a flotilla of eight small boats—23- and 25-footers—and their three-man crews. Guidroz was an E-5 (Bosun's Mate Second Class) at the time, and at least two of her subordinates in this expedition outranked her. She said, "I was nervous for a minute and then [thought] . . . This is what they train us to do," and she set out.[18]

Learning that the lakefront University of New Orleans campus was now "a small island" overrun with 2,200 stranded refugees, she led the group of boats about three miles eastward from the CG station to the seawall near the university arena. Since there were no mooring facilities where the boats could be tied, all they could do was drive the boats' bow far enough up onto the steps to "moor" them, and the only way to hold the boats in place long enough to board the evacuees was to keep the motors running. Given the crowds and slick steps, this was a precarious situation.[19]

Each boat could only take ten passengers—plus the crew. A team of eighteen local firefighters organized the crowd into groups of eighty, ten per line. After they had been searched for weapons, the problem became slowing down the anxious survivors, keeping them from all jumping into the boats at once—a scene not unlike a "Titanic" movie. If too much weight went into the boat at once, the boat would slide off its "step," slam the other boats, and endanger the whole operation. It was a constant struggle to hold back the waves of anxious survivors scrambling to get on the boats. Several times Guidroz and the crews of her boats prevented overly pushy evacuees from boarding until more needy ones were brought on. The elderly and young mothers with infants had priority.[20]

On the second day of the operation, when the crowd was becoming harder to handle, the firefighters backed out, but the routine was repeated over and over again—eighty survivors at a time—and eventually, over the next four days, all 2,200 people were brought off. The evacuees were first taken in the small boats, convoy style, to the CG station at Bucktown, a forty-five-minute trip, then transferred to government vehicles and taken to the FEMA evacuation point at the I-10/610 interchange.[21]

Side trips were necessary to meet the various medical needs of the growing crowd. There was at least one pregnant woman, a man with mental issues who had to be prevented from swimming back to his home for his medicine, and a diabetic in need of insulin. At first there was only one EMT on the scene, plus a few of the Coast Guard personnel who knew CPR, and one nurse who happened to be on hand. Guidroz made attempts, using the uncertain communications net, to call for medical supplies to be airlifted in, but received no immediate response. It was in the course of convoying their charges that they came upon a ladder going up to a second story window in a flooded building. Guidroz tied up the boat, climbed in, and searched for first aid supplies. She found Tylenol and all sorts of other medicines, alcohol, and a supply of water. Guidroz remembered: " . . . we just took all of that with us because there was nothing here for anybody."[22]

In the next hectic days, Guidroz and her crew far exceeded the CG small boat crew fatigue standards, regularly putting in fifteen-hour days.[23] She remembered: "Between stress, the adrenaline, and everything else . . . doing everything from security to launching boats to doing rescues, running COMMS, and so you really didn't sleep that much . . ."[24]

Guidroz did not do this in a vacuum, and her stress levels were not alleviated by her personal losses. She lost her home, car, and possessions—all but her cat—to the storm. But she was not alone: most of the others in the unit were under the strain of either knowing they had lost much, or not knowing what had happened to loved ones and possessions. As senior petty officer on board, Guidroz knew she was key to the effectiveness of the unit, so she continued on: " . . . even though I wanted to break down . . . I had to try to maintain my composure to keep these guys . . . focused."[25]

9

August 31

"The skies are orange"

In what was to become the largest single Coast Guard operation in history, helicopters and other aircraft continued to pour into the devastated area. As early as August 30, the watchwords were seen in a Coast Guard Situation report: "The skies from the Mississippi River to Mobile were orange with Coast Guard aerial overflights conducting SAR."[1]

By Wednesday, the "orange" helos were far from the only participants in the aerial rescue effort. National Guard aircraft were there, plus Marine and Navy helicopters and state and local fliers. The National Guard helo operations had begun the day before with six aircraft. Their first priority was rescuing their own people trapped at the Jefferson Barracks National Guard facility.

With so many helicopters in such a small geographical area, the airspace was soon congested. As Bruce Jones, a CG air station commanding officer put it, "The sky was dark with helicopters . . ." It was an air traffic controller's nightmare. Jones said:

> You know . . . when two aircraft are approaching within a mile it's considered pretty scary stuff. In our case we had helicopters . . . within a few hundred yards of each other. So the idea that anyone could be watching a radar screen providing separation to all those aircraft is simply just not possible. It really relied on the individual aircraft pilots and crew to keep their heads on swivel; to keep alert to avoid a midair collision . . . which they did.[2]

Had an air traffic controller even been able to sort out the aircraft locations, there would still have been the communications congestion. The overhead communications aircraft, given the common 345.0 frequency, was almost impossible to raise: "That radio was so busy that it was almost impossible to get a word in edgewise," said Jones. "But we were able to communicate with other aircraft periodically just by saying 'Hey, aircraft over LSU Hospital, this is so-and-so 200 yards behind you.'"[3]

And nighttime operations added yet another stress level to the aviators' concerns. "Yes," Jones recalls, "it was pretty stressful at night because there were no lights over the city. The towers were unlit. Cell phone towers, radio towers, power lines; all the things that normally would be lit . . . And of course . . . you're flying very, very low." Fortunately, night vision goggles picked up these obstructions, and, Jones said, flyers were first required to fly over the city in daylight to familiarize themselves with the area before taking on night rescue operations.[4]

There were two major concerns for Jones in the air operations: midair collisions and "some sort of crash . . . we wouldn't know about." In normal, everyday air operations, CG pilots were required to call in with their position every fifteen minutes. Thus, if an incident or accident occurred, a maximum of fifteen minutes would pass before an aircraft would be noticed as "missing." Over New Orleans, however, there was no unit anywhere capable of maintaining this kind of hands-on radio guard for the number of aircraft in play. All that could be maintained consistently was notification to the central controller when a particular aircraft entered and departed from the area. Had a helo or fixed-wing aircraft gone missing or crashed without issuing a mayday call, it might not have been noticed until the aircraft failed to return for gas. For the duration of the emergency, no solution was found for this dilemma. Luckily, this worst-case scenario did not occur.[5]

But some of the events that did transpire were harrowing enough. Aircraft CG6034, an HH-60 commanded by Cmdr. Bill McMeekin, flew out of Air Station Mobile at 1:40 A.M.—after waiting some five hours due to a maintenance delay—and set down at the New Orleans Air Station. McMeekin learned that several hundred people were stranded on the roofs of a Best Western motel and nearby apartment complex. Once over the dark city the fog and smoke limited visibility to 1–2 nautical miles, and the ceiling hung at an uncomfortably low 400 feet. Numerous other helicopters with their own missions also battled this poor visibility while trying to keep safe distances. Even with night vision goggles, the conditions were horrendous, and McMeekin was tempted to abort the flight. However, he and his crew persisted and found a relatively obstruction-free route from the Cloverleaf, out over the lake, and back south to the motel/apartment complex.[6]

On the scene, McMeekin found another CG HH-60 making hoists from a building that had been significantly damaged. Flying debris, generated and churned by the rotor wash, endangered both helos and the roof-bound survivors, but McMeekin dropped rescue swimmer Randal Ripley into the dark waters below. On just the first run, Ripley made five 90-foot basket hoists, mostly of the elderly and overweight. Some of the latter were unable to lift themselves out of the basket once in the helicopter and required the flight mechanic's assistance to do so.[7]

The helos were relatively spread out as they operated over the city. However, when it came time for the pilots to land with their charges, congestion became a greater problem as countless helos approached the aerial bottlenecks. When McMeekin arrived at the Cloverleaf drop-off point, he found it a "free-for-all" with CG and Department of Defense aircraft jockeying for space. Two helos were already on deck. McMeekin landed, then had to delay unloading until a third aircraft—a huge military CH53—took off and its rotor wash cleared.[8]

On the second and third runs, the crew of CG6034 decided that although "quick strop" recoveries would be more physically taxing—especially on Ripley the rescue swimmer—they would also be more efficient. The strop method made use of a strap which cinched under the rescuee's armpits and attached to a hook on the swimmer's harness. The crew brought in a total of nineteen survivors over the course of three trips—the five from the first trip's basket hoists and another fourteen via quick strop direct deployment. By the last circuit, conditions had further deteriorated, with visibility down to one mile and 300-foot ceilings. The conditions were nightmarish if nightmares could be said to be pitch black and seen through night vision goggles. When they returned to Mobile at 6:35 A.M. they had been in the air almost five hours, about two of which were spent flying to and from New Orleans.[9]

Thirty-five CG helicopters worked around the clock in this unsafe environment, dealing with life threatening issues and often unstable, desperate people. The dark Gulf Coast skies were replete with hair-raising narratives. A few of the stories from that harrowing Wednesday follow.

Commander James O'Keefe, skippering an HH-60, was directed to evacuate seven critical patients from the Superdome. On arriving, he found that the only "parking space" was between two other moving helos—requiring him to station his crew as lookouts to bring his aircraft in safely. Later, at the destination hospital, he found that the quasi-helipad was not even rated to support the weight of his Jayhawk. Without any real choice in the matter, he executed a light-wheels landing—a tires-on-pavement hover—while the patients were taken off the aircraft. Afterwards, O'Keefe evacuated a 550-pound critically ill patient in a maneuver that required him to hold the aircraft in place for nearly an hour before successfully hoisting the individual.

Also, in cooperation with the local authorities, O'Keefe and his crew inserted an eight-man SWAT team at the Superdome parking lot. But before the day was over, he still had to land his Jayhawk neatly between two buildings nearly as close to each other as the diameter of his rotor blades in order to evacuate a kidney failure patient.[10]

Chief Aviation Survival Technician Martin H. Nelson distinguished himself in one of the many barely forestalled riot scenes of the week when he was lowered to a school roof and came face to face with dozens of desperate people. His first task was to determine who needed to be hoisted first, but he was challenged by openly hostile men demanding to be the first lifted out. By convincing them that he was their only hope, Nelson was able to establish his authority and regain control of the situation before finishing the job at hand.[11]

Swimmer Joel Sayers was also met with unexpected hostility while rescuing a ventilator patient. For unknown reasons, a violent survivor assaulted him, striking him with a bottle. After calming and disarming the man, Sayers was able to rescue the trapped family of the man on the ventilator.[12]

Another crowded scene had a less constructive result. Rescue swimmer Matthew Laub, from Air Station Savannah, began the mission by axing out an entire window to save a family of three. His helo moved on to rescue a large group stranded on a dry "island." Several cabin-loads of survivors were taken off and hoisted up into the helo when the increasingly aggressive crowd became violent, threatening Laub's safety. He had no choice but to call off the effort.[13]

Rescue swimmer William Lawson had over a hundred critically ill patients in a hospital and, because he was on-scene, he became the operational coordinator of the three helicopters making the rescues. Not only did he see to it that all were evacuated, but he personally carried one amputee ten flights up to the waiting helo. Later, back out over the drowned city, he found a couple barely clinging to a makeshift raft. The raft would surely capsize if hit by the rotor wash, so Lawson had the pilot move the aircraft 100 yards from the survivors. Then he swam through the fetid waters to reach the couple and towed them to a safe and dry hoist location.[14]

It was also a day of tremendous efforts for the Coast Guard's first female rescue swimmer, AST3 Sara Faulkner. A nine-year Coast Guard veteran, Faulkner had made two hoists in Mississippi immediately after the storm's passage. Wednesday night her helo located an apartment building with people gathered around a second story balcony. Twenty-five people waited there, but as soon as Faulkner dropped onto the balcony rail for the first pick-up, a woman thrust an infant into her arms. She recalled: "Our rescue devices are too small for babies so I had to hold him in my bare arms . . . and just the look on the mother's face . . . I . . . kicked out from underneath the roof because I didn't have any free hands to even give a signal, and . . . they hoisted me up and we started spinning. And I was so afraid of him wiggling and loosing [sic] my grip on him . . . but he didn't. . . . I did . . . more [hoists] after that . . . but that first one was scary."[15]

All twenty-five survivors were hoisted from the balcony and taken to safety. Faulkner and her crew decided to return to the same location since they "knew the drill" using the balconies. Once back they found that the other survivors had moved as a group to a flooded tennis court. The area was relatively uncluttered and, except for the nasty water, made for good, clear hoists. Using the "quick strop" was the fastest way to bring so many people up.[16]

Faulkner later described one of the difficulties of hoist rescues, which relied for the most part on hand signals:

> probably the hardest was . . . balcony ones, once I got under the roof they couldn't see me and . . . get a signal from me . . . it was kind of blind for the helicopter. They didn't know what was going on and then all of a sudden the flight mech said he would just see, he couldn't see my hand because I had a black glove on and he would just see one little chunk of my wrist pop out from underneath the helicopter and he knew . . . [I can] start hoisting now.[17]

In these unprecedented circumstances, Faulkner found one aspect of CG rescue swimmer training to be the most helpful. "They teach you, 'Don't let these people get the best of you. Even though they're stronger than you or bigger than you, you are the one in control and command.'" Not normally an assertive person, Faulkner took these words to heart. When challenged, she was able to maintain control over the situation and successfully complete the rescues. She said: "I'd have to yell at them and tell them to get back, and 'No, women and children first.'"[18]

Sara Faulkner was decorated by the Coast Guard for her work in Hurricane Katrina. Then, in November 2005 she was named one of the Women of the Year and female heroes of the hurricane by *Glamour* magazine. She traveled to New York City to receive the honor.[19]

As the days passed, Coast Guard aviators continued to astonish with more ways to bring their versatile aircraft where they were needed despite the difficulties of navigating in this environment. In one particular instance of jaw-dropping maneuvering, Lt. Cmdr. David W. Edwards positioned his HH-65 so the rotor blades rotated in the 6-foot clearance *between* the overhanging treetops and the power lines. Maintaining the aircraft in this precarious hover, he moved forward gingerly to deliver the rescue swimmer to the best location for the hoist. Only after all four survivors were successfully lifted aboard could Lt. Cmdr. Edwards sigh in relief. As if that was not impressive enough, Edwards later had to perform an even more daring feat when he encountered survivors in a flooded house. The only way to effectively place the swimmer and basket for the hoist was to fly his helicopter *backwards*—slowly—until the tail rotor was directly beneath a set of power lines—lines which had the additional weight of a downed cypress tree on them. With the rotor wash continually battering the unsteady tree and, by extension, the swaying power lines, Edwards made the hoists. He must have become proficient in this maneuver: he repeated it five times until all the survivors were on the helicopter.[20]

In addition to high risk maneuvers, pilots also made use of unorthodox communications to accomplish their rescues. Lt. Gregory

Houghton, in an HH-65, lowered the swimmer to a second story balcony, losing visual contact with him. Noticing another CG helo within sight, Houghton radioed for assistance. While Houghton hovered above, the crew of the other helo was able to see the rescue swimmer and give Houghton positioning information relayed from the unseen swimmer. The two helicopter crews and the rescue swimmer repeated this unusual but effective process twenty-seven times before all the survivors were out of the building.[21]

The edge of disaster was skirted in another instance where the helo pilot had no way of knowing what was occurring on the ground. Cmdr. Michael McGraw, in an HH-65 at night, lowered the rescue basket bare—without a rescue swimmer. The survivors hauled the basket into their house and apparently assumed the basket would hold all that would fit into it, which was, in this case, three people. With no communication from below, the unexpected weight surprised McGraw and his helo dropped precipitately into an uncontrolled descent. The only way to regain control was to put the nose down and move forward while the flight mechanic rapidly hoisted the basket and survivors. The basket trailing behind and below the helo barely cleared obstacles on the ground, but the exposed evacuees may well not have been aware of the danger they faced. It was a close call, but McGraw regained control and completed the rescue.[22]

We end this day with quotes from AST3 Matt O'Dell's description of what were probably "normal" rescues, considering the circumstances. Having rescued several people in an apartment complex, the helo flew off to take them to a FEMA drop-off point. O'Dell remained behind to prepare more survivors to hoist, and requested that the helo crew return from Station New Orleans with a crash axe so he could hack a breakthrough to the victims. He later said:

> It was kind of nerve racking on the roof, between the squishy spots in the roof (afraid of falling through), the neighbors screaming at me to get them out (and trying to keep them calm), the sweat absolutely pouring off my head and hands

> (sweat in the eyes, hard to see), and the worry of hitting someone underneath the roof that I was slashing through. I found out the true meaning of task saturated. . . . I tore back the shingles with my hands, chopped through the plywood, and punched out the dry wall ceiling. . . . They set up a chair inside, and I reached in and pulled the boy out. Between the adrenaline and the fact the kid only weighed about 130 lbs. he came right up and out. The mom was a different story . . . about 180 or 190 [lbs.]. I had to reach into the hole about two feet to grab her outstretched hands. When I was sure she was ready and that I had a good grip, I gave it the old 1 and 2 and hoo-rah. I got her up to about her waist."

He then had to "pull and roll" the lady the rest of the way onto the roof.[23]

O'Dell was injured that day after locating a family of four on the second floor of a flooded house. He was lowered to the only window giving access to the survivors, but it was aluminum and too small for bringing out the people inside. He found no suitable tool for this obstruction and, as many other Coast Guardsman did in these unique circumstances, he made do with what he had, repeatedly kicking the window frame until it gave way. When he had one of the survivors in the basket, it began sliding down the roof. Instinctively, O'Dell grabbed both the basket and the windowsill, the broken window slashing through the glove into his hand. Nevertheless, he held on until the flight mechanic in the helo regained control of the basket. Then he pulled himself back into the room, cutting his leg.

After the hoists and back on base, O'Dell reported his injuries. He received five stitches in his leg, but refused the stitches for the cut in his hand because putting his hand in a brace would ground him from flying. By day's end, he had thirty-six rescues or assists.[24]

Wednesday also marked the entrance of the Coast Guard into the business of supplying food and water to the evacuees. Capt. Jones contacted higher headquarters with a request that food and water be brought in: "No provisions were made for all these refugees that we had picked off rooftops and put on high ground, we were pretty shocked."[25] Once the authorization was given, the CG officers simply used their government credit cards and purchased pallet-loads of water, sending a C-130 from Clearwater to Dobbins AFB, Georgia to pick it up and deliver it to New Orleans. The first load arrived at Louis Armstrong International Airport on the morning of August 31. It was the first water delivery to the city after the storm.[26]

Subsequently, whenever CG helos were dispatched for SAR, they carried water and MREs for distribution to the multitudes still awaiting transportation and sustenance. This marked a significant change from simple search and rescue operations, but one which was an obvious response to the needs on the ground.[27]

By midweek another overwhelming problem was surfacing: the drop-off points were being saturated. Hundreds of evacuees, freed from the dangers in their homes, were stranded—again—at the Cloverleaf, Lakefront, and other designated areas in boiling heat without food, water, or medical services. Worse, many of the hospitals were overwhelmed and some were not accepting patients—it was all they could do to take care of those already in the facilities. It was a critical dilemma, particularly for the aviators attempting to find a place to offload their evacuees and return for more. The only choice in many instances was for the pilots to land the evacuees against the wishes of the people already at the drop-off zone.[28]

The shortage of medical care was not addressed in a significant way until Thursday—four days after the storm—when the U.S. Air Force brought in a C-141 transport with a complete field hospital and set up at the international airport.[29] Easing the congestion at the drop-off zones and providing even minimal food and water were problems only addressed incrementally throughout the next several days. The Coast Guard by this time had begun fulfilling the latter needs; the difficulty of congestion could only be met by emergency forces on the ground.

September 1

The Watershed Day

September 1, 2005, was the day when the efforts to relieve New Orleans and its vicinities reached a turning point. It was the end of the "golden seventy-two hours" considered by disaster relief experts to be the most critical period for reaching those who had survived the storm. After these first seventy-two hours the chances of people without food or water surviving at all dropped precipitately. From the standpoint of the rescuers, this meant fewer house-top rescues and an increasing chance that the neediest victims were those trapped within the attics and homes, unable to signal for assistance.

On this day U.S. Army Lieutenant General Russell Honore arrived in New Orleans. Honore was the commanding general of the joint task Force set up by the military's NORTHCOM (Northern Command) at Camp Shelby, Mississippi. Accompanying this appointment was the selection of Coast Guard Rear Admiral Robert F. Duncan as the commander of the joint force's maritime component.[1] From the standpoint of the overall rescue and relief effort in New Orleans, this marked the change from a large but uncoordinated effort by various agencies—including the Coast Guard—to one with some sort of common direction. Additionally, for the rescuers this meant that the on-scene communications difficulties were alleviated somewhat by the arrival of the General's forces that brought with them an additional 20,000 handheld radios.[2]

To the average American watching the event unfold from afar, Honore's appearance and can-do attitude was one of the first signs of hope during the disastrous week. The extent of the storm and its disaster was finally in the open. In a televised address, president George Bush stated, "We're dealing with one of the worst natural disasters in our nation's history." After an overflight on Air Force One he remarked to his advisers that "It's totally wiped out . . . It's devastating . . ."[3] These words confirmed the suspicions of many, and were indeed absolute, unfiltered truth.

On the ground, the city was literally full to the brim. As of noon on Wednesday, the waters in New Orleans had reached the same level as Lake Pontchartrain. So the water could rise no farther, but by the same token, there was no place for the water to drain. At this point, the military began dropping huge 3,000-pound sandbags into the various levee breaks, in particular on the 17th Avenue break—a gap over 200 feet long.[4]

Another major change in the city streets was a strong law enforcement response to the growing unrest and lawlessness. Mayor Ray Nagin declared martial law, and then ordered the 1,500-man New Orleans police force to redirect its efforts from search and rescue to peacekeeping. The looting had become an epidemic. The lawbreakers were using inflatable mattresses to float away with the spoils: blue jeans, tennis shoes, TVs, and even guns. In one instance, a forklift had been used to break into a pharmacy; in another, a bus driver had been forcibly removed from his vehicle by thugs. It was rumored—and then reported as fact—that a SWAT team vehicle had been stolen, complete with weapons. Hitherto, the police priority had been search and rescue, and many times first responders had simply avoided confronting the lawbreakers. Consequently, ordinary citizens were arming themselves and challenging looters vigilante-style. Now, the mayor's orders placed the police back in their primary role.[5] This development was good for the Coast Guard, as it relieved them of the predicament of being seen as local law enforcement officers when their most important charge was search and rescue.

The violence, or threat of violence, reached a peak Wednesday evening at Charity Hospital. The facility was overwhelmed by the influx of injured and sick, and finally had to turn away people. That night, sniper fire broke out near the hospital. Shortly thereafter, the National Guard troops around the facility began to pull out. It would seem that this move was inexplicable, but absent other instructions, under the Posse Comitatus Act, the troops were not authorized to shoot fellow Americans.[6]

Also on Thursday, Mayor Nagin ordered a mandatory evacuation of the city, predicting that the city "will not be functional for two or three months." Finally, the first of nearly 25,000 refugees departed from the horrendous scene at the Superdome, where there was no air conditioning, the toilets were backed up, and medical facilities were nearly nonexistent. Buses arrived and they were transported to Houston.[7]

Another milestone of sorts occurred on Thursday. Though many federal troops had been promised for the city, few had arrived, and Mayor Nagin, in a live radio interview had scathingly denounced the feeble federal assistance efforts, specifically mentioning FEMA and the Department of Homeland Security. Fortunately, the Coast Guard was not mentioned in the mayoral diatribe, and indeed had been diligently exerting maximum efforts since the storm had passed.

In the Gulf Coast area, by Thursday the death toll in Mississippi alone was 110. But this total was an "at least" statistic, because many affected areas were still unreachable due to blocked roads and destroyed bridges. There were still many instances when emergency vehicles sped past corpses while making every effort to reach living people still trapped in flooded and crumbling buildings.[8]

⊙

For Coast Guard operations in New Orleans, Thursday was a day of transition. There were changes in key personnel, as well as changes in tactics and strategy. Generally, the changes represented a step up from the somewhat informal arrangements necessitated by the exigencies of emergency, to a more regularized approach: realigning the jobs to be done with more appropriate personnel and equipment newly available for the task.

At Zephyr Field, Lt. Cmdr. Schaffer had made an excellent start as the key CG officer in the Unified Command there. However, by late Wednesday, the Coast Guard contingent had grown significantly, amounting to around 100 people including Disaster Area Response Teams and security personnel, as well as equipment, trailers, etcetera. Schaffer had a twofold responsibility: the first was to coordinate Coast Guard efforts with those of the other agencies in the unified command, and the second task was to direct the CG personnel and units actually on scene. By Thursday, both these jobs were overwhelming and Schaffer requested assistance from above.[9]

In response, Deputy Sector Commander Capt. Mueller and others conferred and hand-picked Lt. Cmdr. Shannon Gilreath to take charge at Zephyr Field. Mueller said, "He [Gilreath] had a strong command presence and he would fit in with the operation . . . and I said to him 'I can't tell you what you're going to be doing exactly . . . but when you get there you're going to understand what needs to happen with the boats and the search and rescue. So go there and do the best you can and we'll send you everything we can.'" As orders go, these were amazingly open-ended, leaving the substance to be filled in by Gilreath as the situations indicated. Given the incredibly poor communications during this period, it was about as specific as his supervisors could get.[10]

To assist Gilreath, Lt. Cmdr. Sean Regan was assigned to head security at the site, in the form of a Marine Safety and Security Team. Regan received nearly the same orders: "You guys are the heavy hitters in the security game. . . . Go down there and take care of our people." The MSST units were relatively new to the Coast Guard and had originally been formed as a direct result of the 9/11 attacks. Each seventy-five-man team received specialized training at the U.S. Marine base at Camp Lejeune, NC in antiterrorism, tactical boat operations, and special weapons.[11]

Once on site at Zephyr Field, Gilreath found literally hundreds of rescuers and support personnel. In addition to CG forces, there were Jefferson Parish police, New Orleans firefighters, state police, and state Wildlife and Fisheries officers. There were also numerous USAR (Urban Search and Rescue) teams from Missouri, Tennessee, Texas, Florida, California, New Mexico, Montana, Arizona, and Colorado. USAR teams are trained to respond in and around collapsed and damaged buildings in urban settings, and the groups are composed of firefighters, paramedics, and other technical specialists. The USAR teams did not have their own boats, but the Environmental Protection Agency, U.S. Geodetic Survey, and Department of the Interior, Fish and Wildlife division provided them.[12] In joint operations with the Coast Guard they operated in CG vessels. At this stage, there were nearly 700 people on site at Zephyr Field dealing with search and rescue, as well as security, in the city.

The search and rescue methods were worked out as follows: the flooded portions of the city were divided into sectors and the search sweeps were to meet the same standards everywhere. There were three search levels: Hasty, Primary, and Secondary. The "Hasty" component involved relatively quick passes through each sector, looking for individuals in need of assistance who were capable of responding to a loud-hailer or voice. The next search level was "Primary," which required the team members to actually touch individual buildings, knocking on windows and doors. And, if there was flooding in the building, rescue personnel banged on the roof and listened for sounds from inside. "Secondary" searches were time-consuming and comprehensive, requiring room-to-room searches covering entire buildings. The goal was to systematically cover each sector with all three types of searches. The "secondary" search would always be the final search, unless a 911 call or other verifying information became available.[13] In addition, the search teams would clearly mark—usually with spray paint—the structures visited to indicate what had been done, thereby preventing redundant efforts.

The areas assigned daily to each search team were determined by intelligence gathered on previous days, as well as other information from Louisiana Fish and Wildlife and local authorities. Further priorities were imposed by the sector's proximity to highways and onramps where boats could be launched. Finally, sections of the city where many civilian boats were already active—such as those of the famous "Cajun Navy" which had deployed on Wednesday—and those with a high incidence of violence against rescue personnel were placed lower in priority.[14]

With strategy and tactics in place, there were still serious issues hampering operations from Zephyr. Security was the primary sticking point. As will be seen, SAR operations were suspended on Thursday due to potentially unsafe conditions for rescuers: shots fired at New Orleans police officers and National Guardsmen were reported, as well as unconfirmed shots fired at helicopters.

Another problem was the lack of transportation to move evacuees from the initial collection points to shelters or staging areas. Buses and other vehicles were repeatedly promised by city, Office of Emergency Preparedness, or Louisiana Fishery and Wildlife authorities, but were only rarely available where they were needed. The results were the notorious and dangerous crowd and riot scenes at various drop-off points across the city.

The third problem at Zephyr Field was logistical: providing toilets, decontamination stations, showers, laundry, fuel, and food and water for the hundreds of workers and responders already gathered there. There were already hundreds on the field. The Coast Guard personnel were sleeping in RVs, tents, in the open, on cots, or with 500 others in a covered practice field. The toilet facilities consisted of five porta-potties and thirty comfort stations with bags. The sewage tanks on the RVs were full, there was barely a day's supply of boat, generator, and vehicle fuel, there were no showers or laundry facilities, and decontamination was a serious concern. Finally, given the growing level of violence, there was still a shortage of weapons and body armor.[15]

At this point there were 135 CG personnel at Zephyr Field, sixty from MSO St. Louis, MSU Baton Rouge, and Aids to Navigation Teams. The latter hailed from Galveston, Sabine, and New Orleans. The seventy-five-man MSST Team from Galveston rounded out the number. There were twelve 16-foot DART boats and six miscellaneous vessels up to 24-foot, both inboard and outboard powered. Besides the MSST unit's weapons, there were only six 9mm handguns and eight sets of body armor available for the Coast Guard contingent.[16]

To maximize security and the effectiveness of the weapons on hand, special tactics were developed. The rescuers would go out in groups of four boats: three DART boats operated by unarmed crews and USAR teams and a fourth vessel manned by two armed individuals and an unarmed coxswain, enabling use of all the DART boats while providing security. Their standing orders were to use weapons for self-defense only, not for law enforcement or property protection. The teams were strongly advised to withdraw immediately if a threatening situation were to occur.[17]

The most significant facet of Thursday's operations was the suspension of search and rescue due to reports of violence against rescuers. This was a decision by the Unified Command: Lt. Cmdr. Schaffer, FEMA, Jefferson Parish, and Louisiana Fish and Wildlife representatives. The key factor leading to this decision was probably the unconfirmed report of shots fired at a rescue helicopter. There has been much controversy over the veracity of that report. At the time, it was taken at face value, but of course media interest played a large part in overdramatizing the situation on the ground in the city.

There was definitely shooting going on, and some casualties. In one instance, private security guards shot two snipers who themselves were shooting at a lock house worker attempting to open a bridge. As to shots taken at helicopters, district attorney Warren Riley stated, "All those stories about people shooting at helicopters weren't true." However, Riley's next sentence in this particular documented interview contradicted this: "There was one guy [who] shot a helicopter in Algiers—A SWAT team went in and got him." But, for the most part, the shooting was not "at" the helicopters. People trapped in attics were shooting weapons to attract attention and help. There were no documented shootings at Coast Guard helicopters.[18]

The ban on SAR was lifted later in the day when the authenticity of the shooting report was brought into question, and some rescue missions were sent out. However, even while the ban was still in effect, the Zephyr Field CG contingent made one sortie: three boats were sent to the ISC New Orleans facility to retrieve personnel medical records.[19]

The SAR cessation also did not affect the efforts staged out of Station New Orleans. Furthermore, the regular boat convoys continued carrying groups of evacuees from the "island" at the University of New Orleans to the pickup points.

⊙

On Thursday, at the third nexus of Coast Guard operations, CGC *Pamlico*, the Chalmette–Algiers ferry/barge operations continued. The numbers brought out dropped from around 2,000 to 1,200 on Thursday because of an endemic problem: lack of buses to transport people from the Algiers terminal to shelters or FEMA transportation hubs.

Two other highlights of the day were the arrival of CGC *Spencer* and another MSST team, the team from New Orleans, with four boats. For a short time, the MSST team provided CWO Lewald with a personal bodyguard. He said, "the Chief parked a guard on me, and . . . it was kind of cool because what I was doing was moving through the crowd to try to calm folks down . . ."[20]

The CGC *Spencer*, a 270-foot, 1,800-ton medium endurance ship capable of handling a helicopter on her flight deck, steamed in from Guantanamo and moored near *Pamlico* early Thursday evening. Her skipper, Commander Robert Tarantino, took over tactical control of the area from CWO Lewald. This change was obviously more mission-appropriate: the *Pamlico*, an unarmed aids to navigation boat was replaced by a fully equipped law enforcement vessel.

The *Spencer* had come prepared. Before leaving Cuba, the crew had stocked up on everything they could find that might be needed in the disaster area: toiletries, baby formula, first aid kits, etcetera. In fact, due to *Spencer*'s normal mission—alien migration interdiction—many such items were already in good supply on board. When the *Spencer* arrived, CWO Lewald went aboard immediately and was certainly glad to turn over the operation to Tarantino.[21]

But Lewald's troops were needy, and many of his Coasties only had the clothes on their backs. Food was in short supply, as were fuel and spare parts for their boats. The *Spencer*'s crew immediately took up a collection—any extra uniforms, coveralls, shirts, etcetera. were gathered and it all went to the *Pamlico*'s hardworking men and women.[22]

The ferry/barge operation continued uninterrupted the next day, with *Spencer* becoming the ICP (Incident Command Post) in lieu of Lewald's vessel, providing support for the twenty-three CG vessels operating from the river. Chief Warrant Officer Lewald later received the Legion of Merit for his leadership during the aftermath of the storm, and, in particular, for those first days when he found himself commanding the Coast Guard's Mississippi River Armada.[23]

⊙

The cessation of search and rescue initiated at Zephyr Field clearly did not apply to many facets of the Coast Guard operations on September 1. Only a partial moratorium was noted in a District 8 situation report: "air ops secured in City Park area SE to French

Quarter due to possible hijacking of SWAT team-DOD vehicle."[24] This sector did not include the areas of heavy flooding from Lake Pontchartrain or the Lower 9th Ward.

In fact, the official take on CG helo operations vis-à-vis the shooting was articulated by Capt. Jones, commanding at the air station, who directed that the aircraft commanders use their own judgment when dangerous situations arose. Thus, the aviators had no across-the-board ban on SAR due to the alleged shooting incidents.[25]

Indeed, air operations seem to have remained at a high level throughout the day, and in fact may have increased in the areas not affected by the prohibition. By this time there were forty-eight aircraft from nine air stations working in the disaster area.[26]

The HH-60 Jayhawk CG6034 commanded by Lt. Zach Koehler went through a typical day operating out of Mobile. Leaving the air station at mid-morning they first delivered a cabin full of MREs and water to the New Orleans Air Station, then picked up Navy SEAL reconnaissance personnel to assist in a survey of the area for appropriate places to launch their RHIs (rigid-hulled inflatable boats). Then they flew Army air traffic controllers to the Cloverleaf.

After these tasks were done, Koehler searched for "targets of opportunity," locating a flooded six-building apartment complex where another HH-60 was already at work. He dropped the rescue swimmer at the opposite end of the complex from the first Jayhawk. The swimmer made rescue hoists from a second floor balcony, bringing several adults and children out of danger. Koehler then delivered them to the Cloverleaf, and when they returned for more, they moved to the next building in the complex. During these hoists, Koehler and his crew saw several people in an adjacent building gesticulating and waving a crude sign reading "Diabetic," so Koehler moved there and deployed the rescue swimmer. Koehler hoisted two diabetics and quickly removed them to the Cloverleaf.

On the third trip, five survivors were found trapped on the rooftop of a building surrounded by trees and debris. These were the last evacuees of the day for Koehler and crew, but it was not the last emergency. Their aircraft flight control systems malfunctioned on final approach to land at Air Station New Orleans. Luckily, this problem did not prevent a safe set-down or hamper their return to Mobile, where they arrived at mid-evening. They had logged 5.5 hours in the air and saved thirty-four lives, including seven children.[27]

The rescue swimmers had another round of hair raising experiences with survivors who, by this point, four days after the storm, were increasingly belligerent and desperate—conditions only exacerbated by the lack of food and water. One of the most notorious situations developed at the Days Inn in east New Orleans. Two CG helos were on the scene, one commanded by Lt. Cmdr. Eric S. Gleason, the other by Lt. Cmdr. Thomas McCormick. They lowered three swimmers to the roof who found a massive crowd of starving, panic-stricken people demanding evacuation. Right at the outset, one man pulled out a loaded pistol and demanded to be the first hoisted. The senior enlisted man on the scene, swimmer AST1 John C. Williams, refused to be intimidated and faced the man down. Once in control, Williams divided the survivors into two groups: the cooperative and the combative. He put the latter under guard while he and the second swimmer circuited the lower floors to make sure there were no more survivors. When all this was done, Williams and the other swimmer supervised the hoisting, bringing off all the evacuees. Williams was later awarded the Distinguished Flying Cross for his actions.[28]

Meanwhile, hovering over the apartments, the pilots and other aircrew members shared a different hazard—nearly zero visibility on scene due to fog and smoke. Gleason's crew rescued thirty individuals in these conditions; McCormick's, 113. By necessity, each helo had to make several trips to deliver their evacuees to safety, and each time they left behind the rescue swimmers, the only ones keeping a lid on the volatile crowds.[29]

Another danger presented itself on Thursday when thunderstorms moved through the area. Even under normal conditions static electricity quickly builds up on metallic objects lowered from a helicopter, and anyone unfortunate enough to touch the object before it is grounded receives the jolt. Now the storms multiplied the danger. As rescue swimmer O'Dell remembered:

> The static electricity in the air built up on the rescue devices so fast that it was producing arcs up to a foot long when it came down to the balconies. The way the balconies were set up with overhanging roofs, the basket could not be put directly on deck and the swimmer had to manually haul it in. It took perfect timing to grab the basket as soon as it hit the guard rail. If you grabbed it too early you received a very painful jolt; too late and the basket would fall . . .

And, he continued: "I tried . . . to time it . . . but then chose to grab it early . . . to expedite the recovery process." He steeled himself for the jolts, and they became part of the job. Not surprisingly, O'Dell reported that his arms were "painfully numb" by the time the day's missions were over.[30]

O'Dell's last mission of the night was at a school building where the survivors threatened him—all the more so when he said he could only take one more person on the trip. He reassured them that more helos were on the way and all would be evacuated. However, once he was back onboard, O'Dell asked the pilots to pass the word: they were to be very careful when hoisting from that particular building.[31]

The rescue basket itself became a tool for some of the hoists during the Katrina effort. AMT2 Daniel J. Hoffmeier, a flight mechanic, was responsible for directing the aircraft's movement during the rescues and deploying or retrieving the basket as needed. In one instance, Hoffmeier took notice of survivors on a second story balcony, but the balcony was covered by a wide overhang. He was unable to drop the swimmer straight down to the site, but he had a solution. He directed the pilot to initiate a back-and-forth motion of the helicopter, creating a pendulum effect—a "controlled swing"—for the swimmer and basket. The swimmer, with trapeze artist timing, waited for the correct moment in the forward swing, grabbed the balcony railing, and pulled himself into the building. The swimmer and crew rescued six people during this process.[32] Once the basket was loaded, the safe departure from the vicinity of the building was no less risky of a venture.

In a true test of professionalism, Commander James S. O'Keefe, skippering an HH-60, ran a mission to a hospital despite a report of shots having been fired there. With 200 patients and staff awaiting evacuation, O'Keefe rallied two other helos to assist. While acting as the on-scene coordinator for the three helicopters, his aircraft and crew worked sixty hoists using night vision goggles. He earned a second Distinguished Flying Cross for his role in the CG disaster response.[33]

Probably one of the most heartrending evacuations was recorded by survival technician Matthew C. Novellino. The mission was from a field medical station in Biloxi which had four seriously ill patients to move to a hospital. One of the four was an elderly patient who went into convulsions and was placed on oxygen during the flight. He passed out from pain several times before the twenty-five-minute flight was over. On the ground and about to be lifted off the helicopter, he looked up feebly and said, "I'm a veteran." Novellino forced a smile to his face and said "What service?" "Coast Guard," answered the man, and with that he was taken away on a stretcher. Novellino and crew saved seventy-four people and two dogs that day, but he would always remember the Coast Guard veteran.[34]

By the end of September 1, the Coast Guard reported a total of 2,859 rooftop rescues by service helicopters since the passage of Hurricane Katrina: 1,259 on Wednesday, and another 1,600 on Thursday.[35]

September 2

The Welcome and the Unwelcome in New Orleans

While the major elements of survivor evacuation continued without letup for the Coast Guard, Friday saw minor dramas acted out. Some warranted national attention, while many others might not have occurred had a national audience been in attendance.

Certainly the city was a live hotbed of drama, contention, and suffering. At the Morial Convention Center, thousands of the bereft festered with only shreds of hope that someone would notice. Elsewhere, some relief could be discerned: the Superdome, cynosure of much negative attention for its overcrowding and unspeakable filth, was finally being evacuated. The long promised buses had arrived and begun their shuttles to points west.

The CGC *Spencer* and *Pamlico*-led barge/ferry transfers from Chalmette to Algiers were interrupted early in the day by smoke from nearby explosions and fires which forced the CG vessels out of the vicinity. By late morning the danger had passed and operations resumed, resulting in over 2,500 evacuees being transported across the river and out of St. Bernard Parish.[1]

Then, for the first time, helicopters were used by Lewald, Tarantino, and the ongoing barge/ferry operation. They had painted a landing zone for MEDEVAC choppers and this was noticed by two Air National Guard CH-53s—the largest helicopters in the U.S. inventory, easily capable of lifting over 10 tons or fifty-three people, loading by way of a ramp in the stern. When they landed on the makeshift pad Lewald was impressed: "It's the biggest thing I've ever seen, and out gets this guy, he's got to be like 6'8". . . . and he's patting me on the head, he said 'I want fifty people per helicopter and don't make me wait.'"[2]

No more encouragement was needed. The ANG helos were lined up on the levee, the Coast Guard coordinated loading the survivors, and in ninety minutes nearly 1,000 evacuees—ten loads per helo—were safely across to the dry side of the river.[3]

Later in the day, another 100 were evacuated from the Canal Street Ferry terminal. In this case, by the CG 41-foot utility boats plus the CGC *Pelican*, a 67-foot patrol boat based out of Abbeville, Louisiana.

The day ended with welcome relief. District 1 (New England) and District 5 (Mid-Atlantic) crews arrived to take over operating the 41-footers, replacing crews who had been at work with little rest for five days in incredibly stressful and unpredictable conditions.[4]

At Station New Orleans another unexpected group was welcomed: the local PGA golf tournament professionals showed up and offered to feed the folks at the station, gratis. Such charity was in great need. In addition to the CG personnel, the station had become a default domicile for an FBI contingent, plus ATF agents, National Guard soldiers, local police, and firefighters, among others. Once they were given the go-ahead, the golfers brought in a portable kitchen and started cooking. Capt. Mueller said: "it was really good chow." Mueller then had second thoughts. He wondered if the scheme was legal . . . a "posh organization feeding us meals." Fortuitously, the next day a VIP tour at the station included the Attorney General of the United States, Alberto Gonzales. On hearing what the PGA group was doing, the attorney general just said, "I want to shake their hands." Mueller assumed this to mean that there was de facto "official" sanction for the providers of good food.[5]

In contrast, one of the more inexplicable events of the day concerned the availability of the Air Guard helicopters. Cmdr. Tarantino dispatched an officer to the beleaguered Morial Convention Center, only a few blocks away to the north, offering to evacuate those individuals using the already prepared landing zone and the ANG helicopters. Furthermore, Tarantino had water and MREs and there were buses available in Algiers to take the evacuees at the convention center to better accommodations. Tarantino remarked, "three times we sent the XO [executive officer] over there to make contact . . . to start moving people . . ." Even without the helos, the Coast Guard 41-foot boats could have been used to shuttle dozens of people each, all night. But the situation at the convention center was in chaos, with no apparent leadership or organization. "They could not get people for us to move," said Tarantino.[6] This was one of the many missed opportunities during the New Orleans saga.

Another sad missed connection involved the DART team from MSO St. Louis. They located and evacuated 200 people from the mid-city area, but by nightfall no transportation had arrived for the evacuees. Not ones to take responsibility lightly, the team members loaded all 200 survivors onto their own vehicles and convoyed them to Louis Armstrong International Airport in hopes of finding them shelter. However, they met with unexpected opposition. At the airport gate a shotgun-carrying Jefferson Parish police officer barred their way, saying, "Turn around, you can't take your evacuees here." After a short argument the officer chambered a round in his weapon and pointed it at them, saying, in so many words, that he would shoot to enforce his authority.[7]

To prevent the standoff from escalating, the DART team backed off and the convoy retraced its steps. They contacted FEMA and the Office of Emergency Preparedness to have the situation rectified, and a few hours later, assuming that the way was cleared, they made a second attempt to gain entry. However, this convoy was also turned away by the local policemen who threatened to arrest everyone in the caravan.

There was no alternative but to drop off the unfortunate evacuees at the I-10/610 location. It was not a good situation, but as Lt. Cmdr. Gilreath said: "we didn't want our people shot."[8]

By day's end, the Coast Guard forces at Zephyr Field had deployed sixteen boats and saved over 300 lives. The Unified Command effort from the field saved over 2,000 lives. Among those assisted by the CG and Unified Command were the inhabitants of a New Orleans East nursing home and hospital. For the first time, CG aids to navigation flat boats were used, brought in from Sabine and Galveston, Texas. Though these were of deeper draft than the flood punts and smaller boats, their extra width made them perfect for handling stretcher patients. The two flat boats were used to evacuate over 100 people.[9]

The evacuation convoys from the University of New Orleans were discontinued on September 2. An Army colonel had observed the situation from his aircraft and volunteered his helicopters to speed the evacuation. With Station New Orleans' assistance, they made fifty helicopter sorties, taking care of about two-thirds of the crowd—around 2,000 evacuees. Another 1,000 remained, many of whom stayed behind because the Army helos would not take their pets. This group was the last taken from the University of New Orleans location by Coast Guard boats.[10]

⊙

At this point in the narrative, I should address an obvious but probably unavoidable imbalance in my coverage of air operations and boat evacuations. The reader will note that there are many descriptions of helicopter and rescue swimmer missions for each day of the emergency, but few depictions of individual Coast Guard boat crew member accomplishments. This is not any attempt to minimize the waterborne aspect of the effort. Certainly both boat and air crews faced life threatening situations daily, even hourly, and due credit should be given both.

The problem is one of sources as well as distinctions between the air and boat operations. The aviators and rescue swimmers made relatively short missions: to the hoist site, execute the rescues as fast as possible, deliver their evacuees, and return for fuel. The hoists were finite units and the entire crew was credited with hoists and the number of rescued per mission. Sometimes, swimmers would be left in place while the helo delivered the previous survivors and/or returned for gas. In any event, the missions were relatively specific and defined. For the writer, the result was easily translated onto paper, assisted by the many medal and award citations, which usually delineated date, time, location, number of hoists, etcetera.

The individual small boat operations—as opposed to major operations such as the evacuation from the University of New Orleans—were entirely different. Boat crews were likely to be out on the water all day, trolling from house to house, then if needed, searching buildings room to room. In some ways their work resembled that of boarding crews at sea: they had little way of knowing what they would meet when they entered a structure or home. Plus, the Coasties' availability on the spot meant they handled tasks often tangentially related to actual rescues: bringing food and water, checking up on survivors who refused to leave their homes, reporting to other authorities if medical assistance was needed, and sometimes facilitating other rescues by relaying information gathered elsewhere. Boat crews faced distinctly different dangers from the aviation fraternity. They also did not have the capability of being hoisted out when a dangerous situation developed. In any event, for boat operations, the official citations are much less specific and rarely accompanied by the date, place, and number rescued. For the most part the citations are of a general nature, employing what became the CG boilerplate paragraphs telling of extended, fatiguing days, horrible, unsanitary water, uncooperative survivors, dangerous obstructions, and so forth. Further, even interviews of the participants, often obtained weeks or months later, showed evidence that their memories tended to overlap and be less specific in detail. In fact, what this implies is that while the boat operators may have faced a lower level of peril than the aviators, they bore up under it and performed their missions for extended periods—often entire days—with little relief.

Consequently, with this problem in mind I have inserted here some of the outstanding boat crew accomplishments, going on the assumption that the specific dates and statistics are not particularly relevant to the deeds being described.

Gunner's Mate Second Class Corey Anderson was a member of the New Orleans Marine Safety and Security Team, and worked eleven straight days as part of the Urban Search and Rescue contingent as well as in the Chalmette–Algiers ferry/barge operation. In addition to providing security for this massive operation, at one point he found himself in Algiers, responding to a report of several elderly people trapped in their home. The home had also been the object of looters. Anderson led a team into the house, cleared it of the looters, and provided food and water to the inhabitants. The team did a second search and found several others in the home, all of whom were handicapped or mentally ill. Anderson provided for their needs until they were rescued. Later in the week, he and two other Coasties entered an eight story building and, working upwards, cleared it of looters. On the top floor they found several elderly survivors, including an HIV/AIDS patient who required special protection.[11]

Boatswain's Mate First Class Anna E. Steel was a member of a DART team from Sector Upper Mississippi Valley operating out of Zephyr Field the first ten days of September after the storm. Steel and her team went house to house, banging on doors and rooftops, poling, paddling, or wading. Sometimes it was necessary to physically carry the aluminum boats over railroad tracks and other dry areas to reach survivors. She became de facto care counselor when the residents were reluctant to evacuate to safety. The 100-plus degree temperatures and saturation point humidity made heat exhaustion a distinct possibility. As it was, she was losing pounds every day from these conditions. She'd increased her fluid intake, but it wasn't helping much. After the work day, "going home" did not mean returning to a comfortable base. For the first few days, she lived in the open; then in tents, with no amenities such as showers, normal toilet facilities, or regular meals. These conditions were common to the Coast Guard boat crews working in the stricken city.[12]

One evening, as nightfall was approaching, BM1 Steel learned of a family trapped in their home. Generally, nighttime operations on the obstruction- and debris-filled waters were particularly risky and, as a rule, not done. Nevertheless, she took on the mission. As Steel and her boat crew approached the house, they smelled natural gas—it was apparent that there were several gas leaks nearby. Any stray spark could trigger an explosion, but she maneuvered the boat to the porch. The front door was swollen shut, and inside a mother and three sons were trapped. Steel's crew removed the door and brought out the family, then very carefully, mindful of the leaks, retraced their path to safety.[13]

Petty Officer Steel worked twelve consecutive fourteen- to eighteen-hour days after the storm. As with the other Coast Guard boat crew members floating in the city streets, the job not only required courage and stamina, but a persistence defying categorization.[14]

There was also Kevin E. Biami, Boatswain's Mate with the Upper Mississippi River sector DART team, who on that first Tuesday, as previously related, rescued a pregnant woman out of the flooded streets just before her water broke. By now he was working out of Zephyr Field, and on one mission learned of an elderly man, with a feeding tube and in a wheelchair, in need of assistance. To even approach the man's home, he had to force his way—unarmed and unarmored—through a hostile crowd, then jump out of the boat into 4 feet of water. Inside the home he encountered a belligerent, intoxicated, linebacker-sized man blocking his way, suspicious of Biami's intentions. He persuaded the enormous man that he was there to help, and he must have been effective because the man became his faithful assistant and immediately turned on the crowd and shut them up. Then he led Biami to the stricken man and his wife, but the wife refused to come. The Coast Guardsman reminded her that she would be needed to tell the doctors what medications her husband needed and only then did she relent. Biami and his corpulent and unlikely helper carried the ailing man out of the house, hoisting him over their heads to prevent the toxic water from contaminating his feeding tube. Biami returned upstairs, carried the lady down to join her husband, and the team took the two to a MEDEVAC pickup point.[15]

Biami spent ten consecutive days in post-Katrina New Orleans as a coxswain (the pilot of a small boat), working with Army, FEMA, state, and local responders. He returned to his home base on September 10.[16]

⊙

Meanwhile, the CG fliers and swimmers continued to expect the unexpected. It was becoming a rule of thumb.

Shortly after Lt. Zach Koehler flew in from Mobile in his HH-60 (CG6038), he rescued ten people in a set of basket recoveries that were in dangerous proximity to trees and power lines. Then, after seeing five people on a flooded tennis court, he let the swimmer down. The situation on the court was more serious than Koehler could have imagined. One of the people was blind and mute. One woman had an infant and another had a severe infection in her leg. The fourth female had collapsed and hovered in and out of consciousness. Each hoist required the utmost in special care, but Koehler and his crew brought them all up without incident. The directions were to bring them to Baton Rouge, despite low fuel. Koehler made the sixty-five-mile trip and his helicopter was met by two ambulances ready to transport the ladies to a hospital.[17]

On Friday, Cmdr. Bill McMeekin and his crew—the backup team during the *Mary Lynn* rescue almost a week earlier—were among the familiar faces in the Gulf Coast skies. They departed from Mobile immediately before the base closed in preparation for the presidential visit and arrived at Air Station New Orleans in company with two other Jayhawks. McMeekin was struck by the crowded landing field. As he followed two CH-53s in to land, he noted that, "all ramps at field now crowded with helicopters and transport aircraft."[18]

Over the city, McMeekin found an ongoing rescue at a large apartment building. Two other helos were already on the scene, hoisting survivors. McMeekin waited his turn and surveyed the surrounding area for other survivors. When he noticed a small white flag fluttering from a hole in an adjacent rooftop, he let the swimmer down. The swimmer enlarged the hole to rescue an elderly gentleman inside and reached down to pull the man off the pile of furniture he had assembled to reach the ceiling. However, after the man was hoisted to the helo's cabin, his breathing became labored. The crew quickly administered oxygen until he stabilized.

McMeekin also spotted a group of survivors on a flooded intersection among power lines. After the crew discussed and dismissed the danger of possibly toxic water, the swimmer was let down again for three hoists. Then one of the evacuees wanted them to move down the street and evacuate his mother from her home. When they found her house, the only available dry drop point was a 5-foot square spot and the lowest they could bring the helo was 80 feet up—the equivalent of threading a needle from a foot away. Despite this, the swimmer went in, located the mother, and reported back that she was fine and would not leave her pets. Her son was relieved and grateful that they had checked on her.

After the two rescues, the apartment building which had been McMeekin's first destination was clear for his aircraft to move into position. Between 80 and 100 people waited for rescue on the flat roof and the swimmer hoisted eight to the helo. With the cabin filled to capacity, they flew to the Cloverleaf drop-off point and then made for the air station to refuel.

The air station was still crowded and McMeekin had to hover-taxi over the grass to the only open space available. They shut down, fueled, loaded water and MREs, and left again.

Their first stop was to deliver food and water to a house they had visited earlier in the day. The only place to deploy the basket was about 12 feet square, but the flight mechanic hit the spot on the nose. The resident unloaded the basket and gave them an "enthusiastic wave" in thanks.

Next they rescued eight people, including two mothers with infants, but first the rescue swimmer escorted them to a clear area in the street, well away from power lines. When the homeowner, now in the helicopter cabin, insisted they lower his house keys back down so the last person in the house could lock up, McMeekin swallowed a tinge of exasperation and humored the man.

But the problem of locking up the evacuee's house would not be the last during this rescue. With the sky so crowded it was inevitable: another helicopter was heading straight for them and McMeekin was still trying to hold at 90 feet for the hoist. The H-3 helicopter—probably a National Guard aircraft—was at nearly the same altitude, but after a few anxious moments, the pilot realized the danger. At about 100 yards out, the H-3 pilot turned a hard right and a near mid-air collision was avoided.

As if things could not get any worse, McMeekin's aircraft experienced a sudden loss of power and dropped 10 feet mid-hoist. McMeekin instinctively went to emergency power and into forward flight—both necessary to regain control—while the flight mechanic rushed to recover the basket and its occupants.

Leaving the rescue swimmer behind, they landed at the Lakefront and inspected the aircraft for the cause of the malfunction. By the time they returned for the swimmer, it was nightfall and he had to show a flare to be seen by the helo crew. They picked him up and returned to the air station.

The power loss indicated a more serious mechanical problem and CG6023 was left on the ground at New Orleans while the crew caught another HH-60 back to Mobile. On the flight were two evacuees: they said their family had been murdered in the street and all they wanted was to find safety. McMeekin and crew finally ended their day at about 10:30 P.M.[19]

Another aircraft commander, Lt. Cmdr. Christian A. Ferguson, was directed to evacuate patients from a hospital, only to find that the landing area was unstable and not likely to support the weight of his helicopter. To compensate, Ferguson held the HH-60 in a hover with the wheels barely touching the surface. As the patients were loaded, he had to adjust altitude and position continually as each patient added more weight to the aircraft.[20]

Rescue Swimmer Mitchell A. Latta was also forced to make instant, drastic decisions. He was hoisted down to rescue a woman in chest-deep water, and as she grabbed him she immediately collapsed. He attached her to the quick strop and signaled for the hoist, but when she cleared the water, he saw that her legs were tangled in a garden hose. Immediately he signaled to be dropped back into the water, and swam below the waters to untangle the hose, saving the woman's life.[21]

Rescue Swimmer O'Dell—who earlier in the week received injuries to his hand and leg while rescuing a family of four from a flooded house—described an incident that particularly impressed itself upon him during Friday's operations. He was especially appreciative of the man involved:

> One man on top of a school with hundreds of people on and in it, who refused to be hoisted so that he could be down there to help keep people in order and hopeful on top of the roof. . . . Nobody asked him to, he just did it, he took the initiative and recognized the (rescuers) needed the cooperation of the giant mob. . . . He saw us (RSs) getting mobbed and threatened . . . and decided to help. I wish I knew what became of him . . .[22]

Another woman impressed O'Dell at the airport where she awaited transportation. She was carrying a small office supply box—"the kind you see people carry in movies when they have just been fired." O'Dell learned that the box contained everything she owned, the only few things she had left. But she smiled at him because she "still had her life to be thankful for."[23]

⊙

The final event which must be included in this day of all-too-real encounters in the inundated Crescent City had more to do with politics and public relations than emergency rescues. After President Bush's poorly received flyover of the area in Air Force One, he arranged for a tour on the ground in the disaster area. As will be related in the chapter on operations farther east on the Gulf, the president began at Mobile, visiting the Coast Guard air station and air training command there, then moved on to Biloxi, surveying damage from a helicopter en route. He landed at Station New Orleans, where CWO Brooks was in charge. The president had a press conference there, and then shook hands with all present. This was a powerful morale boost for the exhausted and nearly overwhelmed Coast Guard personnel, most of whom were still subsisting on MREs and sleeping in tents.[24]

In the course of the New Orleans visit, the president viewed the 17th Street levee break as well as FEMA and other agencies at work at Louis Armstrong International Airport. For good or ill, the airport was under a security lockdown for the duration of his visit.[25] It is possible that the severe, armed "welcome" afforded to the Coast Guard evacuee convoy mentioned earlier in this chapter may have been related to this lockdown.

It would seem that this was a day of mixed messages—the "welcome" sign was not for everyone, everywhere in New Orleans. The disaster area equivalent of the "fog of war" still hung over the beleaguered city.

September 3

Flying Boats over New Orleans

Saturday marked nearly a week since Katrina's landfall. It was a day of notable expansion in the Coast Guard effort, as well as consolidation and, of course, further improvisation.

CG units from across the nation continued to send helicopters. There was even international support as Canada supplied two B-412 helos to backfill for local search and rescue needs at Air Station Cape Cod, allowing the CG aircraft to fly to the southern disaster area. Additionally, the CG Atlantic area contributed another four HH-60s, from Clearwater and Elizabeth City.[1]

There were nineteen Coast Guard HH-60s on the scene by Saturday, plus twenty-five HH-65s. Five HU-25 Falcons and several C-130s served in support roles. The Coast Guard Auxiliary, always prepared to participate in their parent organization's work, also contributed thirteen small private aircraft and their pilots to the effort.[2]

The Auxiliary is a volunteer organization, with their only remuneration being the cost of fuel and mileage for their aircraft and boats. They were present throughout the Katrina and Rita efforts, offering their services both in the air and on the water with several small planes—a Cessna 210, a Mooney, and a Beechcraft, among others, from units in Louisiana, Texas, Alabama, and Florida. Capt. Mueller, New Orleans sector deputy commander, said: "we had to move people to get things done but you didn't want to take a rescue helicopter because there weren't enough helicopters to go around . . . so you'd jump in an Auxiliary . . . and they'd fly you . . ."[3]

One of the Auxiliary pilots, Jim Finley, worked seven consecutive days in the aftermath of the storm from his Cessna 210. One of the major needs was to provide flights for key CG personnel from New Orleans to Alexandria and Baton Rouge, particularly when a Coast Guard representative was needed at joint force meetings.[4] In a post-Katrina interview, Capt. Jones, commanding the CG air efforts, said, "the Auxiliary provided extensive logistic support. . . . The air Auxiliary did a tremendous job as they always do."[5]

⊙

With forty-four Coast Guard helicopters on scene (minus the HH-60 which had landed at Lakefront airport with mechanical problems) the pace of rescues mushroomed. By 4:00 P.M. on September 3, there had been 385 aircraft sorties in the previous twenty-four hours. On average, this amounts to about fifteen flights per hour, or one dispatched every four minutes. Each aircraft was averaging eight sorties through the day. This brought the total number rescued by air to about 9,500.[6] Looking at the whole effort, in addition to the CG aircraft, the Department of Defense (National Guard and other agencies) had another forty-four helicopters on the scene, plus nine fixed wing aircraft.[7] These statistics do not include survivors rescued by local, parish, and private agencies.

On the water, Unified Command teams were deployed from Zephyr Field, mainly to Lakefront, East New Orleans, mid-city, and Chalmette. Zephyr Field-based Coast Guard forces were augmented by the arrival of DART teams from Sector Ohio Valley, which included MSU Pittsburg, MSU Huntington, MSU Paducah, MSU Baton Rouge, and other reserve and Auxiliary boats. Three more flat aids to navigation (ATON) boats arrived from St. Louis units. By the end of the day, the CG forces at Zephyr had nearly doubled to over 120 people, including at least thirty new security personnel.[8] This total did not include the MSST team.

Fortunately, the influx of new troops, most of whom were housed at the CG station, was accompanied by critically needed equipment and logistical support. The station eventually played host to over 250 Coasties, plus personnel from other agencies.[9] The DART teams, in particular, brought weapons and body armor, and the arrival of their RVs meant they did not put additional pressure on the living arrangements in and around the crowded station. The group from Baton Rouge contributed tents, underwear, and toiletries—all of which were needed. Finally, FEMA arrived with portable toilet units, fuel seemed to be more readily available, and one group brought in a couple solar showers.[10]

The importance of the CG security units cannot be overstated. In addition to the MSST units, there were TACLETs (Tactical Law Enforcement Teams), LEDETs (Law Enforcement Detachments), and the MSU (Marine Safety Units). During the day, thirty MSST members from New Orleans and Galveston joined FEMA DART teams dispatched into the city. This contingent rescued over 200 survivors. Throughout the day, there were twenty armed escort teams sent out, twelve of which were to protect logistic and supply runs. A FEMA representative arrived and stated that, had it not been for the CG waterborne security units, "rescue efforts would have been halted and innumerable people would not have been saved."[11]

Saturday saw an innovative approach to waterborne rescues. Two National Guard CH-47 Chinook helicopters became available for joint operations. The Chinook is a twin-tandem-rotor, heavy lift transport helicopter capable of carrying thirty to fifty troops or 14 tons of cargo. They were loaded with four CG flood punts complete with trailers, ATVs, equipment, and MSST security personnel and dispatched to Chalmette. They were intended to set down at the Chalmette Slip, but a navigational error put them near the St. Bernard Civic Center.[12]

Despite the mix-up, the teams improvised well. They located eighty-five people in flooded houses. None, however, could be convinced to evacuate, so the CG personnel supplied them with food and water for their stay. The effort was definitely not in vain. It set a precedent for later operations to reach areas of the city otherwise inaccessible by water. The method was safer and more efficient than conducting primary searches by going rooftop to rooftop by air alone.[13]

Also, in Chalmette, rescue team surveys resulted in the discovery of the massive oil spill at the Murphy Oil Meraux facility, about a mile south of the Chalmette Ferry Slip. The upshot of this was the evacuation of fifty individuals from the danger zone. These people were taken out by truck to Chalmette, then by ferry across to Algiers.[14]

By the end of the day, the Unified Command was responsible for 2,000 lives saved. The Coast Guard at Zephyr Field had sent out seventeen boats with teams who were responsible for 325 lives saved.[15]

On the river at 8:00 A.M., CGC *Spencer*, under Cmdr. Tarantino, positioned CG personnel on both sides of the Mississippi, anticipating the arrival of buses at Algiers Point. A security unit was also dispatched to the Canal Street Ferry, near the Convention Center, to assist loading of displaced residents. The transfer was halted when about 250 people had been ferried over because the promised buses did not arrive, but not before another 200 survivors were brought in by ferry from a senior citizen center. By this time there were over 300 senior citizens on site, awaiting transportation. Twelve people with severe medical needs were MEDEVACed. Finally, the buses pulled in and the loading began. Along with the evacuees who had already been at Algiers point, some 750 were moved out by bus and helo. When the CG raised questions about the bus delay, they were informed by the Army escort personnel that Algiers Point was the fourth in the queue to receive buses being parceled out by city emergency authorities.[16]

But there was still no shortage of evacuees awaiting transportation from Chalmette. Local officials estimated that over 2,000 remained, many of whom had been brought in by National Guard buses. The ferry/barge operation continued and all of these were safely at Algiers Point by the end of the day.[17]

The CG river fleet was reinforced on September 3 by CGC *Greenbrier*, a 75-foot river buoy tender from Natchez, Mississippi. *Greenbrier* brought in DART teams and boats, and coordinated their dispersal over the levees into the flooded areas. They encountered seventy-five survivors during the day. However, all but one refused assistance, part of an emerging trend.[18]

While the river contingents dealt with masses of evacuees, the airborne CG specialized in small numbers, many with special needs. Lt. Zach Koehler in HH-60 CG6013 flew from ATC Mobile on a night mission. He was sent to locate an assisted living home with two diabetics and other elderly people in need. In order to direct his aircraft to the exact location, he communicated with a resident of the home by way of a phone patch. Guided by the resident's directions, he found the four-story, flat topped structure, and the rescue swimmer was immediately deployed. One survivor was already on the roof and quickly hoisted in. Then the swimmer entered the facility and identified those most in need of airlifting. Outside, the aircrew searched for a more accessible, dry, lift site, finding a parking lot across the street. Three people were hoisted from the lot, and the swimmer then requested saws and an axe to break into a locked room where a survivor was thought to be trapped. No one was in the room, but the swimmer satisfied his duty by checking.

Meanwhile, across the street, a man and a pregnant woman approached the helo requesting assistance. Both were hoisted out, along with a fourth elderly person, and all were taken to a hospital.

Later, Koehler and crew hoisted at least another five people from a housing complex before calling it a night and returning to Mobile at about 2:30 A.M. During the 6.7-hour night vision goggle mission they rescued fourteen people.[19]

Not everything went according to plan in the air. In one instance, mentioned briefly earlier, swimmer Kenyon Bolton was left on site as his aircraft departed to deliver survivors to a drop-off point. As the helo pulled away, the rotor wash blew an elderly man into the toxic waters. Bolton immediately pulled him out. Once on dry ground, the two were in for a nasty surprise: hundreds of fire ants were also interested in reaching high ground. For the next half-hour Bolton frantically removed hundreds of the insects from his body as well as the old man's body. The task was particularly daunting as the man's skin had begun to shed from being immersed in the water for several days.[20]

Bolton continued the work of saving lives in the disaster area after this, but he was later medically evacuated against his wishes for "injuries sustained by native wildlife while performing search and rescue operations."[21]

Mechanical failure turned one mission into a nightmare for Cmdr. Michael McGraw, co-pilot Lt. Cmdr. Jacob E. Brown, and their HH-65 crew. In this night operation, McGraw located twenty survivors clinging to the roof of a flooded school bus. Having no choice, McGraw was forced to hover near a billboard, power lines, and a nearby fire blowing smoke and ash into the cockpit. Two successful hoists were made, but on the third the hoist mechanism failed with survivors still hanging in mid-air. Through the smoke and limited visibility and avoiding various unlit towers and obstructions, he navigated 6 miles to a safe drop-off point for the air-bound evacuees. It may well have been the most exciting ride of their lives, but one which McGraw would rather have avoided. This was Lt. Cmdr. McGraw's final mission during Katrina. Since August 29 he had flown nineteen hours—most of them at night—over the devastated landscape, and rescued fifty-one people.[22]

To wrap up the aviation scene for September 3 are two success stories. Rescue swimmer Jay M. Leahr was deployed to a hotel, and found himself in the midst of an angry crowd. He ignored their hostility and volunteered to search floor by floor for survivors, locating over seventy in the blacked out structure. Eventually, over 300 people were rescued from the building.[23]

Swimmer Timothy R. Fortney was lowered to a University of New Orleans neighborhood to search for survivors. After nearly an hour treading the waters, and employing the assistance of a local man with a light boat, Fortney gathered and hoisted out eight victims of the storm. Later, he located a ninety-year-old couple trapped in their house. He carried them through the waters to the hoist site, and they were lifted to safety.[24]

⊙

By the end of September 3 the Coast Guard effort in Sector New Orleans was massive, in terms of both people and machines. There were 1,344 CG members in the New Orleans area, working in both support and response roles. There were twenty-eight CG cutters on scene, as well as fifty-two aircraft, both fixed wing and rotary wing. On the ground there were three MSST units, two TACLETs, and one Port Security Unit. Two Civil Engineering units were there doing damage assessments at the Coast Guard facilities. Additionally, there was a National Strike Force twenty-eight-man team at Alexandria to deal with chemical and oil spills.[25]

It was estimated that about 9,500 survivors had been rescued by the Coast Guard, either by air or water.[26] Of course, it should be kept in mind that because of the nature of the water rescue mission, only approximate numbers could be generated, and it is not clear whether this statistic included the hundreds of survivors being brought out on the Chalmette/Algiers ferry operation.

September 4

The Tide Peaks

Sunday, September 4 marked two milestones. First, a full week had passed since Katrina's landfall. Second, it was the peak day for the Coast Guard rescue effort since the storm passed.

By Sunday there were 2,502 Coast Guard members working in Katrina-related operations, including 295 reservists called up for the emergency. In addition to twenty-six CG cutters and sixty-two aircraft, there were 111 small boats of all sorts. These statistics also include the personnel and equipment working in Sector Mobile. (Operations along the Gulf Coast east of New Orleans will be dealt with in a later chapter.)[1]

Boat operations out of Zephyr Field and Station New Orleans were systematically moving through the city. A major effort involved DART swift water rescue teams with CG and FEMA members, escorted by sixty MSST security personnel. They worked their way along the streets, hacking through roofs as needed to free trapped survivors. Over 340 people were assisted throughout the day. At this stage in the rescue efforts, many of the survivors were refusing to leave the area and their homes, but they accepted water and MREs. Communications among CG and other units were still weak, and, by the end of the day, one of the teams was unaccounted for and a search was necessary to bring them in.[2]

A second helicopter-transported small boat mission was dispatched on Sunday. Again, a communications breakdown hampered the outcome. Groups from MSST Galveston and Station New Orleans, with their boats, were dropped at various sites in Chalmette and the Lower 9th Ward. Afterwards, the Galveston MSST reported that in central Chalmette, ten people were evacuated while six elected to remain in their homes; in west Chalmette, two were evacuated and fifty-eight refused to leave; and in the Broad Street area, twenty-five remained while 152 were evacuated. In the hard hit 9th Ward, sixty-three remained in the city and none were evacuated. By the day's end, 152 citizens were assisted in place while 164 were rescued.[3]

The helicopter-transported small boat DART group was supposed to be withdrawn from the area the same way it arrived—by helicopter—but the mission was marred by misunderstanding and, again, poor communications. The helicopter did not arrive at the prearranged time and place, and a second attempt to retrieve the team was aborted at nightfall. Once again, they had to improvise, commandeering two trucks and driving themselves back to the command center.[4]

New and old problems surfaced in boat evacuation operations. The waters began to recede in the city, making operation and launch of deeper draft boats more problematic. The threat of violence continued to hamper missions, with an MSST team encountering twenty-five people, some with guns, in a flooded building. An effective "officer presence" contributed to deescalating the threat level, and the structure was successfully evacuated. In the Lower Garden District, another DART team had to withdraw from the area when shots were fired nearby. The official policy continued to be that withdrawal from the scene was preferable to any potential confrontation with hostile, armed civilians.[5]

On the positive side, especially for the morale of the Coast

Guard, the New Orleans police reported that the criminals loose in the city feared the Coast Guard more than they did the local and state police. It was commonly believed that the CG people were SWAT trained. Consequently, when the CG arrived, armed and protected by body armor, lawbreakers "wade[d] the other way"—though these same people did not hesitate to confront NOPD or state police. This was an accurate evaluation of the MSST teams who were trained in law enforcement and weapons, but broadening it to include the Coasties in general did not hurt the service image and probably made their jobs easier.[6]

Another law enforcement group on site at Station New Orleans was an eight-man FBI contingent sheltered and fed at the station. The CG also provided boats, personnel support, and replenishment for the fifty-man FBI unit in downtown New Orleans.[7]

But there were negative impacts, as well. CG troops in the rescue effort developed health issues. Two Coasties required treatment for heat exhaustion and were sent to local hospitals. Another four or five were treated on site by corpsmen and given IV fluids. Several others were caught just in time in the early stages of heat stress and forced to sit out for a time. Most of the affected Coasties were new to the area and not acclimated to the extreme heat, humidity, and unrelenting pace of the work. In the excitement of lifesaving they neglected to look after their own fluid intake.

Injuries from rotor wash were another occasional problem.[8] This had been a constant problem for the rescue swimmers and the survivors on the ground and rooftops. It was not uncommon for people to be literally blown into the water, and flying debris—shingles, for instance—was a constant worry. The pilots were always balancing the need to hover high enough to mitigate the problem for the evacuees and swimmers, while avoiding trees and other tall obstructions. On the other hand, the higher the hover, the more vulnerable the hoist would be to wind conditions—both expected and unexpected.

As has been noted, the rescuers were encountering an increasing number of people electing to remain in their dwellings, and the groups of evacuees were growing smaller. Medical experts maintained that even by Thursday it was unlikely that anyone could have survived if they were trapped without power and supplies in overheated and dangerous attics or upper floors. However, one of the day's rescues confounded this expert opinion. Lt. Cmdr. Gilreath reported that one DART boat team searching in the vicinity of the CG station "turned off their motor to listen and they heard . . . a little faint tapping sound . . . and it was an elderly man . . . on the second story. There are bars over the window so they can't get out . . . They [the team] get somebody to cut a hole . . . and go in . . ." The elderly man was with his eighty-seven-year old mother, who was bed-constrained and up to her neck in water. They had been trapped there since Monday. The circumstances went beyond those of mere chance: here were several Coasties in a boat, trying to reach as many survivors as possible, and yet they just shut down their motor and simply "listened." On the other hand, the old gentleman in the house had no doubt heard the motor beforehand and strained to reach the window, hoping and praying his tapping would be heard.[9]

At the Chalmette Slip, activity continued to drop off as more individuals elected to remain in the city. Groups of twenty or so each arrived; around 100 people were moved from Chalmette to the Algiers Point ferry terminal. It was estimated that nearly 6,000 residents had been evacuated thus far via the Algiers/Chalmette ferry operation.[10]

On the Coast Guard's "domestic" front on board the CGC *Spencer*, a CISM (Critical Incident Stress Management team) arrived on Sunday. A chaplain and his assistant arrived and held mass at the ferry terminal and aboard the *Spencer*. Later, the Navy's USS *Tortuga*, a huge landing ship/dock craft with a complete flight deck and crew facilities moored on the river nearby.[11] Cmdr. Tarantino and his executive officer coordinated operations with the Navy ship, and the weary Coasties were offered full access to berthing, showers, laundry, medical care, water, and more. Conversely, the Coast

Guard offered the Navy support for search and rescue operations, security teams, and evacuee processing.[12]

By the end of Sunday, CG small boat surface rescue efforts with their twenty-seven operative vessels yielded 320 saved lives. The Unified Command—including CG elements—reported that 808 lives were saved.[13]

⊙

Air operations were unrelenting over the city. By Sunday, helicopters and crews from nine different air stations were involved, with aircraft being utilized constantly and aviators flying their maximum hours until regulations ("bag limits") forced them to take breaks between flights. The two main staging areas were the air stations at Houston and Mobile. The usual pattern involved the aircraft coming in to Air Station New Orleans with MREs and water, refueling, then departing for a specific task or to "freelance" looking for survivors.

One of the unique characteristics of the CG helo effort was the interchangeability of crewmen. Whenever a helicopter was ready to go to the city, the next available rescue swimmer not on mandatory down time and on the roster was summoned for the flight. It was not unusual to have members from four different air stations operating one Jayhawk or HH-65. Standardized training and procedures made the massive post-Katrina effort remarkably efficient, particularly in the air operations.

The experience of Cmdr. Anthony Vogt was typical in some ways, but unusual in others. Vogt was engineering officer at Air Station Clearwater, in charge of the base's seven HH-60s and four C-130 Hercules transports used for Katrina operations. Until September 4, Vogt had operated out of Clearwater, but on September 4 he flew to New Orleans to test fly one of the Clearwater HH-60s which had been grounded for repair. When the aircraft was ready, he gathered a crew, enlisted the next available swimmer, and was soon over the city freelancing search and rescue. The crew included co-pilot Lt. Mark Lay, also from Clearwater, AET2 Brian

Marcotte from Elizabeth City, AST1 Dave Gray of Corpus Christi, and AMT3 Ahmed Elfarrah from Mobile.[14]

They were called for a few evacuations, but found themselves in close proximity to eight other helos, so they continued on, surveying the adjacent blocks. For the first time, Vogt saw the extent of the devastation: wreckage, debris, human bodies, dogs and cows on levees, and a man "tied to a chimney" (no explanation was given for the latter). They monitored a call for an aircraft required at the Convention Center to pick up seventy people that needed to be taken to the airport. It was after dusk and no Department of Defense aircraft were available, so Vogt flew out to the center.[15]

The first group picked up at the Convention Center was escorted by National Guard troops carrying M-16s. Vogt said, "We thought they may be dangerous. They [the National Guard troops] said they were OK." Vogt's crew said the group looked to be in "bad shape." The group was transported and dropped off without incident, and Vogt returned for a second load of survivors destined for the airport. On approaching the airfield for the second time, they noticed an HH-65 "playing chicken" with an Air Force C-17 transport. The latter was landing on an east-west runway, while the former was approaching the same runway from the north. Vogt quickly realized the impending catastrophe and radioed the helicopter pilot to tell him the landing site was on the south side of the runway. Rather than going around, the HH-65 flew directly across the runway in front of the huge C-17—at night.[16] In the workaday aviation world, such an incident would have warranted an investigation.

After the second delivery was completed, Vogt returned to Mobile, the crew dispersed, and Vogt turned in for the night. The following morning he learned from the flight mechanic that the interior of the helicopter was "full of blood and excrement" and that one of their passengers had been beaten up before coming on board.[17] It seemed that Vogt had probably not gotten an accurate description of his passengers the previous day at the Convention Center.

Garbled communication had a part in another rescue that day. Aircraft CG6040 under Lt. Cmdr. Eric Johnson was en route from Mobile to New Orleans with forty-five cases of MREs and two cases of water when he was directed to pick up an appendicitis patient at Garden Park Hospital and fly them to a Mobile infirmary. After picking up the patient at the hospital, Johnson navigated to the correct latitude and longitude for the infirmary and landed at the medical facility, but the swimmer was told by hospital personnel that they were at the "wrong" hospital. Further inquiry elicited the fact that the "infirmary" was on the other side of the building. Despite the fact that there were two ambulances on site, hospital personnel refused to take the patient to the other side. Johnson had no choice but to fly around to the "correct" facility to drop off the patient.[18]

Next, he responded to a Navy Seahawk requesting a basket-capable helo to pick up a 400-pound, non-ambulatory man on the first floor porch of a four-story building nearby. Only the two top steps to the porch were above water, and there were power lines running 10–15 feet parallel to and in front of the structure. They lowered the swimmer by harness to the top steps—a target about 2 feet square—from a hoist altitude of 80–100 feet. The flight mechanic directed the helicopter expertly, placing the swimmer on the porch step, inches from the water. The basket was lowered and the man was taken to the airport and EMS care.[19]

The remainder of Johnson's mission involved three CNN reporters taken on at the Superdome to videotape several hoist operations. After they were returned to the air station, Johnson and crew flew to base Mobile, ending their day.[20]

That night an HH-65 went on an unusual mission involving yet another 100-foot hover. After Lt. Steven C. Priebe learned of a man trapped in his attic, he located the house and lowered the rescue swimmer to the rooftop. The swimmer, axe in hand, first hacked an aperture in the roof, then radioed that the evacuee was too dehydrated and weak to climb out. Priebe directed the swimmer to enlarge the hole to accommodate the entire basket. From 100 feet up—the height of a ten-story building—using night vision goggles,

Priebe and the flight mechanic delivered the basket through the hole in the roof. The swimmer loaded the evacuee into the basket when he noticed one of the dangers of a high hover. The hoist had already begun, but a CH-53 Super Stallion was flying over and its rotor wash created a vortex. In an instant, Priebe's helo lurched with a nearly disastrous loss of lift, dropping with the unsettling sound of the turbines unspooling above. He went to emergency power to retain his position and the altitude necessary to complete the lift. In incidents such as this, it is necessary to remember that helicopters have no wings, and thus no possibility of gliding to an unpowered landing: everything depends on the rotor. This was Priebe's last Katrina mission. He saved 136 lives and put in twenty-eight hours in the air, most of them at night.[21]

September 5–15

The Tide Recedes

The second week after the passage of Hurricane Katrina proved to be a turning point in the storm's aftermath as the emergency transmuted into methodical house-to-house rescue and relief. By September 15 the response phase of the CG operation had run its course. Many of the units—surface and air—had been or were being demobilized and returned to their home bases.

In the city of New Orleans several events served to mark the transition from a city reeling from disaster to one that silently suffered its aftereffects. By this time, the Superdome and the Morial Convention Center—the two places where national attention had focused and which had become exemplars of both the natural and manmade disasters—had been evacuated. Some 400 busloads of evacuees left the Superdome, for the most part to Houston, Texas, with the last group out of the facility by late Saturday, September 3. It took three days to empty the building. The Convention Center evacuation which began on Friday was also completed by Saturday.

Its 15,000–20,000 miserable inhabitants were ushered out by the Louisiana Army National Guard.[1]

Several of the other major evacuee gathering places had also been emptied: the long-running Chalmette Slip/Algiers Point ferry operation was done. The crowd at the University of New Orleans had long since been removed by boat and helicopter. The last of the city hospitals were evacuated by late on Friday, September 2; accomplished by joint National Guard, local authority, and Coast Guard operations.[2] The I-10 interchange was emptied by Saturday afternoon.

Moreover, the floodwater had begun to recede. Sandbags by the hundreds had been dropped or piled in place. Helicopters, including National Guard and Coast Guard aircraft, had plied the levee gaps with "Super Sacks," each containing 8 tons of Gulf coast sand. Over 2,400 of these had been lowered, under Corps of Engineers direction, into the breaches, resulting in the closure of the openings which had allowed the inundation of the city. On September 5, the largest breach, that of the 17th Street levee, was filled. It was the last of the breaks; the pumps were engaged to drain the city.[3]

The federal government pumped more help into the town, dispatching a force without the soiled reputation of certain other federal agencies. The U.S. Army's 82nd Airborne Division, famous for its D-Day exploits and respected as a real "can-do" outfit, received the go-ahead from President Bush on Saturday morning at 10:00 A.M. A task force of 3,600 was en route from Fort Bragg in North Carolina by four o' clock that afternoon, boarding transport aircraft even as other elements of the division were bound for Afghanistan and Iraq.[4]

To many, the arrival of these crack troops signaled that the crisis was over and quelled the average citizens' fear of the lawbreakers in the streets. As one observer put it, with the coming of the 82nd troops, "the cockroaches that had caused the problems ran for cover."[5] Throughout the rest of the week the Coast Guard teamed up with the 82nd Airborne in systematic searches of the city.

The week also saw significant developments related to the Coast Guard, in its role in the aftermath of the hurricane, in its leadership, in its realignment of mission and, eventually, in the drawdown of forces in the storm-ravaged area.

Since the beginning, the Coast Guard's outstanding role as a first responder to the hurricane was national news. It began as early as the day after the storm, when CNN viewers saw a "middle-aged woman climb from a rooftop into a basket that was then winched into a helicopter hovering a hundred feet in the air." The same day, *New York Times* associated photographer Vince Laforet hopped a helicopter ride over the city and snapped photos of CG helicopters pulling women and children off rooftops. His "emblematic photo of a Ninth Ward woman, floodwaters beneath her, being pulled out of the sludge by an orange Coast Guard helicopter, dangling in a basket" made the front page of the *Times* on Wednesday, September 29. It became one of the great photos of 2005.[6]

The visual images were only the beginning of the extensive media coverage. On Tuesday, September 6, Stephen Barr, a columnist for the *Washington Post* wrote: "Coast Guard's Response to Katrina a Silver Lining in the Storm." In this article he lauded the service in no uncertain terms, calling it a "model agency" and, indeed, one which should serve as an organizational template for "fixing what's wrong elsewhere in Homeland Security."[7]

Two days later, the *Washington Times* followed this up with "More than a Coast Guard," an equally complimentary piece that began: "The Coast Guard faced many of the same challenges as other government agencies in responding swiftly to Hurricane Katrina—and yet it was able to outperform all of them." It went on to praise the service for its training, flexibility, and relative freedom from hierarchical bureaucracy.[8]

Finally, the *Times* saluted Secretary Michael Chertoff's selection of CG Chief of Staff Vice Admiral Thad Allen as deputy to FEMA's "embattled Michael Brown." This selection, said the paper, was particularly appropriate "given the Coast Guard's institutional efficiency." Brown had come under increasingly vehement public criticism for the obvious shortcomings in the FEMA response to Hurricane Katrina.[9]

Vice Admiral Allen had been named deputy primary federal official (PFO) for the Katrina task force on September 5. He arrived in New Orleans on September 6 and, on September 9, Secretary Chertoff moved him up to PFO for the Hurricane Katrina effort.[10] He would become commandant of the Coast Guard in May 2006.

The selection of Admiral Allen was a positive move by the federal government to meet the challenges of the post-Katrina effort. Admiral Allen, in a later interview with the author, said he felt particularly suited to the job. He stated that "every single assignment" he had had in the Coast Guard came to bear on this new task. In his thirty-plus year career, he had dealt with operations of major seaports, handled significant oil spills and their environmental impact, dealt with nationally significant search and rescue events, and also worked extensively with other government agencies at the state, federal, and local levels—particularly with regards to law enforcement. Most importantly, the admiral had been on-site commander during an "incident of national significance" drill in New Orleans in 2002, so when Allen walked into the Baton Rouge emergency management center on Tuesday, September 6, a week and a day after Katrina, he already knew some of the local first responders personally.[11]

Allen later described some of the immediate needs and problems he had to address as he came into the job. Among them was the necessity of applying the federal response to local needs without preempting the prerogatives of local government. This was a delicate job and the task was ameliorated by a similar attitude on the part of General Honore. Consequently, after the city was divided into sectors for search and rescue operations, Honore and Allen implemented a plan in which the federal emergency agency representatives submitted their plan of action for the next day's SAR and relief efforts to the state and local officials for their perusal, response, and approval. Furthermore, when search and rescue sweeps were made through the city, the teams were, as far as possible, composed of both federal and local personnel. When decisions were made about actions to be taken at a home or other structure, the federal responders—Coast Guard, National Guard, Army, and Marines—deferred to the local officials.[12]

When Admiral Allen entered onto the scene, there was a visible shift of emphasis from disaster response to recovery. Allen's goals ranged from the short-term (draining the city, repairing the levees, searching each and every home for survivors, recovering bodies, assessing environmental safety issues, and removing massive fields of debris) to the long term (obtaining temporary housing for the displaced, funneling federal aid money to the individuals in need, and rebuilding the city).[13]

Admiral Allen gained national attention during his tenure as the principal federal official for Katrina, and, later, Hurricane Rita. His leadership and success were duly noted and lead directly to his selection as the next Coast Guard commandant.

⊙

On September 9, National Public Radio broadcast *Coast Guard Praised for Katrina Response*. This piece echoed the criticism that other agencies had been "slow to react" to the storm, while the Coast Guard was already "plucking people off rooftops."[14] Indeed, there was nearly universal praise for the service's role in the hurricane response.

While the praises eddied through the receding waters, the Coast Guard activities continued and, as the number of evacuees declined, new priorities arose.

On September 5, a "dramatic drop off in rescues" was noticed. The number of people who now opted to remain in their dwellings was rapidly increasing, no doubt encouraged by the increased security provided by the Army as well as the prospect of soon seeing their streets dry again.

Led by Commander Robert Tarantino on CGC *Spencer*, the flotilla had completed the Chalmette/Algiers Point ferry and Chief

Warrant Officer Robert R. Lewald, the original leader of the task, and *Pamlico* were reassigned to more familiar work. *Pamlico*, along with tenders *Greenbrier* and *Clamp* plus the two 55-foot ATON buoy tenders, were shifted to the command of Sector New Orleans where they were directed to resume aids to navigation work on the Gulf and inland waterways.[15]

The gap created by the reassignment of the aids to navigation vessels was partially filled by the September 5 arrival of an unusual group from District 9—the Great Lakes. After some discussion with the district chain of command, a group of ice boats descended to the city. These vessels are a version of the airboats common in the Florida Everglades. They are flat bottomed, with a light draft, powered by a stern, deck-mounted propeller. Lacking an underwater propeller, they are capable of sliding over the ice on the Great Lakes. By the same token, they were able to operate in shallow water for rescues in the New Orleans streets. Given the amount of debris in the New Orleans streets-turned-waterways, it followed that these boats would be useful additions to the rescue forces.[16]

The iceboat contingent consisted of three boats along with forty-two Coast Guardsmen. The crews were from the shores of Lakes Michigan and Erie: units from Michigan, Ohio, and New York. The group set up temporary camp at the Naval Support Facility in New Orleans and was placed under the direction of Cmdr. Tarantino.[17]

The utility of the ice boats was immediately apparent to the newly arrived 82nd Airborne, and joint operations were planned the same evening the District 9 group arrived. The first joint sortie went out to Orleans Parish the next morning.[18]

The iceboats proved their usefulness, particularly in reaching confined areas where helicopters could not operate. Their numbers were augmented by five conventional boats and they ranged about Central New Orleans. Each crew was comprised of a CG coxswain, one CG security member (MSST, TACLET, or PSU), plus two Army personnel. In about four days of operation, this group was credited with clearing thirty buildings, saving 126 lives, and rescuing fifty animals. Included in these numbers were three crewmembers of a downed aircraft.[19]

However, a question arose concerning the safety of the iceboats. Their high-mounted fans tended to aerosolize the polluted water, creating the potential for breathing hazards. The boats remained in the area for a few more days, utilized in numerous non-rescue roles, and the team was demobilized on September 18.[20]

Parallel with the ice boat operations, search and rescue continued from Zephyr Field. DART units now consisted of teams including 82nd Airborne troops, usually in place of USAR members. As with the iceboats, each four-man boat crew consisted of a CG coxswain in body armor, one armed CG security person, and two soldiers—the latter with unloaded weapons. Sorties with the 82nd began on September 7 when all twenty-four CG boats were dispatched into the city.[21]

Three other boats were sent to suburbs east of New Orleans, including Rigolets, about 15 miles northeast of the city on the strait connecting Lake Borgne, Lake Catherine, Lake Pontchartrain, and Venetian Isles. This area had experienced a storm surge comparable to that which had demolished the Pearl River area. Reports were coming in about survivors previously missed by rescuers.

Altogether twenty-seven vessels were dispatched, spending a total of 216 hours. Five lives were saved during the day.[22]

Through September 15, the number of surface sorties into the gradually drying city declined, along with the number of rescues. The one odd day was September 9, when there were 156 rescues and ninety-three sorties. On September 8, there were fifty-eight rescues, with the number declining to zero on September 15. Two hundred seventy-five survivors were brought in during these eight days.[23]

The decline in rescues was accompanied by a realignment of priorities. Sector New Orleans and District Eight surface units were making the transition from search and rescue to waterways management and pollution response. Coincidentally, FEMA reported that all of the primary searches in the city would be completed by September 15.[24]

◎

The air effort also experienced a downturn in rescues. The number of flights remained high for a time, but the numbers rescued rapidly declined. On September 5, there were forty-three helicopters, eight fixed-wing aircraft, and fourteen CG auxiliary planes working in both New Orleans and the Gulf coast areas.[25]

The numbers make the situation obvious. On September 4, there were 275 people rescued by CG helos; the next day the number was 115. By September 8, the daily number was 7. From September 5–8 192 lives were saved.[26]

One pilot's work during the period illustrates the decline in rescues. Lt. jg. Adam Spencer, normally stationed at Air Station Clearwater, flew various HH-60s on September 5, 7, 9, 11, and 12. The first mission was to provide transportation for passengers to New Orleans. In two missions on September 7, totaling 7.8 hours flying time, three survivors were picked up from an exit ramp and taken to a trauma unit. Two days later, a 6.5 hour flight involved logistics and transporting FEMA and engineering personnel to survey storm damage. On September 11, Admiral Duncan, commander of the Eighth CG District, was taken to USS *Iwo Jima* for breakfast with President Bush. The next day, Spencer flew Duncan on a damage assessment overflight. These rather humdrum tasks illustrate the fact that a decline in rescues freed up more helicopters for routine work.[27]

Two other pilots' itineraries for September 5 probably show more "normal" operations for that day. The busiest was Lt. Steven E. Cerveny. He located a family of five in an area near Six Flags amusement park, the swimmer was deployed to the front porch, and the survivors were hoisted to safety. Apparently this area had been overlooked in earlier rescue sweeps, and many people were still in their homes without water or power. On several occasions, however, the swimmer returned empty handed because the survivors refused CG assistance. Later in the day, Cerveny flew six people from landing zones to the airport, and delivered 1,200 lbs. of water and food from the air station to Sector New Orleans.[28]

The arrival at the sector landing zone was met with another difficulty. The landing area was crowded with pre-staged sandbag bundles—in the process of being taken to drop on the broken levees—and Army helos were continuously rotating through and picking up the bundles, carrying them externally on slings. The crowding was such that Cerveny opted to find an alternate landing site before setting down.[29]

Lt. Martin M. Simpson flew in cases of water from Mobile, each time loading his aircraft to its maximum gross weight, and dropping them off at various overpasses and bridges. For the balance of the mission Simpson and his crew moved from house to house. By the end of the day, twelve survivors were hoisted to his aircraft.[30]

It was a day of rather unusual rescues. One of the larger hauls was eight survivors extracted by swimmer Bradford Simmons. Simmons' first problem was to move the people from a nearly inaccessible apartment building to a suitable hoist point. He improvised a raft for and then both the co-pilot and the second rescue swimmer were sent down to help carry the non-ambulatory to the basket. Among the eight were a diabetic, an elderly man, and a woman without use of her legs. Later in the day, on a second mission, only a single survivor was rescued.[31]

One of the least profitable missions was by rescue swimmer Eric Biehn, who was to deliver supplies to a home and family. When the helo approached, there was no response seen in the house, but the helo crew had no way of knowing if there were people inside, incapable of responding, or not. Biehn deployed to a tree, carrying a load of MREs and water. From there, he climbed through a window and searched the dwelling. Finding no one home, he deposited the water and MREs and left via the window and tree limb.[32]

Swimmer Tom Emerick turned in another unusual narrative, not without a bit of humor, or at least comic relief. It was his first rescue of the night and it involved a tricky descent among telephone lines to gain entry into a dwelling through a high window. Inside, he found an elderly man and his dog. The man had been waiting three days for rescue and said not to worry about the dog: he expected the SPCA would come along later for the canine. The gentleman was hoisted out and taken to the airport.[33]

The second sortie, Emerick said, was "a bit crazy" and difficult to manage. They saw a man in neck-deep water pushing a canoe up to a house's front porch at night, but when the helo approached the rotor wash flipped the canoe over. Then, Emerick was dropped on a telephone line due to poor communication with the hoist operator. Another attempt put him into the stinking, neck-deep water. On the third try, Emerick finally landed at the porch and a short interview with the canoe-man aroused his suspicions. He claimed to be sick and refused to be hoisted. Emerick did not think he acted sick, and usually, sick people were anxious to be hoisted out. And what sick man would be out pushing a canoe in neck-deep water at night? Finally, Emerick convinced him to leave and sent him away with a supply of MREs and water.

But then the owner of the house, drunk and semi-dressed, confronted Emerick, yelling that the canoe-man was the local heroin addict who was looting all the neighborhood houses, and he wanted Emerick to arrest him. Emerick calmed the man down and convinced him to evacuate. They went back into the house first, navigating by flashlight through debris and empty liquor bottles, to get clothes for the old man. In his closet the man rummaged around "like he's getting ready for church and picking out his best outfit." All the while, the HH-65 was still hovering, using gas, and the pilot was anxious to leave. The old man put his shoes on calmly, and said not to worry about running out of gas, he would pay for it. Emerick was thoroughly exasperated, but he managed to get him to the porch. The "looter" had returned. A fistfight ensued between the looter and the old man and Emerick ordered the looter to stand in the corner. Amazingly, the looter did what he was told, and Emerick hoisted the owner off the porch. Once onboard, Emerick discovered that the survivor had a massive leg infection and by the time they arrived at the airport, the man had to be carried from the aircraft. Emerick later learned that the canoe-man was indeed a looter. After that, he said, he didn't "feel so bad about the rotor wash overturning his canoe." Afterwards, Emerick made several other flights, but "most of the people were waving us off signaling that they didn't need any help."[34]

The next day, September 6, also saw a limited number of hoists and survivors. Rescue swimmer Steven R. Garcia was lowered down to a nursing home and by the time he assessed the occupants and moved them to a hoist point his helo was at "bingo" fuel (minimum for return to base), so they called for another HH-60 to hoist the nursing home residents out. On a second mission one survivor was hoisted from a balcony, and two others refused to be evacuated.[35]

Another swimmer, Matthew I. Bayne, made his third and last helo hoist deployment. On September 3, he had rescued one man from a rooftop, and then his aircraft transported eighty-nine people from the Convention Center to the airport. The next day was fruitless—none of the survivors they found wanted to be rescued. En route back, while flying over a rural, fenced field, the crew noticed seven horses, and Bayne was hoisted down, where he delivered two bales of hay to the equine survivors.[36]

Bayne's final mission was on September 6. Most of the night flight yielded no survivors, but a flashlight signal brought them to an apartment building. He was dropped onto the roof, yelled for the survivors, hoisted three out, and they were flown to the airport.[37]

Due to the decrease in tempo of operations, some of the helicopters and crews began to demobilize and return to their home bases. On September 7, for instance, HH-65s from Miami, Savannah, and Atlantic City, and an HH-60 from Elizabeth City all departed from New Orleans.

This concludes the portion of the narrative dealing with Hurricane Katrina search and rescue in the New Orleans area. The recovery and relief efforts in the city continued on a lesser scale throughout the next several days. Then the unwelcome news of Hurricane Rita served to reinstitute Coast Guard operations in the area. The Rita operation will follow in a subsequent section.

To complete the Katrina story, the Coast Guard efforts centered on Sector Mobile and the shattered Gulf Coast will follow, as well as a survey of the environmental and waterways tasks of the service.

Sector Mobile Deals with the Destruction

While the New Orleans Katrina drama played out in the headlines, the people of the Alabama and Mississippi coastal areas struggled to deal with their own misery. The main distinction between the New Orleans disaster and that further east was the water: the Gulf coast shore was certainly submerged, but, as with a tsunami, the water receded, leaving the destruction exposed but at least accessible by dry land. Therefore the Coast Guard response here was much more mundane, and called for fewer of the specialized skills for which the service is known.

Capt. James D. Bjostad, commanding Sector Mobile, had established the Mobile Incident Command Center-Katrina prior to the storm, and with his deputy, Capt. Edwin M. Stanton, began reconstituting the Mississippi/Alabama coast after the storm's passage. Under this command were the stations at Pascagoula, Gulfport, Mobile, Panama City, Destin (Florida), Pensacola, Dolphin Island, and Base Mobile. Vessels, including those from elsewhere brought in for the emergency, included cutters *Razorbill, Pompano,*

Shamal, Tornado, Decisive, Saginaw, Wedge, Oak, Joshua Appleby, Barbara Mabrity, and *Cypress*. In addition, there were two port security units (PSU 308 and PSU 309), one MSST unit from Kings Bay, Georgia, four aids to navigation teams, and numerous small boats.[1]

To organize cooperation with local and state authorities in planning the CG response, Capt. Stanton placed liaison personnel at the area emergency operations centers. These included regional Mississippi EOCs in Jackson, Harrison, and Hancock counties, plus the state EOC in Jackson. In Alabama, they were in the Mobile County EOC and the state EOC at Clanton.[2]

Building on cooperation with local and state entities, Stanton and his deputies integrated the CG effort, in particular with overwhelmed state and local law enforcement units. As the two port security units—the Kings Bay MSST contingent and CGC *Decisive*—arrived in the area, they were quickly employed effectively along with the local CG units already on scene. The cutter became a communications platform for the effort.[3]

In the background, Stanton and his staff established the critical logistics "train" to provide necessities for the operations both in New Orleans and along the Gulf coast. Freight haulers and other government agencies were quickly brought into the system, providing food, water, medicine, and fuel for the area. In spite of the complete disruption of the delivery infrastructure, there was never a significant fuel shortage during the response period, thanks in part to the CG logistics effort.[4]

On the aviation side of the story, we saw the beginnings of air search and rescue in a previous chapter. On August 30, Mobile-based aircraft numbered fifteen: five HH-65s, seven HH-60s, and three HU-25s. Sixty sorties had been flown since Katrina passed, totaling 180 hours of flight time and rescuing about 150 survivors. Evacuees were being taken to hospitals, the Aviation Training Center, and a local football field.[5]

Of course, ATC Mobile was the staging area for search and rescue flights to New Orleans. In many instances, helos began their missions with sweeps along the Mississippi and Alabama coast. Whether they continued on to the city depended on what they found on the devastated Gulf shores. Capt. Stanton, as deputy incident commander, directed that the HH-60s—with larger load capacity and longer range—be given priority over the shorter-legged HH-65 Dolphins for New Orleans missions. The HU-25 Falcons were sent over the Gulf on sensor and survey missions, searching for four missing oil platforms.[6]

One of the key units on the Gulf was the station at Gulfport. As seen in a previous chapter, the buildings were totally destroyed, but CWO Steve Lyons, commanding the unit, immediately set to work. He began the necessary cleanup on the station and patrols were instituted on the coast, from Ocean Springs, Mississippi, just east of Biloxi, to the Pearl River, including the hard-hit Bay St. Louis area as well as the barrier islands.[7]

The Gulfport crews began search and rescue less than twenty-four hours after the passage of the storm, launching two boats from an unobstructed boat ramp at Ocean Springs, Mississippi. In the process of searching for survivors, Lyons and his team surveyed the ruined coast meticulously, noting hazards to navigation and items of interest—sunken fuel tanks, fishing vessels, and other debris.[8] In the days to come CG teams would revisit these with an eye to reestablishing safe coastal waterways.

On September 1, despite the destruction of the Gulfport station, it was the site of the joint local, state, and CG emergency operations center. The same day, CG vessels including cutters *Shamal* and *Bonito,* as well as several small boats, began systematic patrols along the Mississippi coast.[9]

The Gulfport operation further expanded on September 5, and was then designated the Mississippi Coastal Recovery Base, Gulfport. This entity included the Harrison County EOC, Coast Guard PSU 308, MSST Kings Bay, a contingent of Navy Seabees, the Alabama Department of Natural Resources, the Florida Department of Fish and Wildlife, groups from Indiana and Michigan, two airboats from the Charleston police department, and the support of Congressman Gene Taylor. Alongside the Coast Guard cutters, at least seventy small boats operated under the control of this body.[10] Two of the cutters, CGC *Razorbill* and CGC *Pompano*, immediately began working shore-side relief in the Gulfport area.[11]

In addition to the Gulfport-based CG units, other security contingents, aids to navigation teams, and CG cutters and boats came to the aid of the beleaguered Gulf Coast residents. These included the ANT team from Charleston and PSU 309 from Ohio.

The two major needs along the devastated coast were security and delivery of relief supplies. Looters became common, particularly in the casino towns where smalltime operators hoped to find slot machines and gambling money. Of course, running water was nearly nonexistent and hospitals were short of insulin and other critical medicines.

In the nearly demolished town of Bay St. Louis, the most pressing needs were at the Hancock Medical Center and the Emergency Operations Center. The hospital had lost power not long into the storm and supplies were running out: oxygen, insulin, food, linen. Overcoming these difficulties, the hospital treated over 800 people during the first three or four days after the storm. The Coast Guard brought insulin and obtained power generators, which were flown into Hurlburt Field, north of town, on two C-130 aircraft.[12]

On September 3, security needs were addressed at the Hancock County Emergency Operations Center with the establishment of a CG command post on site. This included a boat mooring facility, a contingent of the Kings Bay MSST, and one boat. This was later expanded to three boats.[13] Similarly, PSU 308 was dispatched to Harrison County (Gulfport) with six boats to assist in security patrols.[14]

One of the most tragic situations encountered by the CG relief force was that of the local Vietnamese-owned and operated fishing fleet, operating out of Biloxi and vicinity. The plight of this group was exacerbated by the language barrier—many simply did not know the intensity of the storm that would strike them.

Hundreds of their vessels were destroyed, sunk, or damaged in the storm. Furthermore, many—including entire families—remained on board their vessels as the storm raged. Biloxi's Back Bay was home to many of the fishermen, and several boats had been lashed together and moored securely, or so they thought, before the storm. Katrina's storm surge took them all, en masse, eastward until their momentum slammed them into a concrete bridge. There they remained, with families on board, after the storm passed.[15]

When the Coast Guard found over 200 of these people, they were destitute and stranded: their floating homes wrecked. Over the next few days Coast Guard units, including PSU 309—a CG reserve port security unit with personnel from six Midwestern states, and based at Port Clinton, Ohio—handed out MREs to over 200 survivors. Then they brought in over 50,000 pounds of relief supplies.[16] Similar relief efforts were extended to trapped shrimpers at Pass Christian, by crewmembers from CGC *Decisive*.[17] To this day, the Gulf Coast Vietnamese fishing community has not completely recovered from Hurricane Katrina.

The major role of Sector Mobile after Hurricane Katrina was internal to the Coast Guard, as a staging area for the aviation element of the New Orleans search and rescue effort. In effect, the CG airfield at Aviation Training Center Mobile was the funnel through which both fixed wing aircraft and helicopters moved to the city.

The two key people in organizing the ATC in-house response were Capt. David R. Callahan, commanding officer of the training center, and CWO Kenneth P. Hardenbrook, chief of the training center's Aviation Engineering Support Branch. These men successfully undertook a massive, unprecedented job, on short notice, with little room for error. Compounding the achievement, they were operating from a storm-damaged base, with significant problems in the major flight line and maintenance structures.

By the end of the Katrina effort, thirty-six Coast Guard helicopters had been operated on a twenty-four-hour a day basis, in addition to innumerable aircraft from other agencies. This involved maintaining the aircraft and meeting supply, parts, and fuel needs. On top of this were very practical day-to-day considerations, such as finding parking room for the aircraft and ensuring that maintenance could be done when and where needed. In the airspace, as well as on the runways and taxiways, there was the utmost need to operate with safety, which in turn required good management of air traffic control and flight line safety issues.

To keep the aircraft operational, a massive task force of Coast Guard maintenance and support crews was brought in. Personnel from over twenty agencies also arrived to maintain their aircraft. In a matter of days, over 2,000 people were added to the population of the base. Even though it was only on a temporary basis, the condition of the base did not make things easy. Meeting the day-to-day needs of these support personnel added an immense logistical challenge to the operation, most of which was handled by Capt. Callahan, as well as by Capt. Stanton and their subordinates.

Coast Guard aircrews, aviation mechanics, and other support personnel came in from every CG aviation unit in the service. It was Capt. Callahan's job to work them all into a cohesive team and provide a seamless backdrop for the largest Coast Guard aviation operation in history.

In the end, it was a monumental achievement, resulting in 1,193 sorties by CG aircraft, amounting to over 2,200 hours flying time. The human results were more impressive: 4,812 lives were saved by aircraft and crews operating out of Mobile.

The Coast Guard at Mobile was nationally highlighted with the visit of President Bush and other dignitaries on September 2, four days after the storm. The president set up shop in an ATC hangar and met with Governor Haley Barbour of Mississippi, Alabama governor Bob Riley, and Michael Brown, director of FEMA. President Bush praised the Coast Guard in a short televised speech: "I am incredibly proud of our Coast Guard. We have got courageous people risking their lives to save life." The president then shook hands all around, including those of all the CG personnel in attendance. It was at this venue that the famous "Brownie, you're doing a heck of a job" statement was made. From Mobile, President Bush continued on by helicopter to Biloxi, then New Orleans, where Air Force One met him for the return from the hurricane front.[18]

Restoring the Gulf Coast Waterways

Once the search and rescue emergency was under control the Coast Guard could turn its attention to the waterways disaster. As was outlined in an earlier chapter, the hurricane had brought the Gulf Coast and Mississippi River maritime system to a virtual standstill. Derelict vessels and oil platforms, drifting barges, demolished bridges, oil and chemical spills, and masses of waterborne debris inhibited river and Gulf transportation, and destruction of most of the buoys and markers made even small boat operations hazardous—and no less dangerous for the 1,000-foot, deep draft oil tankers and container ships which formed a major part of the commerce in New Orleans and associated ports.

To centralize the Coast Guard response to these issues, the service established the Maritime Recovery and Restoration Task Force (MRRTF), based in St. Louis. The senior officer charged with implementing the task force operations was the captain of the port for New Orleans, Capt. Frank Paskewich.

At the outset, early in September, the Coast Guard effort was hampered by the damage to the service's Gulf Coast and river aids to navigation units. The stations at Venice, New Orleans, and Gulfport were destroyed, as well as the New Orleans ATON office and the equipment and supplies stored at Integrated Support Command in the city.[1]

There were hundreds of Gulf, intercoastal, and river buoys and markers missing, destroyed, or damaged. On September 2, the cutter *Decisive* made a survey of the 40-mile stretch from Pascagoula to Gulfport and found that twenty-eight buoys or other aids were missing, seventeen from the Gulfport ship channel alone. Five were gone from the Intracoastal Waterway between the two cities, as well as five from the Pascagoula ship channel. It was a quick survey that did not even take into account the aids which were damaged, inoperable, or out of position.[2] And this was hardly the worst of it because the maximum storm damage was west of Gulfport.

Given the enormous scope of the problem, it was imperative that buoys and markers be hauled in from other CG ATON units all over the country. The buoy tender *Cypress*, for instance, was loaded with "as many Aids to navigation supplies as she could physically carry" and steamed in from Houston. Additionally, the other districts—particularly District Seven—sent in men, buoy tenders, and boats, as well as their spare buoys and markers to assist until the situation was stabilized.

Even before work could begin, detailed surveys of the waterways were undertaken. The Coast Guard did photographic and sensor overflights and sent cutters on fact-finding missions immediately after the storm. Then, the Army Corps of Engineers, NOAA survey vessels, and commercial tug companies all cooperated to assess the scope of the problem. The information they gathered included cataloging obstructions in the waterways, above and below water. Particularly of concern was shoaling of the bottom caused by the storm and surge. This sometimes reduced depth by as much as 20 feet, with obvious implications for the draft of vessels able to use the waterways. Once collated, this material enabled the Coast Guard to determine where to concentrate their efforts.[3]

The highest priorities were the Mississippi River north of the city, the Intracoastal Waterway near and through New Orleans, and the lower Mississippi south of the city to the Southwest Pass. In these areas over 80 percent of the aids were destroyed, "hundreds of them," according to Capt. Paskewich. Other critical areas were the ship channel at Pascagoula—which leads to the naval shipyard as well as the huge Chevron refinery—and the port of Mobile.

Probably the largest assembly of CG buoy tending forces in history was gathered to put these waterways back into operation. Among the vessels of the CG "black hull fleet" were the buoy tenders and construction tenders *Hatchet, Greenbrier, Clamp, Pamlico, Wedge, Harry Claiborne, Barbara Mabrity, Cypress, Joshua Appleby, Oak,* and *Saginaw,* plus the crew from the dry-docked *Axe.* Aids to navigation teams and personnel showed up from Charleston, Jacksonville, Corpus Christi, Portsmouth, Cleveland, Galveston, Sabine, and Port O'Connor, all operating out of Morgan City, Louisiana until the CG stations destroyed or mangled by the storm were reopened.[4]

The process began with the river north of the city. Fortunately, there was little damage there and it was soon open to the barge traffic from the heartland. The Intracoastal Waterway in the city was also reasonably clear. *Pamlico* was dispatched from New Orleans to clean up and drain station Venice, then her crew retrieved supplies and any usable buoys and markers before returning to work the Intracoastal Waterway and Mississippi River Gulf Outlet.[5]

To work the lower Mississippi, the aids to navigation team from station Venice was employed, along with *Pamlico, Hatchet, Harry Claiborne,* and *Greenbrier.* The latter relayed additional supplies and buoys from Morgan City southward. The *Pamlico* and others began working their way northwest, repairing and replacing aids—shore-based and floating—on both sides of the river. Meanwhile, the *Wedge* and crewmembers from *Axe* were building eight range towers and twenty-five other navigational markers on the Pascagoula ship channel.[6]

With time constraints and pressure building it was necessary to limit the initial restoration to the critical aids: mainly the deep channel and hazardous obstruction markers. These allowed traffic to restart, as long as the larger vessels remained within the marked deepwater parameters. The lower Mississippi reopened to deep draft traffic on Friday, September 2. At that juncture, the maximum depth was 35 feet, and only to be used in daylight operations. This depth was gradually increased, and by September 29 there were no operational limits to deep draft vessels under normal circumstances.

In Pascagoula, the port opened for 36-foot draft vessels on September 7.[7] In the meantime, to enable the critical flow of gasoline to consumers in the Florida Panhandle, shallow draft barges were used to relay the fuel to tank ships and expedite the shipment of fuel along the Intracoastal Waterway until the channel was cleared for deeper draft tankers.[8]

At Mobile, buoy tenders *Wedge* and *Saginaw* were dispatched to work ATON in the bay and ship channel. By September 5, the Mobile bar was open to a 47-foot depth, the Theodore channel was open at 37 feet, and Mobile River was open at 40 feet.[9]

By September 20, when the Coast Guard began to gear up for Hurricane Rita, the Gulf coast ports were for the most part back to normal, at least in terms of buoys and markers. Some were still awaiting dredging to increase the size of vessels which could enter, or removal of wrecked or grounded vessels. Ships at Biloxi, for instance, were forced to navigate around three sunken ships. The Coast Guard—plus the Canadian Coast Guard's loaned buoy tender *Sir William Alexander*—had worked on 1,202 buoys and markers.[10]

The removal of wrecks remained an ongoing task, for which the Coast Guard was at least partially responsible. However, the owners of defunct vessels sometimes try to avoid the costs involved in salvage and defer action until faced with fines or other penalties imposed by the Coast Guard and local port authorities. If the wreck is considered a hazard to navigation or source of pollutants, then the arm of the law can be more effectively applied to the responsible party—the owner, contractor, or operator of the vessel. That is, if the responsible party can be identified. Conversely, if the wreck is not posing a risk to vessel traffic and not a source of toxic pollutants, the owner's liability and responsibility is reduced.

To deal with the post-Katrina situation, the Coast Guard organized a Wreck Removal and Salvage (WRS) group. This was composed of Coast Guardsmen from Sector Mobile and Sector New Orleans, the U.S. Navy Supervisor of Salvage, the U.S. Army Corps of Engineers, and leaders of professional commercial salvage entities. Their goal was to complete a "risk-based assessment of all maritime casualties," with an eye toward confining the allocation of high-cost heavy lift cranes and barges to the most risky wrecks. Detailed criteria for determining the risk factors were developed and applied to each wreck.[11]

A complete survey of the wrecks and hazards would be beyond the scope of this work, but highlights from the September 2005 WRS report may give the reader an idea of the prevailing conditions at the time.

There were 187 active cases—twenty-seven were deemed imminent pollution threats and/or hazards to navigation and five were slotted for immediate prosecution. In the Lower Mississippi around Venice, there were over 100 vessel casualties, including four capsized fishing vessels, the latter with potential for pollutants aboard. These 100 vessels did not include over 300 barges on and in the river and other waterways.[12]

Another aspect of the post-Katrina Coast Guard response was that of pollution and environmental cleanup. As noted previously, there were several major oil spills, with over 8 million gallons contaminating rivers and tributaries. Personnel from three of the CG National Strike Force teams were brought in to handle the situation and cleanup. Fortunately, most of the spills were mitigated by local containment and the contaminants did not reach the river. On the other hand, the responders were faced with remote locations, poor communications, impassible roadways, and lack of local temporary housing. And of course they met the usual natural inhabitants of the Louisiana swamps and bayous: snakes, alligators, and mosquitoes.[13]

The federal on-scene coordinator was Cmdr. Ronald Cartin. His unified command, covering Louisiana, Mississippi, and Alabama, consisted of personnel from twenty different agencies—federal, state, and private organizations. Over 1,000 responders were on hand as well as thirty-five contractors, helicopters, Maritime Administration vessels for berthing and command centers, thirty-four oil recovery barges, and over a hundred small boats. More than 31,000 feet of booms and forty-four skimmers were used to restrain and suck up the oil.[14]

As of the end of September—after the hiatus caused by Rita—over 3 million gallons had been recovered. An additional 1.7 million gallons had evaporated and 1.5 million gallons naturally dispersed. Capt. Paskewich stated, "Any oil that escaped the booms flowed inland, away from the river levees. Only a few minor oil sheens thin enough to evaporate in the sun have appeared on the river."[15]

The amount of work, materials, and men involved in pollution cleanup can be gauged from a few examples. A spill of unknown amount originated from a 20-inch pipeline rupture at a Shell Oil facility, creating a 6-mile-long sheen. Ordered to the site were 3,800 feet of containment boom, two fast response boats, two airboats, one deck barge, four small boats, two barges set up as housing for personnel, and one command and control barge with a crane. At a Chevron facility, a spill of approximately 200 barrels required five skimmers, 11,000 feet of 18-inch containment boom, 10,000 feet of sorbent boom, four airboats, two tugboats, and eleven small boats, plus a 210-foot ship to house the fifty-nine people on the site.[16]

The Murphy Oil spill mentioned earlier was still in the process of being removed. At this point there were four vacuum trucks, four barrel trucks, and 1,500 feet of containment boom in use. Air quality monitoring equipment was also in use at the site.[17]

The variety of hazardous materials encountered after a storm of this magnitude was incredible. In Biloxi, a fiberglass manufacturing facility was found to have drums containing dimethyl ethyl aniline, cobalt, and methyl ethyl ketone peroxide. 728 drums of unknown and possibly dangerous liquids, 170 compressed gas containers and cylinders, and 13 petroleum cells were found at various sites in Sector Mobile.[18]

By the end of September, the job was not nearly complete. Cleanup operations continued at nine spill sites, while gross oil removal had been wrapped up at only four sites. There was also a twelve-member team still investigating over a hundred storm-related oil discharges throughout the area.

As a final addendum to the cleanup, the debris left by the storm had to be dealt with. The amount was enormous. Just at Base Mobile, 200 tons of debris completely covered the area. To deal with marine debris cleanup, the Coast Guard—including a team of reservists led by Capt. Stanton at Mobile—spearheaded the operation. This involved both mapping the problem and prioritizing the removal. Some 500 vessels, as well as hundreds of tons of refuse and debris both above and below water were taken away. By September 2008 this massive task was substantially completed.[19]

17

Hurricane Rita and a Conclusion

The previews on the weather channel were ominous: another hurricane was wallowing around the Gulf packing Category 5 winds, bearing west from Key West and then north toward the Texas/Louisiana border. It was enough to set the already shell-shocked population moving northward, and an estimated 2 million people evacuated from coastal Texas alone.[1]

For the Coast Guard, the familiar evasions before the storm began, with ships and personnel heading either west to Brownsville or east to Mobile and New Orleans. All the Hurricane Katrina salvage projects were halted as their crews also made for high ground. Three large ships being salvaged near Venice were restrained in place with huge anchors—sufficient to prevent the hulks from breaking loose and becoming navigational hazards. The two heavy lift crane barges were also sent away for the duration.[2]

In Mobile, the lessons of Katrina were already coming into play:

large flatbed trucks were pre-staged just out of the storm's path and loaded with generators, food, water, and at least eighteen flood punts. Across the region nineteen aircraft and thirty-six helicopters were readied for post-storm rescue operations. The Coast Guard participated in several medical evacuations in Texas even as the storm approached the coast. From Washington, Secretary Chertoff announced the appointment of principal federal officials for the impending disaster, Hurricane Rita. CG Rear Admiral Larry Hereth was named principal federal official for operations in Texas and Vice Admiral Allen for those in Louisiana.[3]

The mass evacuations and sudden drop in wind velocity took the fatal edge off Hurricane Rita. It struck the coast just east of Sabine Pass, Texas carrying with it 100 mph, Category 3 winds, but it reverted to tropical storm levels just 35 miles north of Beaumont, Texas, only twenty-four hours after landfall. The storm surge ranged from 6–20 feet, the lowest in Galveston, the highest in southwest Louisiana, where in some instances the waters refilled Katrina-soaked towns and parishes. Vermilion, Iberia, and St. Mary's Parishes were inundated. The storm surge affected areas as far east as Lake Pontchartrain and Slidell. In all, there were only seven fatalities directly attributed to the storm.[4]

Initially, the CG response plan was based on the worst of the storm going into Texas, but the night before storm predictions showed that the storm's center would be farther east, hitting southwest and south central Louisiana. The Coast Guard strategy was immediately adjusted to fit the circumstance. Coast Guard helicopters again flew in right behind the storm in 60–70-knot winds, and again began the harrowing routine of plucking people off rooftops.[5]

The first rescue by CG helicopters was a pregnant woman with a child in Port Fourchon, Louisiana. The helo pilot, Lt. Roberto Torres—a Katrina veteran—commented that "Most of the town was already underwater from Katrina and what wasn't got flooded by Rita."[6]

Some 500 survivors were rescued in the areas south of New Orleans, some by CG helicopters. Many were evacuated to Abbeville, Vermilion Parish, where the Coast Guard and local officials designated a local high school parking lot as a drop-off point. There the evacuees were met by local police and fire departments and relief personnel, as well as food, water, and medical supplies.[7]

One of the outstanding Coast Guard responders in Rita was BM1 Karyn Boxwell, executive officer at the aids to navigation station, Dulac, Terrebonne Parish, in south Louisiana. Shortly after the storm's passage she drove into the area and fortuitously encountered the fire chief of Grand Caillou, who requested federal assistance from Boxwell. His concern was for the population of the mostly low-lying rural communities south of Houma which were flooded due to levee breaks.[8]

Bosun's Mate Boxwell immediately phoned her supervisor, who was out of town at the time, then contacted Sector New Orleans. Coast Guard superiors at the sector designated Boxwell as the on-scene commander for rescue operations in south Terrebonne Parish. She now had two tasks: the first was actual on-scene search and rescue, and the second was to coordinate the search and rescue efforts of the helicopters and boats in the area. Familiar with the locality, she was able to contact over 250 people personally—by whatever means possible—up to and including boating to their homes. She determined which survivors were in need of rescue or had special health issues. Under her direction, three special needs medical cases were brought out by helicopter.[9]

The following day the Coast Guard made seven helicopters available for the area. Working with the Terrebonne authorities and Louisiana and Arkansas National Guard troops, Boxwell directed the helos as needed, both in Terrebonne and adjacent Vermilion parish. Another three special needs individuals were hoisted out that day. One of them was an Alzheimer's patient who showed signs of severe dementia when it came time to hoist her into the helo. BM1 Boxwell joined the woman in the basket to calm her on the

150-foot lift, and then she was lowered back down. By the end of the second day, BM1 Boxwell had assisted some 800 people, over 300 on a personal basis, reaching many of them as coxswain of an 18-foot boat that navigated the debris-filled watery landscape.[10]

There were 138 rescues by the Coast Guard, plus fifty-three medical evacuations after Hurricane Rita. Again, during this disaster, the service's flexibility was demonstrated in the overall approach to the actual situation on the ground. In the initial planning stages, the Department of Defense joint task force designated staging locations for the evacuee drop-off, where they could be met by relief personnel and have their immediate needs taken care of. Given the expected landfall of the storm, most of the drop-off points were in Houston and other places in Texas. However, when the storm veered eastward the Department of Defense would not relocate the drop-off points according to the path of the storm. The Coast Guard was expected to fly the survivors to the originally designated points, despite the fact that these locations were some two hours round trip from the actual disaster scene in southern Louisiana. Coast Guard officials protested that efficient evacuation required quick, nearby drop-off points for the benefit of the survivors, particularly those with medical needs. This would also enable short turnarounds for the helicopters, facilitating more frequent rescues with a given fuel load.[11] After making some headway with the DoD, the Coast Guard was able to establish local drop-off points such as the Abbeville high school mentioned above. All the service had to do was establish contact with the local first responders and quickly implement a plan interfacing CG rescuers with local authorities and relief organizations.

Rescues continued in the wake of Hurricane Rita until September 27, when there was only one survivor saved and two medical evacuations. Shortly thereafter, the Coast Guard forces gathered for Katrina and Rita were able to wind down their emergency operations, demobilize, and return to their home stations.

This marked the end of an extraordinary and unprecedented

month for the U.S. Coast Guard. The hurricane season of 2005 would not be soon forgotten in the annals of the Coast Guard.

⊙

For a small and generally decentralized service, the Coast Guard effort during Hurricane Katrina went far beyond anything seen to date. In wartime, Coast Guard personnel are often dispersed among Navy personnel; in peacetime only massive natural disasters bring together large numbers of service members. The Great Mississippi Flood of 1927 was the largest effort at the time, bringing out 650 men and 128 vessels. Hurricane Floyd in 1999 was probably the largest concentration of men and resources since the flood, involving twenty-seven helicopters and support personnel.

In contrast, the Katrina effort was one of the largest search and rescue operations in U.S. history. And, for the Coast Guard, it was by far the largest such operation to date. The peak number of Coast Guard members—including auxiliarists and reservists—in the effort was 4,500, on September 16. The aggregate total was over 5,000.[12]

In terms of equipment, there were forty-two cutters involved as well as 131 small boats (under 65'). Sixty-two aircraft (forty-three helicopters and nineteen fixed wing) and fourteen auxiliary small planes participated in the effort. The helicopters amounted to about 40 percent of the entire Coast Guard inventory, and came from every CG air station—as far away as Kodiak, Alaska, and Barber's Point, Hawaii.[13]

Officially, the total number of persons saved (rescued, evacuated, or assisted) by the Coast Guard, for both hurricanes, was 33,735—which includes 138 for the second storm. In an average year, the Coast Guard rescues around 5,500 people; thus the Katrina/Rita operations concentrated six years worth of rescues into the two weeks of post-storm operations. Coast Guard helicopters were responsible for saving 12,535 individuals. Based on flight hours, this amounted to one person for every fourteen minutes flown. Small boats and their crews saved 21,200 people, including 9,400 hospital evacuations. The latter were in joint operations with the Department of Defense and other agencies. In the entire period from the onset of Katrina to the cessation of operations for Rita—nearly a month—the Coast Guard had no casualties or serious injuries, and no aircraft accidents.[14] In terms of size, scope, and results, it was an impressive performance.

However, in the post-Katrina assessments there were still lessons to be learned. Some of shortcomings of the CG response were evident in the "evasion" stage. When the CG unit personnel evacuated, they carried very little with them, assuming that the station and its equipment would survive. Katrina destroyed this assumption. As a result, in preparation for Hurricane Rita, more supplies and equipment were pre-staged out of the storm's path. In the long run, a project was begun whereby entire communications setups and other operational necessities were to be made completely portable. All could be trailered out of danger during the approach of the storm, and then just as easily returned to the station afterwards. This would minimize the downtime caused by a storm and enable a return to nearly normal operations with little or no gap.[15] As another part of the pre-storm preparations, certain critical supplies were to be acquired in large numbers, including more body armor and weapons, as well as emergency tools such as axes.

The two major public critiques were of the communications breakdown and what was considered the "disorganized" CG early response over New Orleans—before the grid system was in effect. The communications problem was, of course, not unique to the Coast Guard after the storm, and there are currently projects underway to address the issue, in particular the use of mobile communications vans.[16]

Captain Joe Castillo, chief of District Eight Operations commented: "Initially we are going to go to where the people are that need saving. We're not going to spend a lot of time to make sure we've gone through a grid when we can see people over there that need help. You've got to do them first and then it's your secondary effort where you're going through in a bit more methodical approach."[17]

Captain Jones, commanding officer at Air Station New Orleans, maintained that, with literally thousands of simultaneous search and rescue missions, there would have been no way to micromanage "individual aircraft on individual rescue cases."[18]

In contrast, FEMA was criticized for an announcement made the Monday after the storm directing all emergency responders from outside the region to stay home until specifically asked to come to the scene. They said, "The response . . . must be well coordinated between federal, state, and local officials to most effectively protect life and property."[19]

The priorities of each agency are evident: whether to spend precious time organizing a response or respond immediately to the need at hand. The former is the bureaucratic approach; the latter, the Coast Guard approach. Whether a more organized effort would have been better can only be determined by the numbers. How many additional lives could have been saved during those first few days? Given the fact that the Coast Guard was throwing all they had into it, and that the helicopters were not coming into the landing zones empty or light, that speculative number will remain an imponderable.

⊙

At sea and on the waterways, there were 1,799 aids to navigation destroyed or damaged. Most of these were repaired or replaced by late October. Some 2,900 shipwrecks were left behind by the storm and 113 offshore oil platforms were destroyed, with fifty-two damaged. About 9.4 million gallons of oil were spilled. Seven were major incidents. Most of the spills were associated with onshore refining and pipeline facilities, rather than offshore platforms.[20]

It would be difficult to conjure up appropriate superlatives for the men and women of the Coast Guard and their work in these two storms. And the conditions under which they worked were far from easy: over 28 percent of the CG workforce either lost their homes or sustained severe property damage. Five hundred eighty-two men and women of the Coast Guard lost their homes due to Katrina, and another sixty-nine suffered the same from Hurricane Rita. The number of CG Auxiliary personnel who suffered similar losses is not known.

And of course, Coast Guard stations in the path of the storms were destroyed or damaged. Station Gulfport was totally demolished, and those at Grand Isle, Dauphin Island, Pascagoula, Venice, Mobile, and New Orleans suffered severe damage in some cases.[21]

Since September 2005 the laurels have been heaped upon the Coast Guard for its performance during the hurricanes. It should be noted that, at one and the same time, what made the Katrina story unique was also what made the situation particularly appropriate for the Coast Guard. The breaking and overtopping of the levees transformed New Orleans from a hurricane site to a flood zone. Houses and hotels, garages and warehouses, suddenly became "sinking" boats and ships, many with desperate people on their decks. It was the ultimate rescue at sea, and that is what the men and women of the Coast Guard train for and excel at.

After the mopping up was done, many eyes turned on the Coast Guard and wondered how they did it. The little service shone when other agencies simply wallowed in indecision and bureaucratic mire. Some of the reasons for the excellence of the CG response were uncovered in subsequent congressional hearings. Admiral Duncan and Captain Paskewich testified early on and many of their main points summarized "how they did it."

The first factor is almost too obvious. The Coast Guard bases, stations, and facilities are *there*: they have local knowledge of the rivers, lakes, and infrastructure. Unlike other agencies which "come in" for the emergency, the local Coast Guard is already on hand. This factor enables them to quickly establish working relationships with local authorities, and reduces their learning curve when it comes to reacting quickly to a fast-moving emergency.

Second, the multi-mission nature of the service enables them to switch from the mundane daily missions, such as inspecting small boats and fixing damaged buoys, to search and rescue or relief work, quickly and efficiently.

Third is the service-wide uniformity of training. The results of this were seen daily during the storm's aftermath. Coast Guardsmen from all over the service came together for the mission and were able to work together efficiently. This was evident and particularly necessary in the aircrews. These men and women had lives hanging by large threads from their aircraft, and there was little room for misunderstanding or inefficiency.

Fourth was the efficient delegation of responsibility to the lowest levels. Coast Guard personnel are trained to take responsibility early in their careers. Admirals do not command small boats; petty officers do. The Katrina emergency saw men such as Chief Warrant Officer Lewald commanding a substantial flotilla and women such as Boatswain's Mate Jessica Guidroz in charge of boat convoys and enlisted crewmembers senior to her own rank. This ability also made it possible for service members to act appropriately despite total communications breakdowns that left them without instructions from headquarters.

Fifth was the culture of service. As first responders, service must be the priority. When all others take cover, the Coast Guard must act. As with the old lifesaving service men who rarely had work to do on nice days, in an emergency or natural disaster the Coast Guard is there, and the ingrained culture impels them to action. As Captain Jones put it: "We wouldn't dream of NOT taking action."[22]

The encomiums heaped on the service after the storms were so numerous that one has a difficult task sorting out the most apt. An article in the September 8, 2005, *Washington Times* made this comment:

> For the Coast Guard there was no calm before the storm. Its members were busy before the storm hit preparing for deployments and have been working around the clock since. Its service in the hours after Katrina descended on New Orleans has been the one bright spot to an otherwise dismal government response.

Author Douglas Brinkley, in his book *Great Deluge*, is consistently in awe of the Coast Guard men and women. "They did it all one person at a time. And with virtually no exceptions, they treated the suffering with respect. They didn't wear their humanity on their patches, it was in their hearts."[23]

A 2006 FEMA news release began: "Each day" the Coast Guard "anticipates saving 15 lives, assisting 117 people in distress and investigating 20 vessel collisions or groundings. . . . Since hurricanes Katrina and Rita plowed through Louisiana there have been no average days." The article ended with: "The U.S. Coast Guard lives for above average days."[24]

⊙

With the approach of the fifth anniversary of the storm in 2010, it is appropriate to conclude here with recent remarks by Admiral Thad Allen, commandant of the Coast Guard, regarding Katrina itself, as well as the storm's ultimate effect on the service, both present and future.

In an interview with the author, when Commandant Allen was asked to describe the long term effects of the storm, he began with the immediate results of the storm and its aftermath.[25]

The sequence, of course, began with Allen's appointment as principal federal official in September 2005. While still performing this duty, Allen was called back to Washington by Secretary Chertoff to be interviewed for the position of commandant of the Coast Guard, a term which would begin in May 2006.

Fresh from the site of the largest hurricane disaster in U.S. history, Allen brought with him ideas and plans inspired by what had gone right and wrong in New Orleans. On the basis of these proposals, Allen was selected for the ultimate Coast Guard leadership position.[26]

Probably the single most obvious result of the storm and aftermath was Admiral Allen's concept of the Deployable Operations Group (DOG). In Katrina, as with other national incidents, the CG response had always been "brokered by field commanders," who plucked assets—units, aircraft, personnel—as needed, or as they came available from their geographic districts, to send into the disaster area. There was no preset plan or concept for these deployments.[27]

Under the DOG concept, when the next Katrina or similar disaster strikes, the Coast Guard will be able to set up a command and control network, pre-position supplies and assets, and bring in the forces in a "package"—all in advance of the storm. Furthermore, the Coast Guard will be able to more effectively work with FEMA, as well as other government and volunteer agencies. The CG response will be part of a national rescue system headquartered at Tyndall AFB, Florida, coordinating the CG efforts with those of the other services and agencies.[28]

Hand in hand with the DOG concept, the service is developing and implementing improvements in their communications structure to avoid the problems endemic at the outset of Katrina. Specifically, the goal is complete interoperability of CG communications with those of the Department of Defense, as well as eliminating dependence on non-service communications systems.[29]

Lastly, Commandant Allen reiterated the need to retain and encourage the key part of the Coast Guard culture that was so evident and so vital during Katrina and Rita: the principle of on-scene initiative. It is set forth in the Coast Guard Publication 1, which states in part that CG personnel on-site are given latitude "to act quickly and decisively within the scope of their authority, without waiting for direction from higher levels in the chain of command."[30]

In conclusion, looking at the Coast Guard in the past, Hurricane Katrina exemplified "Semper Paratus" in the very best sense. By the same token, the storm may well have been the chrysalis for a future service where the motto is meaningful on every level, from the individuals in the boats and in the air, to the quality and efficiency of the Coast Guard organization as a whole.

Acknowledgments

The key to the writing of this book was the United States Coast Guard Historian's Office at CG Headquarters, Washington, D.C. From the outset, chief historian Dr. Robert Browning, Jr. and his staff have been uniformly supportive and helpful. Thanks go particularly to Jeff Bowdoin, who handled the Katrina Archive and Freedom of Information Act request, and Scott T. Price, Assistant Historian, whose previous work on the Katrina story made his advice and suggestions invaluable. Thanks to Bill Thiesen, Atlantic Area historian, for assistance in finding interviewees in the New Orleans area. Thanks also to Chris Havern in the historian's office and Arlyn McDaniels, Coast Guard Curator, for their support.

To write the book from some semblance of knowledge I made trips to New Orleans and the Gulf Coast in 2007 and 2008. I visited District Eight headquarters in New Orleans, Station Grand Isle, Station Gulfport, Sector Mobile, and Air Station Mobile. In particular, I would like to thank the commanding officers at Grand Isle and Gulfport, Lt. Cdr. William Gibbons and CWO Steve Lyons, respectively, for their time and courtesy. At Mobile, Capt. Edwin

Stanton and Capt. David R. Callahan were generous with their time and the information they had to share.

On a more personal basis, thanks to Mike Lichtensteiger for looking over the manuscript, and Keven Foster, of the National Park Service, for good advice and leading me to other sources of information.

And I must extend my thanks to Dennis Noble, another historian and a retired Coast Guardsman. His advice and suggestions for this project were invaluable.

Additionally, thanks to the individual Coast Guard members whom I had the privilege to interview, personally and by telephone. Their enthusiasm, professionalism, and dedication to the service were outstanding, and represent the best of the U.S. Coast Guard today.

Finally, thanks to Admiral Thad Allen, Commandant of the Coast Guard, for allowing me a portion of his time to interview him at CG headquarters earlier this year.

Donald L. Canney

Notes

Chapter 1. Round One

1. The *Mary Lynn* narrative is compiled from: Tully, Tasha, PA1, "First Into The Fray," *Coast Guard Magazine*, Issue 4, 2006: 32; Krueger, Curtis, series in St. Petersburg *Times,* Aug. 30, Oct. 23, 24, 25, 26, 27, 28, 2005; *Night Flight: SOS Coast Guard Rescue*, Discovery Channel; and USCG Summary of Action for the Distinguished Flying Cross: LTJG Catherine D. Gross.

2. Time Line, Katrina, USCG Historian's Office; SITREP (Situation Report) One TS Katrina (251600Z Aug. 5), USCG District Seven

3. Time Line, USCG Historian's Office.

4. Time Line, USCG Historian's Office; SITREP Five, Hurricane Katrina, (271600Z Aug. 5) USCCG Dist. seven: 2.

5. SITREP Five, Hurricane Katrina, (271600Z Aug. 5, USCG Dist. Seven: 2).

6. Interview, Capt. Frank Paskewich, USCG Katrina Archive: 3

7. Ibid: 2.

8. Ibid: 4.

9. Katrina Time Line, CG Historian's Office.

10. Interview, BM2 Ronald Mancuso, CG Katrina Archive: 2; Interview by author, Lt. Cmdr. William Gibbons, Station Grand Isle, May 2007.

11. Interview by author, CWO Steve Lyons, Station Gulfport, May 2007; Downs, SN Lauren, "Before and After," *Coast Guard Magazine*, Special Edition, 2005: 62–63.

12. Interview, CWO Robert Lewald, CG Katrina Archive: 3–4; SITREP two, Sector New Orleans, (280204Z) Aug. 5; *Coast Guard Air Station New Orleans: Initial Response to Hurricane Katina.*

13. Interview by author, Capt. Edwin Stanton, Sector Mobile, May 2008.

14. Time Line, CG Historian's Office; Brinkley, Douglas, *The Great Deluge*: 126, 132.

15. Web Site: Nola.com (New Orleans *Times-Picayune*), *The Katrina Files, Time Line*; Website: www.Infoplease.com, Hurricane Katrina Time Line.

16. Brinkley: 237, 321.

Chapter 2. Round Two

1. Brinkley: 133; Sector New Orleans SITREP Twelve (310614Z) Aug. 5: 7.

2. Interview by author, Lt. Cmdr. William Gibbons, commanding officer, USCG Station Grand Isle, LA, May, 2007; Website: ncdc.noaa.gov (National Climatic Data Center, National Oceanic and Atmospheric Administration).

3. Website: lapage.com and louisiana.speaks-parishplans.org.

4. Website: epa.gov (U.S. Environmental Protection Agency)

5. Website: quickfacts.census.gov (U.S. Census Bureau);louisiana.speaks-parishplans.org

6. Website: ncdc.noaa.gov.

7. Website: louisianaspeaks-parishplans.com.

8. Editors of New Orleans *Times-Picayune, Katrina*, maps on 46–51; Brinkley: 219.

9. Websites: rand.org (The Rand Corporation); Louisianaspeaks-parishplans.com.

10. Website: Louisianaspeaks-parishplans.com

11. Website: wunderground.com (Weather Underground) "Katrina's Surge," parts 7–10.

12. Ibid.

13. Ibid.

14. Interview by author, Capt. Edwin Stanton, commanding officer, USCG Sector Mobile, May 8, 2008.

15. Brinkley: 177.

16. Visit by author to Gulfport, May 2006.

17. Brinkley: 174.

18. Brinkley: 176.

19. Brinkley: 173.

20. Website: cnn.com, (Cable News Network) Sept. 4, 2005; cdc.gov (Centers for Disease Control).

21. Websites: weather.com; uspolitics.about.com.; cdc.gov.

Chapter 3. "There's Thousands of Them"

1. Interview, Katrina Archive, Capt. Bruce Jones: 3–5.

2. Ibid.; "First 12 Hours," USCG document, *Coast Guard Air Station New Orleans Initial Response to Hurricane Katrina.*

3. Interview, Jones: 5.

4. Ibid.: 4; LaGuardia-Kotite, Martha, *So Others May Live*: 212–214.

5. Summary of Action Report and Citation for Air Medal, Laurence D. Nettles; website: hurricanearchive.org; Hurricane Digital Memory Bank, Moreau, Bobbie, "Untitled," Oct. 2, 2007.

6. Summary of Action Report/Citation, Nettles; O'Berry, Mike, "Full Force," *Coast Guard Magazine,* Special Edition, 2005: 11–12; Summary of Action Report and Citation for Air Medal, Lt. Craig E. Murray.

7. Summary/Citation, Nettles; Summary/Citation, Murray; Citation, Distinguished Flying Cross, Lt. David M. Johnston; Interview, Katrina Archive, Laurence D. Nettles.

8. Summary/Citation, Nettles; Summary/Citation, Murray.

9. *Coast Guard Initial Response*: 2

10. Ibid.

11. *Coast Guard Initial Response:* 2; Citation/Summary, Air Medal, Lt. Roberto H. Torres; Citation for Distinguished Flying Cross, Lt. Cmdr. Thomas F. Cooper.

12. Interview, CG Katrina Archive, Capt. Frank Paskewich, p.13; Citation for DFC, Lt.Cdr.Mark Vislay, Jr.

13. Interviews, CG Katrina Archive, Paskewich: 13–14; and Capt. Robert Mueller: 6–7.

14. *Coast Guard Initial Response*: 2.

15. *Coast Guard Initial Response*: 3; Summary of Action, Gordon: 1–2; interview, Katrina Archive: 3.

16. Gourley, Scott R., "The Coast Guard and Hurricane Katrina," *Coast Guard Magazine, Katrina Issue*: 17, 19.

17. Interview, Katrina Archive, Capt. Steve Taylor: 22–23.

18. Ibid.

19. Gourley: 19.

20. LaGuardia-Kotite, Martha J., *So Others May Live*: 215.

21. Citations for Distinguished Flying Cross, Joel M. Sayers and Patrick M. Gorman; Cangemi, NyxoLyno, *A Coast Guard Story, Hurricane Katrina: The U.S.Coast Guard at Its Best*: 37.

22. Cangemi: 37.

23. Citation for Distinguished Flying Cross, Lt. Cmdr. Scott E. Langum.

24. LaGuardia-Kotite: 214–215.

25. Ibid.

26. Ibid.: 215.

27. Ibid.: 215–216.

28. Creacy, Darrel, and Carlito Vicencio, *The Real Guardians*: 85–100.

29. Ibid.: 39–40, 100–101.

30. Ibid.: 40.

31. Ibid.: 40.

32. Ibid.: 41, 101–103.

33. Ibid.:37–38.

34. Summary of Action, Meritorious Service Medal: CWO Dan Brooks; interview, CG Katrina Archive, BM2 Jessica Guidroz: 6; interview by author, BM2 Christopher Hebert, Station Grand Isle, May, 2007; interview by author, Lt. Cmdr. William Gibbons, Station Grand Isle, May, 2007.

35. Summary of Action, BM2 Jessica Guidroz: 2

36. Interview, Guidroz: 6

37. Interview, Guidroz: 7; interview by author with BM2 Christopher Hebert.

Chapter 4. The Maritime and Environmental Disaster

1. O'Berry, Mike, "Full Force," *Coast Guard Magazine*, Special Issue, 2005: 14.

2. Website: ops.fhwa.dot.gov. (Federal Highway Administration, Department of Transportation.) Table. 2–7. Largest U.S. Seaports.

3. Hearing, *Always Ready*: the Coast Guard's Response to Hurricane Katrina . . . before Senate Homeland Security and Governmental Affairs Committee, Nov. 9, 2005: 20 (Capt. Frank Paskewich Testimony).

4. Website: sfgate.com, *San Francisco Chronicle*, Oct. 15, 2005. "Chevron Refinery Back in Production."

5. Ibid.

6. *Frequently Asked Questions Related to Coast Guard's Response to Hurricane Katrina and Rita,* USCG Document, Katrina Archive.

7. Ibid. O'Berry, "Full Force": 15.

8. O'Berry, "Full Force": 15.

9. CG Report, *Salvage Engineering Response Team* (09182005). CG Katrina Archive.

10. Gourley, "The Coast Guard and Hurricane Katrina": 21.

11. *Frequently Asked Questions . . . ;* "Katrina Stats and Facts," *Hurricane Katrina, The U.S. Coast Guard at its Best,* p.47.

Chapter 5. First Responses

1. Citation for Air Medal, Lt. Cdr. William E. Sasser, Jr.; Citation, Air Medal, Lt. Cdr. Thomas S. Swanberg; Citation, Distinguished Flying Cross, Cmdr. Michael P. McGraw.

2. Citation, Air Medal, Lt. Cdr. David W. Edwards.

3. SITREP Seven, Sector Mobile, (R30187Z) Aug. 5: 2.

4. Interview by author, CWO Steve Lyons, Station Gulfport, May, 2007.

5. Quoted in Brinkley: 173.

6. Interview by author, Lt. Todd Behney, Station Gulfport, May, 2007.

7. Interview, CWO Lyons.

8. Interview by author, Capt. David Callahan, ATC Mobile, May 8, 2008.

9. Interview by author, Capt. Edwin Stanton, Sector Mobile, May 8, 2008.

10. Summary of Operations, CG 6038, Aug. 29 to Sept 3, 2005: 1.

11. Website: military.com. Helms, Nathaniel R., "With the U.S. Coast Guard Responding to the Hurricane Katrina Disaster," Sept. 9, 2005: 2–7.

12. Ibid.

13. Interview, CG Katrina Archive, Lt. jg. Amber Jack: 4–5.

14. SITREP Seven, CG Lantarea, (302352Z) Aug. 5: 7.

15. Ibid.: 2.

16. Interview by author, Capt. David Callahan, ATC Mobile, May 8, 2008.

17. Citations, Air Medal, Lt. Cornelius E. Cummings, Lt. Charles E. Webb; Lt. John F. Druelle, and Lt. Joseph W. Klatt.

18. Interview by author, Capt. Edwin Stanton; Sector Mobile SITREPs Seven and Ten (30, 31 Aug. 2005).

19. Summary of Action for the Meritorious Service Medal, CW03 Kenneth P. Hardenbrook: 2–3.

Chapter 6. Wet Tuesday in New Orleans

1. Interview, Katrina Archive, Lt. Cmdr. Daryl Schaffer: 2.

2. Ibid: 3; interview, Katrina Archive, CWO Carter Owens: 3

3. E-mail, Katrina Archive: Lt. Cmdr. Daryl Schaffer to Cmdr. Robert Hayes, Oct. 10, 2005; interview, Schaffer: 6.

4. These ten Coast Guardsmen were recipients of the Higgins and Langley Memorial Award for Swiftwater Rescue in 2006.

5. Interview, Schaffer: 7.

6. Interview, Schaffer: 3.

7. Interview by author, BM2 Hebert, Grand Isle, May, 2007.

8. Ibid.; interview, Katrina Archive, BM2 Jessica Guidroz: 11–12

9. Ibid.: 13.

10. Ibid.: 14.

11. Ibid.: 14–15.

12. Ibid.: 16.

13. Interview, Hebert; Harless, PA3 James, "Station Crew Stays the Course following Katrina Devastation," *Coast Guard Magazine*, Issue 4, 2006: 16–17.

14. Summary of Action for Meritorious Service Medal, BM2 Ryan McKay: 1.

15. Interview, Katrina Archive, Lt. Shannon Gilreath: 3; After Action Report, Katrina Archive, S. Gilreath; Summary of Action for Meritorious Service Medal, BM2 Ryan A. McKay: 2.

16. Interview, Gilreath: 3.; Summary, Meritorious Service Medal, McKay: 2.

17. Summary of Action, Meritorious Service Medal, BM2 Kevin E. Biami: 3.

18. After Action Report, Lt. Cmdr. Shannon Gilreath.

19. Summary of Action, Biami: 3.

20. Summary of Action, Meritorious Service Medal, PO Gerald Eubanks: 1.

21. After Action Report, Gilreath, Aug. 30, 2005; SITREP Two: MSO St. Louis (P302234Z), Aug. 5.

22. After Action Summary, MSU Morgan City: 1; Timeline, Katrina Archive, Aug. 29–30: 1; SITREP One: (R012228Z), Sept. 5, FOB (Forward Operations Base) NOLA to District Eight: 1.

23. Interview, Katrina Archive, CW03 Robert D. Lewald: 4–5.

24. Ibid.: 1–2.

25. Ibid.: 5.

26. Interview, Katrina Archive, BMCS Steven Noyes: 5–6.

27. Interview, Katrina Archive, BM2 Ronald Mancuso, Station Grand Isle: 2.

28. Interview, Noyes: 7; interview, Lewald: 6.

29. Brinkley: 351.

30. Interview, Lewald: 7.

31. Interview by author, Lt. Cmdr. Gibbons.

32. Ibid.

33. Ibid.: SITREP Three, Station Grand Isle (P111504Z), Sept. 5: 1–2; Harless : 17.

34. Citation, Douglas A. Munro Award for Inspirational Leadership: Navy League to CBM George M. Williams, July 14, 2006.

35. Websites: usatoday.com: *New Orleans Toxic Soup*; democracynow.com (U.S. Centers for Disease Control Report), Sept. 8, 2005.

36. Interviews, Katrina Archive, BMCS Steven Noyes: 22; Lt. Cmdr. Daryl Schaffer: 6.

37. Summary of Actions, AST3 Nettles.

38. Citation, Achievement Medal, AST3 Kenyon Bolton.

39. Citations, Air Medal, Lt. Cornelius E. Cummings and Lt. Roberto H. Torres; Citation, Distinguished Flying Cross, Cmdr. Michael P. McGraw.

40. Fawcett, Paul, "Ice Boat Summer," *Coast Guard Magazine*, Katrina Issue: 31.

41. Websites: underwatertimes.com; sciencedaily.com

Chapter 7. Wet Tuesday II

1. Interview, Katrina Archive, Capt. Robert Mueller: 10; 23–24.

2. Interview, Gilreath: 12; interview, Katrina Archive, Capt. Neil Buschman: 13, 23; Interview, Katrina Archive, Capt. Bruce Jones: 5.

3. Interview, Katrina Archive, Capt. Joe Castillo: 10.

4. Summary of Action for Distinguished Flying Cross, Lt. jg. Catharine Gross; Award Summary, William F. McMeekin; Citation, DFC, AST3 Bret A. Fogle.

5. Summary of Operations, McMeekin: 3.

6. Ibid.

7. Ibid.; Award Summary, Randal L. Ripley.

8. Citation, Air Medal, Lt. Cmdr. Thomas S. Swanberg.

9. Citation, DFC, AST1 Timothy R. Fortney.

10. Citation, DFC, AST3 Mitchell A. Latta.

11. Citation, DFC, AST1 Jason A. Shepard.
12. Citation, DFC, AST3 Jay M. Leahr.
13. Citation, Shepard.
14. Citation, Air Medal, James M. Guidry.
15. Summary, DFC, Matthew Laub: 2.
16. Citation, DFC, AST1 John C. Williams.
17. Citation, DFC, Lt.Cmdr. Scott E. Langum.
18. Citation, Air Medal, Lt. Cmdr. Christian A. Ferguson.
19. Citation, Air Medal, Lt. Cmdr. Eric S. Gleason.
20. Summary of Actions, AST3 Matt O'Dell: 2.

Chapter 8. Wednesday, August 31

1. Log Summary, CGC *Pamlico*; interview, Lewald: 7–8.
2. Interview, Noyes: 9.
3. Interview, Lewald: 8–9.
4. Interview, Lewald: 9; Log Summary, *Pamlico*.
5. Interview, Lewald: 10; interview, Gilreath: 4.
6. Interview, Lewald: 10; Summary of Action, Lewald: 1.
7. Interview, Lewald: 11.
8. Ibid.: Log Summary, *Pamlico*.
9. Log Summary, *Pamlico*: 2; Zephyr Field After Action Report: 2.
10. Log Summary, *Pamlico*: 2.
11. Zephyr Field After Action Report: 2; interview, Gilreath: 4.
12. Interview, Schaffer: 3.
13. Ibid.: 3–4.
14. Ibid.: 8.
15. E-mail, Daryl Schaffer to Robert Hayes, Oct. 10, 2005, Subject: Zephyr Field.
16. SITREP One, FOB New Orleans (R012228Z), Sept. 5: 1–3.
17. Summary of Actions, Brooks: 2.
18. Summary of Actions, BM2 Guidroz: 1; Guidroz telephone interview by author, July 23, 2008.
19. Summary, Guidroz: 2; Guidroz telephone interview.
20. Interview, Guidroz: 17–18.
21. Telephone interview, Guidroz.
22. Interview, Guidroz: 26.

23. Summary of Action, Meritorious Service Medal, BM2 Jessica Guidroz: 1.

24. Interview, Guidroz: 1; Pueschel, Matt, "Coast Guard Threw 'Everything it Had' into Katrina Evac, Rescue." Website: usmedicine.com, January, 2006: 6.

25. Interview, Guidroz: 21.

Chapter 9. August 31

1. SITREP Six (300715Z), Aug. 5: CG District Eight: 1.
2. Interview, Jones: 16.
3. Ibid.
4. Ibid.: 17
5. Ibid.
6. Summary of Operations, McMeekin/CG6034: 5.
7. Ibid.: Summary of Actions, Randal Ripley: 3.
8. Summary, McMeekin: 5–6.
9. Ibid.
10. Citation, DFC, Cmdr. James S. O'Keefe.
11. Citation, DFC, Martin H. Nelson.
12. Citation, DFC, Joel M. Sayers.
13. Summary, DFC, PO Matthew Laub: 1
14. Citation, DFC, William E. Lawson.
15. Interview, Katrina Archive, AST3 Sara Faulkner: 7.
16. Ibid.: 3–4.
17. Ibid.: 5.
18. Ibid.: 4.
19. Ibid.: 1.
20. Citation, Air Medal, Lt. Cmdr. David W. Edwards.
21. Citation, DFC, Lt. Gregory A. Houghton.
22. Citation, DFC, Cmdr. Michael P. McGraw.
23. Summary of Actions, AST3 Matt O'Dell: 3.
24. Ibid.: 4–5.
25. Interview, Katrina Archive, Capt. Bruce Jones: 20.
26. Ibid.
27. Ibid.: 21.
28. Ibid.
29. Ibid.

Chapter 10. September 1

1. Gourley, "The Coast Guard and Hurricane Katrina": 21–23.

2. Interview by author, Commandant Thad Allen, February 23, 2009.

3. Website: MSNBC.com: "Thousands feared dead from Katrina's wrath; stadium evacuation begins." Sept. 1, 2005: 2.

4. Brinkley: 405.

5. MSNBC.com, "Thousands feared dead": 1.

6. Brinkley: 486–487. In fact, in an emergency an order from the state governor can bypass this restriction on the National Guard. The U.S. Coast Guard is the only U.S. military service exempt from the act.

7. MSNBC.com: "Thousands feared dead": 1; Brinkley: 268.

8. MSNBC.com: 3.

9. Interview, Katrina Archive, Schaffer: 10.

10. Interview, Katrina Archive, Mueller: 15.

11. Website: uscg.mil/hq

12. Gilreath, After Action Report, Sept. 1.

13. Ibid.

14. Ibid.: Brinkley: 376.

15. Ibid.

16. Ibid.

17. Ibid.

18. Brinkley: 277, 365.

19. Gilreath, After Action Report.

20. Interview, Lewald: 12.

21. Interview, Katrina Archive, Cmdr. Robert Tarantino: 4–5.

22. Ibid.

23. Summary of Action, Legion of Merit, CWO Robert R. Lewald.

24. SITREP Eleven, District Eight, Sept. 1, 2005: 1.

25. Interview, Capt. Jones: 19

26. SITREP Eleven: 1.

27. Summary of Actions, Lt. Zach Koehler: 1.

28. Citations, Air Medal, to Lt. Cmdr. Thomas McCormick and Lt. Cmdr. Eric S. Gleason; Citation for DFC, AST1 John C. Williams.

29. Citations, Gleason and McCormick.

30. Summary of Actions, O'Dell: 5.

31. Ibid.

32. Citation, Air Medal, AMT2 Daniel J. Hoffmeier.

33. Citation, DFC, Cmdr. James S. O'Keefe.

34. Narrative, AST3 Michael C. Novellino: 4–5.
35. CG Katrina Archive, Timeline.

Chapter 11. September 2

1. Log, *Pamlico*, Summary: 1
2. Interview, Lewald: 12.
3. Log, *Pamlico*, Summary: 1; interview, Lewald: 12.
4. Log, *Pamlico*, Summary: 1.
5. Interview, Mueller: 29.
6. Interview, Tarantino: 10–11.
7. Interview, Gilreath: 15.
8. Ibid.
9. After Action Report, Gilreath/Zephyr Field: 7.
10. SITREP One, CG FOB New Orleans: 4.
11. Summary of Action, Corey Anderson: 1, 3.
12. Summary of Action for Meritorious Service Medal, BM1, Anna E. Steel: 1–3.
13. Ibid.
14. Ibid.
15. Summary of Actions for Meritorious Service Medal, BM2 Kevin E. Biami: 1–4.
16. Ibid.
17. Summary, Lt. Zach Koehler: 2.
18. Summary, McMeekin: 8–10.
19. McMeekin narrative from Summary: 8–10.
20. Citation, Air Medal, Lt. Cmdr. Christian A. Ferguson.
21. Citation, DFC, AST3 Mitchell A. Latta.
22. Summary, AST3 O'Dell: 7–8.
23. Ibid.
24. Interview, Capt. Mueller: 11; Interview, Capt. Paskewich: 27.
25. Brinkley: 559–560.

Chapter 12. September 3

1. Gourley: 27.
2. SITREP Sixteen, District Eight (030931), Sept. 2; U.S. NORTHCOM OPERATIONS, Sept. 3, 2005: 3.

3. Interview, Capt. Mueller: 36; Johnson, Jennifer, PA2, "Flying High," *Coast Guard Magazine*, Katrina Issue, 2005: 45.

4. Interview, Mueller: 36.

5. Interview, Jones: 17.

6. Gourley: 27.

7. SITREP Twenty, Sector Nola (031232), September 5.

8. After Action Report, Zephyr Field/Gilreath: 7.

9. Summary of Actions, Meritorious Service Medal, CWO Dan Brooks: 2.

10. Ibid.

11. SITREP One, FOB NOLA: 5.

12. After Action Report, Zephyr Field/Gilreath: 7.

13. Ibid.: Summary of Action, Meritorious Service Medal, DC1 Brett Wickett 3.

14. After Action Report, Zephyr/Gilreath: 7.

15. Ibid.

16. CGC *Spencer* Patrol Summary (132202Z) Sept. 5: 2–3.

17. Ibid.

18. Ibid.

19. Summary of Actions, Lt. Zach Koehler: 2–3.

20. Citation, CG Achievement Medal, AST3 Kenyon Bolton.

21. Ibid.

22. Citations, DFC, Cmdr. Michael P. McGraw and Lt. Cmdr. Jacob E. Brown.

23. Citation, DFC, AST3 Jay M. Leahr.

24. Citation, DFC, AST1 Timothy R. Fortney.

25. Time Line, USCG Katrina Archive.

26. Ibid.

Chapter 13. September 4

1. Timeline, Katrina Archive.

2. SITREP One, FOB NOLA (011118Z), Sept 5: 6

3. Ibid.

4. After Action Report Zephyr Field/Gilreath: 8.

5. Ibid.

6. SITREP One, FOB NOLA: 6

7. Ibid.

8. After Action Report, Zephyr Field/Gilreath: 9.

9. Interview, Gilreath: 22.

10. CGC *Spencer* Patrol Summary (132202Z) Sept. 5: 3.

11. *Tortuga* had been built at Avondale shipyards in New Orleans. Ironically, the vessel's launch had been moved up due to the arrival of Hurricane Gilbert in late 1988.

12. *Spencer* Summary: 3.

13. After Action Report, Zephyr/Gilreath: 9.

14. Citation, Meritorious Service Medal, Cmdr. Anthony J. Vogt.; Summary of Actions, Cmdr Anthony J. Vogt: 3.

15. Summary, Vogt: 3.

16. Ibid.

17. Ibid.

18. Summary of Actions, Lt. Cmdr. Eric Johnson: 6

19. Ibid.

20. Ibid.

21. Summary of Actions, DFC, Lt. Steven C. Priebe: 3, 4.

Chapter 14. September 5–15

1. Brinkley: 634–637.

2. Brinkley: 636–637; 617.

3. Brinkley: 526; 617.

4. Brinkley: 615.

5. Brinkley: 616–617; Terry Ebert, Department of Homeland Security, quoted in Brinkley: 617.

6. Brinkley: 235–237; 324.

7. Website: washingtonpost.com: Septmber 6, 2005: Barr, Stephen. "Coast Guard's Response to Katrina a Silver Lining in the Storm."

8. Website: washingtontimes.com, Sept. 8, 2005, "More than a Coast Guard."

9. Ibid.

10. Gourley: 28, 30.

11. Interview by author, Admiral Thad Allen, CG commandant, Feb. 23, 2009.

12. Ibid.

13. Kitfield, James, "Allen Wrench," *Coast Guard Magazine*, Katrina Issue: 38.

14. Website: npr.com, Sept. 9, 2005.

15. *Spencer*, Patrol Summary: 4

16. Fawcett, Paul, "Ice Boat Summer," *Coast Guard Magazine,* Katrina Issue: 31.

17. CG Commandant Brief, Great Lakes Search and Rescue Detachment (SARDET).

18. Ibid.

19. Ibid.

20. Ibid.: Memo from CG Historian Scott Price, May, 2008.

21. After Action Report, Zephyr Field/Gilreath: 11.

22. Ibid.

23. SITREPs, Sector NOLA, 29, 30; 9, 10 Sept. 5; SITREPs, District Eight, 23, 26, 27, 28, 29, 30:(Sept. 8, Sept. 11–15)

24. SITREP Twenty-Nine, District Eight, Sept. 14: 2.

25. Press Release, Sept. 5, 2005, District Eight Public Affairs.

26. CG Air Station New Orleans, "Initial Response to Hurricane Katrina," Oct. 5, 2005: 4–5.

27. Summary of Actions, Lt. jg. Adam Spencer: 1–2.

28. Summary of Actions, DFC, Lt. Steven E. Cerveny: 2.

29. Ibid.

30. Summary of Actions, DFC, Lt. Martin M. Simpson: 2.

31. Summary of Actions, AST3 Bradford W. Simmons.

32. Summary of Action, Air Medal, AST1, Eric Biehn: 2.

33. Narrative, AST1, Tom Emerick: 1.

34. Ibid.: 2.

35. Report, AST1 Steven R. Garcia: 2.

36. Report, AST Matthew I. Bayne.

37. Ibid.

Chapter 15. Sector Mobile Deals with the Destruction

1. SITREP Seven: Sector Mobile, Aug. 30, 2005: 2.

2. Summary of Action, Legion of Merit, Capt. Edwin M. Stanton: 2.

3. Ibid.

4. Ibid.

5. SITREP Seven, Sector Mobile, Aug. 30, 2005: 2.

6. SITREP Ten, Sector Mobile, Aug. 31, 2005: 3.

7. Summary of Actions, Meritorious Service Medal, CWO Steve Lyons: 1.

8. Ibid.

9. SITREP Twelve, Sector Mobile, Sept. 1, 2005: 3–5.

10. SITREP Nineteen, Sector Mobile, Sept. 5, 2005: 1; Interview, CWO Steve Lyons.

11. SITREP Twenty-Three, District Eight, Sept. 8, 2005: 11.

12. Interview by author, Capt. Edwin Stanton, Sector Mobile, May 8, 2008; Brinkley: 165–169.

13. SITREP Fifteen, Sector Mobile, Sept. 3, 2005: 2.

14. SITREP Twenty-One, District Eight, Sept. 9, 2005: 4.

15. McKinley, Scott, "A Helping Hand," *The Reservist*, Vol. 52, Issue 7–2005: 36.

16. Ibid.

17. SITREP Twenty-Three, District Eight, Sept. 8, 2005: 11.

18. Interview, Capt. Paskewich: 27; Brinkley: 547–549.

Chapter 16. Restoring the Gulf Coast Waterways

1. Interview, Katrina Archive, Capt. Paskewich: 26.

2. ATON Survey, CGC *Decisive,* Sept. 2, 2005.

3. Ibid.: 18.

4. Ibid.: 19; SITREP Nineteen, District Eight, Sept. 5, 2005: 3; Marinelli, Anthony, "An Army of ANTs," *Coast Guard Magazine,* Katrina Issue: 83.

5. *Pamlico* Log Summary: 3.

6. Marinelli: 83.

7. SITREP Twenty-Two, District Eight, Sept. 7, 2005: 4.

8. Interview, Capt. Stanton, May 2008; Summary of Actions, Capt. Stanton: 2.

9. SITREP Nineteen, District Eight, Sept. 5, 2005: 4.

10. SITREP Thirty-Four, District Eight, Sept. 19, 2005: 1–2.

11. SITREP Eleven, NOLA Salvage, Sept., 2005: 1.

12. Ibid.: 2.

13. Lutz, Mike, "Oily Aftermath," *Coast Guard Magazine*, Katrina Edition: 71–73.

14. Ibid.

15. Ibid.

16. SITREP Twenty-Two, District Eight, Sept. 7, 2005: 2.

17. Ibid.

18. Ibid.

19. Citation, Legion of Merit, Capt. Edwin M. Stanton; interview by author, Capt. Stanton, May, 2008.

Chapter 17. Hurricane Rita and a Conclusion

1. Website: *Houston Chronicle*, Feb. 12, 2008.

2. SITREP Thirty-Six, District Eight, Sept. 21, 2005: 3.

3. SITREP Forty-Three, Sector NOLA, Sept. 21, 2005: 12; website, *Houston Chronicle*, Feb. 12, 2008; Website: nhc.noaa, Hurricane Rita: 2.

4. Website: *Houston Chronicle*, Feb. 12, 2008.

5. Interview, Capt. Jones: 22.

6. Website: www.foxnews.com, Hurricane Rita Response.

7. Interview, Capt. Jones: 22.

8. Interview, BMCS Steven Noyes: 26.

9. Ibid.: 27.

10. Ibid.:27–28; Citation, Meritorious Service Medal, BM1 Karyn M. Boxwell.

11. Interview, Capt. Jones: 22.

12. Frequently Asked Questions, Dec. 6, 2005, CG Katrina Archive.

13. Ibid.

14. Ibid.: 2.

15. Interview by author, CWO Lyons, Station Gulfport, May, 2007.

16. *Always Ready*, Senate Committee Hearing, Adm. Duncan testimony: 77.

17. Interview, Katrina Archive, Captain Joe Castillo, District Eight chief of operations: 13.

18. Interview, Capt. Jones: 5.

19. Michael Brown, as quoted in Brinkley: 254.

20. Ibid.: 5, 7.

21. Collins, Adm. Thomas H., commandant of the Coast Guard, Foreword, *Hurricane Katrina: The U.S. Coast Guard at its Best*: 3; testimony of Rear Admiral Robert F. Duncan, *Always Ready: The Coast Guard's Response to Hurricane Katrina.* Hearing, Senate Homeland Security and Governmental Affairs Committee, Nov. 9, 2005: 15.

22. Ibid.:1–3.

23. Brinkley: 214.

24. Website: fema.gov. "No Average Days for the Coast Guard in Louisiana," March 28, 2006: 1–2.

25. Interview by author, Commandant Thad Allen, Feb. 23, 2009.

26. Ibid.

27. Pine, Art, "Admiral Allen's Blue Tsunami," Naval Institute Proceedings, August, 2008, Vol. 134/8, www.usni.org.: 2–3.

28. Ibid.: Interview, Allen.

29. Ibid.

30. Coast Guard Publication 1: 42.

Bibliography and Note on Sources

Of course the major source for a book about the U.S. Coast Guard is the service itself. In fact, the Coast Guard Historian's Office in Washington D.C. is the central location of most of the Coast Guard and its predecessor agencies' records. Furthermore, a dedicated electronic Katrina archive was created in the Historian's Office for the official records of Hurricane Katrina and Hurricane Rita. These records include oral histories of people ranging from admirals downward.

Though all unclassified government documents are available to the general public, Katrina documents were not available to me until I had submitted a FOIA (Freedom of Information Act) request. This required a letter describing what types of documents and materials I desired, the inclusive dates, reasons for requesting the material, etcetera. No master list of the material in the archive is available.

Once the FOIA was submitted there was a three-month delay while it was being processed. The result was a CD containing the material I had requested. That is, a selected portion of the entire collection. For instance, of the approximately 200 interviews, about forty were available to me; many were as yet not transcribed.

Consequently, this book is not the definitive work on Hurricane Katrina. Only when all the pertinent records are available, without having to resort to the FOIA process, will a comprehensive history of the Coast Guard after the storm be possible.

In the following bibliography, I have started with the material received from the USCG Katrina Archive, via the FOIA request. The bibliography cites the types of documents I have used, while the individual note will cite the specific document in question. For example, I list "District Eight" SITREP in the bibliography, while the individual SITREP, by number and date, is in the notes.

Following this are the items available to the general public, as well as interviews I did with various individuals in two trips to the Gulf Coast and one to Coast Guard headquarters in Washington DC.

Coast Guard Katrina Electronic Archive

Situation Reports (SITREPS)

Atlantic Area (LANTAREA)
CGC *Decisive*
CCG *Harriet Lane*
CGC *Shamal*
CGC *Spencer*
District Seven
District Eight
Forward Operating Base New Orleans
Marine Safety Office, St. Louis
Pollution Sitreps
Salvage Sitreps
Sector Mobile
Sector New Orleans (NOLA)

Station Grand Isle
Zephyr Field

Time Lines

Coast Guard Hurricane Katrina Archive Time Line
First Twelve Hours Response/ Air Station New Orleans

Logs

Katrina CGC *Pamlico* Logs
Station Gulfport

Commandant Briefs

Great Lakes Search and Rescue Detachment (SARDET)
Aids to Navigation Brief September 26, 2005

Summaries and After Action Reports

ATON Survey, September 2, 2005
Forward Deployment Summary: MSST Galveston
Lt. Cmdr. Shannon Gilreath/Zephyr Field
MSU Morgan City
Summary of Operations: HH-60 CG6038, August 29–September 2, 2005

Medals, Awards Citations, and Summaries of Actions

Air Medal
Coast Guard Achievement Medal
Commendation Medal
Distinguished Flying Cross
Legion of Merit
Letters of Commendation
Meritorious Service Medal

Katrina Archive Oral History Transcripts

Capt. Neil Buschman, Area Operations Officer, Atlantic
Capt. Joe Castillo, Chief of Operations, District Eight
AST3 Sara Faulkner
Cmdr Patrick Flynn, ISC New Orleans
Cmdr. Shannon Gilreath, commanding officer, Marine Safety Unit, Baton Rouge
EM2 Rodney Gordon, Air Station New Orleans
BM2 Jessica Guidroz, Station New Orleans
Lt. jg. Amber Jack
Capt. Bradley Jacobs, chief of operational forces, Atlantic Area
Capt. Bruce Jones, commander, Air Station New Orleans
CW03 Robert David Lewald, commanding officer, CGC *Pamlico*
BM2 Ronald Mancuso, Station Grand Isle
Lt. Iain McConnell, Air Station Clearwater
Capt. Robert Mueller, deputy commander, Sector New Orleans
BMCS Steven Noyes, Station Dulac, LA
CWO Carter Owens, ISC New Orleans
Capt. Frank Paskewich, sector commander, NOLA
Lt. Cmdr. Daryl Schaffer, Integrated Support Command, New Orleans
Cmdr. Robert Tarantino, commanding officer, CGC *Spencer*
Capt. Steve Taylor, aviation force manager, Atlantic Area

Miscellaneous Katrina Archive Documents

"Always Ready": The Coast Guard Response to Hurricane Katrina before Senate Homeland Security and Governmental Affairs Committee, November 9, 2005.
E-mail: Lt. Cmdr. Daryl Schaffer to Cmdr. Robert Hayes, Oct. 10, 2005.
Evening Update: 02 Sept 2005, NORTHCOM Operations
Frequently Asked Questions: Katrina Archive
Government Accountability Office, July, 2006: "Observations on the Preparation, Response, and Recovery Missions Related to Hurricane Katrina," Report#06–903,

Press Releases: CG Public Affairs
Report: Salvage Engineering Response Team

Miscellaneous Documents: Coast Guard Historian's Office

"Coast Guard Operations During Natural Disasters and Events of National Significance."

"Costliest Hurricanes, United States, 1900–1992."

"Deadliest Hurricanes, United States, 1900–1992."

Kaplan, H.R., "Camille Revisited."

Teletype Rescripts from CG District Eight: Hurricane Camille, August 19–22, 1969.

Books

Annual Report of the U.S. Coast Guard, 1922.

Brinkley, Douglas. *The Great Deluge.* New York: William Morrow, 2006.

Canney, Donald L. *U.S. Coast Guard and Revenue Cutters, 1790–1935*. Annapolis: Naval Institute Press, 1995.

Creasy, Darrel, and Carlito Vicencio. *The Real Guardians.* Houston: Dude Productions, 2006.

Evans, Stephen, *The United States Coast Guard, 1790–1915.* Annapolis: Naval Institute Press, 1949.

Gourley, Scott R. "The Coast Guard and Hurricane Katrina." In *Hurricane Katrina: the U.S. Coast Guard at its Best.* Tampa: Faircount LLC, N.D.

Insight Guide. *New Orleans.* Maspeth: Langenscheidt Publishers, Inc., 2003.

Johnston, Robert Erwin. *Guardians of the Sea.* Annapolis: Naval Institute Press, 1987.

LaGuardia-Kotite, Martha J. *So Others May Live.* Guilford: The Lyons Press, 2006.

Moore, Richard, and Jay Barnes. *Faces from the Flood: Hurricane Floyd Remembered.* Chapel Hill: University of North Carolina Press, 2004.

Smith, Horatio D. *U.S. Revenue Cutter Service, 1789–1849.* Washington D.C.: U.S. Coast Guard, 1989.

The *Times-Picayune. Katrina.* New Orleans: The *Times-Picayune* Press, 2006.

Periodicals

Downs, Lauren. "Before & After." In "Katrina: The Gulf Response." Special Issue, *Coast Guard Magazine* (2005): 62–63.

Fawcett, Paul. "Ice Boat Summer." In "Katrina: The Gulf Response." Special Issue, *Coast Guard Magazine* (2005): 30–31.

Johnson, Jennifer. "Flying High." In "Katrina: The Gulf Response." Special Issue, *Coast Guard Magazine* (2005): 44–45.

Lutz, Mike. "Oily Aftermath." In "Katrina: The Gulf Response." Special Issue, *Coast Guard Magazine* (2005): 70–73.

McKinley, Scott. "Sending the Reserve." In "Katrina: The Gulf Response." Special Issue, *Coast Guard Magazine* (2005): 28–29.

Newlin, Kelly. "Ingenuity keeps Helos humming." In "Katrina: The Gulf Response." Special Issue, *Coast Guard Magazine* (2005): 22–23.

O'Berry, Mike. "Full Force." In "Katrina: The Gulf Response." Special Issue, *Coast Guard Magazine* (2005): 10–16.

Schofield, Matthew. "Iceboats." In "Katrina: The Gulf Response." Special Issue, *Coast Guard Magazine* (2005):

Coast Guard Magazine, Issue 4, 2006.

Gulf & Rivers Connection, USCG District Eight, Fall, 1999.

The Reservist, V01.52, Issue 7–05.

Interviews By Author

Admiral Thad Allen, Commandant of the Coast Guard

Lt. Todd Behney, Station Gulfport

Captain David R. Callahan, ATC Mobile

Lt. Cmdr. William R. Gibbons, Station Grand Isle

BM2 Christopher Hebert, Station Grand Isle

CWO Steve Lyons, Station Gulfport

BM2 Ronald Mancuso, Station Grand Isle
Capt. Edwin M. Stanton, Base Mobile

Websites and Articles

"A Look back at Hurricane Camille," www.usatoday.com

Barr, Stephen. "Coast Guard's Response to Katrina a Silver Lining in the Storm," Sept. 6, 2005, www.washingtontimes.com

———. "More than a Coast Guard," Sept.8, 2005.

"Chevron Refinery Back in Production," *San Francisco Chronicle*, Oct. 15, 2005, www.sfgate.com

www.cnn.com (Cable News Network)

"Coast Guard Rescue Operations Continue," Sept. 2, 2005, www.about.com:usmilitary.

U.S. Centers for Disease Control Report, Sept. 8, 2005, www.democracynow.com

Helms, Nathaniel R. "With the U.S. Coast Guard Responding to the Hurricane Katrina Disaster," Sept. 9, 2005, www.military.com

Houston *Chronicle*, www.houstonchronicle.com

www.hurricanearchive.org

"Hurricane Katrina Timeline," www.infoplease.com

"Hurricane Rita Response," www.foxnews.com

Krueger, Curtis. "A glow in the mist," Oct. 25, 2005, *St. Petersburg Times*, www.sptimes.com

———. "A long, long, night," Oct. 26, 2005, *St. Petersburg Times*, www.sptimes.com

———. "Coast Guard rescue crew braves Katrina's winds," Aug. 30, 2005, *St Petersburg Times*, www.sptimes.com

———. "The flying frogman," Oct. 27, 2005, *St. Petersburg Times*, www.sptimes.com

———. "Gambling in the Gulf," Oct. 23, 2005, *St. Petersburg Times*, www.sptimes.com

———. "The Race to Save the Mary Lynn," Oct. 24, 2005, *St. Petersburg Times*, www.sptimes.com

———. "Water under the dam," Oct. 28, 2005, *St. Petersburg Times*, www.sptimes.com

"Louisiana Page," www.lapage.com
www.louisiana.speaks-parishplans.org
National Climatic Data Center, www.ncdc.noaa.com
"New Orleans . . . The New Atlantis?," Jan. 21, 2000, www.sciencedaily.com
"No Average Days for the Coast Guard in Louisiana," www.fema.gov
www.quickfacts.census.gov
"Persons of the Week: Coast Guard Rescue Teams," Sept. 2, 2005, www.abcnews.go.com
Ripley, Amanda. "How the Coast Guard Gets It Right," Oct. 23, 2005. www.time.com
"The Katrina Files," *New Orleans Times-Picayune*, www.nola.com
Wilson, Jim. "New Orleans Is Sinking," Sept. 2001, www.popular Mechanics.com
"Thousands feared dead from Katrina's Wrath; stadium evacuation begins," Sept. 1, 2005, www.msnbc.msn.com
www.underwatertimes.com
U.S. Coast Guard website, www.uscg.mil
U.S. Environmental Protection Agency, www.epa.gov
www.uspolitics.about.com
www.weather.com
Williams, Jack. "Answers: Hurricane Betsy Hits Florida, smashed New Orleans in 1965," www.usatoday.com
www.wunderground.com

Index

Page numbers in italic refer to illustrations.

Donald L. Canney is a historian and author of six books on American Naval and Coast Guard history. Mr. Canney was registrar of collections for the U.S. Coast Guard museum program before retiring in 2006. His books include *Lincoln's Navy* and *Africa Squadron: the U.S. Navy and the Slave Trade, 1842–1861*. He currently resides in Ohio.

New Perspectives on Maritime History and Nautical Archaeology

Edited by James C. Bradford and Gene Allen Smith

Maritime Heritage of the Cayman Islands, by Roger C. Smith (1999; first paperback edition, 2000)

The Three German Navies: Dissolution, Transition, and New Beginnings, 1945–1960, by Douglas C. Peifer (2002)

The Rescue of the Gale Runner: *Death, Heroism, and the U.S. Coast Guard*, by Dennis L. Noble (2002); first paperback edition, 2008

Brown Water Warfare: The U.S. Navy in Riverine Warfare and the Emergence of a Tactical Doctrine, 1775–1970, by R. Blake Dunnavent (2003)

Sea Power in the Medieval Mediterranean: The Catalan-Aragonese Fleet in the War of the Sicilian Vespers by Lawrence V. Mott (2003)

An Admiral for America: Sir Peter Warren, Vice-Admiral of the Red, 1703–1752, by Julian Gwyn (2004)

Maritime History as World History, edited by Daniel Finamore (2004)

Counterpoint to Trafalgar: The Anglo-Russian Invasion of Naples, 1805–1806, by William Henry Flayhart III (first paperback edition, 2004)

Life and Death on the Greenland Patrol, 1942, by Thaddeus D. Novak, edited by P. J. Capelotti (2005)

X Marks the Spot: The Archaeology of Piracy, edited by Russell K. Skowronek and Charles R. Ewen (2006, first paperback edition 2007)

Industrializing American Shipbuilding: The Transformation of Ship Design and Construction, 1820–1920, by William H. Thiesen (2006)

Admiral Lord Keith and the Naval War against Napoleon, by Kevin D. McCranie (2006)

Commodore John Rodgers: Paragon of the Early American Navy, by John H. Schroeder (2006)

Borderland Smuggling; Patriots, Loyalists, and Illicit Trade in the Northeast, 1783–1820, by Joshua M. Smith (2006)

Brutality on Trial: "Hellfire" Pedersen, "Fighting" Hansen, and the Seamen's Act of 1915, by E. Kay Gibson (2006)

Uriah Levy: Reformer of the Antebellum Navy, by Ira Dye (2006)

Crisis at Sea: The United States Navy in European Waters in World War I, by William N. Still Jr. (2006)

Chinese Junks on the Pacific: Views from a Different Deck, by Hans K. Van Tilburg (2007)

Eight Thousand Years of Maltese Maritime History: Trade, Piracy, and Naval Warfare in the Central Mediterranean, by Ayşe Devrim Atauz (2007)

Merchant Mariners at War: An Oral History of World War II, by George J. Billy and Christine M. Billy (2008)

The Steamboat Montana *and the Opening of the West: History, Excavation, and Architecture*, by Annalies Corbin and Bradley A. Rodgers (2008)

Attack Transport: USS Charles Carroll *in World War II*, by Kenneth H. Goldman (2008)

Diplomats in Blue: U.S. Naval Officers in China, 1922–1933, by William Reynolds Braisted (2009)

Sir Samuel Hood and the Battle of the Chesapeake, by Colin Pengelly (2009)

Voyages, The Age of Sail: Documents in Maritime History, Volume I, 1492–1865; Volume II: The Age of Engines, 1865–Present, edited by Joshua M. Smith and the National Maritime Historical Society (2009)

Voyages, the Age of Engines: Documents in Maritime History, Volume II, 1865–Present, edited by Joshua M. Smith and the National Maritime Historical Society (2009)

H.M.S. Fowey *Lost and Found*, by Russell K. Skowronek and George R. Fischer (2009)

American Coastal Rescue Craft: A Design History of Coastal Rescue Craft Used by the United States Life-Saving Service and the United States Coast Guard, by William D. Wilkinson and Commander Timothy R. Dring, USNR (Retired) (2009)

The Spanish Convoy of 1750: Heaven's Hammer and International Diplomacy, by James A. Lewis (2009)

The Development of Mobile Logistic Support in Anglo-American Naval Policy, 1900–1953, by Peter V. Nash (2009)

Captain "Hell Roaring" Mike Healy: From American Slave to Arctic Hero, by Dennis L. Noble and Truman R. Strobridge (2009)

Sovereignty at Sea: U.S. Merchant Ships and American Entry into World War I, by Rodney Carlisle (2009)

Commodore Abraham Whipple of the Continental Navy: Privateer, Patriot, Pioneer, by Sheldon S. Cohen (2010)

Lucky 73: USS Pampanito*'s Unlikely Rescue of Allied POWs in WWII*, by Aldona Sendzikas (2010)

Cruise of the Dashing Wave*: Rounding Cape Horn in 1860*, by Philip Hichborn, edited by William H. Thiesen (2010)

Seated by the Sea: The Maritime History of Portland, Maine, and Its Irish Longshoremen, by Michael C. Connolly (2010)

The Whaling Expedition of the Ulysses*, 1937–1938*, by LT (j.g.) Quentin R. Walsh, U.S. Coast Guard, edited and with an Introduction by P.J. Capelotti (2010)

Stalking the U-Boat: U. S. Naval Aviation in Europe during World War I, by Geoffrey L. Rossano (2010)

In Katrina's Wake: The U.S. Coast Guard and the Gulf Coast Hurricanes of 2005, by Donald L. Canney (2010)